Treating Black Wom With Eating Disorders

The first of its kind, this edited volume provides in-depth, culturally sensitive material intended for addressing the unique concerns of Black women with eating disorders in addition to comprehensive discussions and treatment guidelines for this population.

The contributing authors—all of whom are Black professionals providing direct care to Black women—offer a range of perspectives to help readers understand the whole experience of their Black female clients. This includes not only discussion of their clients' physical health but also of their emotional lives and the ways in which the stresses of racism, discrimination, trauma, and adverse childhood experiences can contribute to disordered eating. Through a wealth of diverse voices and stories, chapters boldly tackle issues such as stereotypes and acculturative stress.

Clinicians of any race will gain new tools for assessing, diagnosing, and treating disordered eating in Black women and will be empowered to provide better care for their clients.

Charlynn Small, PhD, is a licensed clinical psychologist at the University of Richmond in Virginia. She received her PhD at Howard University and is an advocate for eating disorders awareness.

Mazella Fuller, PhD, is a psychiatric social worker at Duke University. She attended Smith College for social work in Northampton, Massachusetts, and completed her clinical training at University of Massachusetts, Amherst.

"The intersection of clinical expertise, lived experience, and compassion is where therapeutic magic, otherwise known as sound, evidence-based care that seeks to liberate not pathologize, happens. The clinician authors of *Treating Black Women with Eating Disorders: A Clinician's Guide* have harnessed that magic and make an invaluable scholarly contribution which broadens the much needed evidence base and knowledge on this topic. A must read for every mental health provider who works with and cares about the well being of Black women and their self actualization."

Nerine Tatham, *MD, General Psychiatrist,*
Diplomate in Psychiatry, American Board
of Psychiatry and Neurology

"Dr. Small and Dr. Fuller have compiled an essential reading list about the nuances of treating Black women struggling with eating disorders. This groundbreaking work starts a very necessary conversation that not only expands our understanding of the recognition, assessment and treatment of eating disorders among Black women, but deepens our understanding of the core nature of eating disorders for all as disorders rooted in experiences of marginalization and voicelessness."

Norman H. Kim, *PhD, National Director for Program*
Development, Reasons Eating Disorder Center

"Thirty-eight years after Gilligan's ground-breaking book *In a Different Voice* asserted that all people aren't male, Small and Fuller enlighten the eating disorders' world that all women aren't Caucasian. Twenty in-depth chapters cover every topic imaginable, written with passion, insight, expertise and lived experience. Research outcomes blend beautifully with poignant case studies and tools for treatment. More than just a 'what to do' book, this is a heartfelt treatise on how to 'feel', to inhabit another's world, to broach issues of race and identity and build the therapeutic alliance crucial to providing patients with the quality treatment they deserve."

Adrienne Ressler, *LMSW, CEDS, F.iaedp,*
Vice President of Professional Development
at The Renfrew Center Foundation

"Most clinicians are not trained on the needs of marginalized populations. The authors help to fill that important gap from their extensive experience in the eating disorder field treating Black women, and their own personal experiences as Black clinicians. I hope that all therapists will read this book and strive to improve their cultural humility in their treatment."

Millie Plotkin, *MLS, Informationist,*
Eating Recovery Center

"While we know that eating disorders do not discriminate, Black women are virtually invisible in many of the current eating disorder treatment manuals. With this groundbreaking book the authors have substantially enriched the eating disorders field by shining the light on the important work of Black professionals treating Black women suffering from eating disorders. This is an essential read for any eating disorder clinician treating Black women and serves as a helpful resource for all clinicians who desire to increase cultural competence and empathy."

Gayle E. Brooks, *PhD, CEDS-S, VP & Chief Clinical Officer,*
The Renfrew Center of Florida

Treating Black Women With Eating Disorders

A Clinician's Guide

**Edited by Charlynn Small
and Mazella Fuller**

NEW YORK AND LONDON

First published 2021
by Routledge
52 Vanderbilt Avenue, New York, NY 10017

and by Routledge
2 Park Square, Milton Park, Abingdon, Oxon, OX14 4RN

Routledge is an imprint of the Taylor & Francis Group, an informa business

Library of Congress Cataloging-in-Publication Data
A catalog record for this book has been requested

ISBN: 978-0-367-82065-7 (hbk)
ISBN: 978-0-367-82064-0 (pbk)
ISBN: 978-1-003-01174-3 (ebk)

Typeset in Times New Roman
by Apex CoVantage, LLC

MIX
Paper from
responsible sources
FSC FSC™ C013985
www.fsc.org

Printed in the United Kingdom
by Henry Ling Limited

For my children, Chuck and Taylor Dionne, and in memory of my parents, Charles and Martha Robison.

Mazella dedicates her work to her wonderful husband, Al, and in loving memory of her grandmother, Mazie B. Tune, and great-grandmother, Lillie Pearl Bynum.

Contents

Acknowledgments

I couldn't have done this work without the encouragement of my brothers, Sheldon and Charles, my beloveds Teresa and Donny, Aunt Mary, Lissa Brown, B John, Vicki Ruff, my Sands, Tamura Lomax, and my supportive University of Richmond colleagues, including Peter LeViness, Tina Cade, Steve Bisese, Eric Grollman, Bert Ashe, Gill Hickman, and Lucretia McCulley.

Mazella acknowledges her colleagues at Duke CAPS.

Together, we gratefully acknowledge the powerful voices of Black women, including Blanche Williams, our brilliant contributors and mentors, and all of those marvelous women who are now flourishing and building community.

Foreword

Becky Thompson

It is a joy to read this book, to hold it in my hands knowing that it is about the serious business of saving Black women's lives. As we witness the continued assault on the integrity, intelligence, and accomplishments of Black girls and women in the United States, Charlynn Small and Mazella Fuller offer a marvelous antidote to despair, a roadmap for healing that Black women and their allies have been waiting for—for decades. This is a book to celebrate, the first to offer an expansive understanding of clinical work that can support Black women who are healing from eating problems. Edited by two internationally recognized clinicians with more than a half century of professional work between them, *Treating Black Women With Eating Disorders* promises to transform research and treatment in life-giving ways, offering teachers, parents, clinicians, faith-workers, students, and social justice activists new and vital tools for healing at the level of the mind, body, and spirit.

In the opening pages, co-editor Charlynn Small asks a profound question: "Are Black women eating because we're hungry or because something's eating us?" Right away, the editors shift the gaze from eating problems among Black girls and women as individual pathologies to recognizing them as responses to a range of social injuries, from the historical and contemporary damage of slavery to undermining Black women's beauty; from racist social media sites to doctor's offices that only include images of White people's bodies on the walls and in educational literature. In response to clinicians who hold onto the archaic notion that Black women don't get eating problems (even though research documents that Black girls/women are as or more likely than White women to develop eating problems) and the pernicious ways that the mundane, extreme violence of racism is overlooked and discounted in US society, this book insists that we listen to Black women as they vow that their lives matter. And will continue to, into the future.

Among the many innovations this twenty-chapter collection offers is an up-to-date assessment of why putting Black women at the center of focus in eating disorders research and treatment will reinvigorate the field as a whole. Once eating problems are understood as ways girls and women cope with a range of socially induced stressors, it is then possible to create treatment (action) plans that take into account the complexity of women's lives. Innovations include attention to how and why it may be helpful to get fathers and other family members involved in treatment (based on experience with healing in Jamaica). And there is an important chapter on new research on links between polycystic ovary syndrome and eating disturbances that is particularly important given POS's prevalence.

The book also offers crucial writing on historical trauma as a weight that can twist women's appetites and unravel a sense of a safe connection to the world. Jacqueline Conley offers timely lists of YouTube channels that include focus on Black girls and women with eating problems alongside discussion questions for clinicians working with these sites in therapy. There are exemplary questions that clinicians may consider asking to invite layered conversations about colorism, hair, and body shape as well as suggested guidelines for walking clients away from cycles of binging, shame, and secrecy. As I read this treasure trove of guidelines for creating therapeutic settings that are alive with healing, I imagine billboards and three-dimensional sculptures adoring clinical walls, where the knowledge and wisdom of Black women's lives could be projected, walls for the healing arts.

With its exemplary attention to historical/cultural context, this book gives us nuanced understandings of why many Black women shy away from seeking treatment—not only the damage of systematic racism practiced in Tuskegee Institute (1932–1972) but also high infant and pregnancy mortality rates, the unethical treatment of Henrietta Lacks (1951), the torture of Black women in the name of gynecological discovery, and the disrespect of Black women seeking health support currently.

Given this history, it is remarkable that Black women are willing to continue seeking care, a fortitude that the editors recognize must be matched by cultural humility and race- and gender-conscious treatment on the part of clinicians. In her remarkable chapter, Warrenetta Crawford Mann offers advice for White clinicians: "Resist the urge to minimize, justify, diminish and reframe every emotionally destructive experience Black women have had to hold onto." To Black women clinicians, she advises that both the clinician and client meet their fears and misunderstandings collaboratively. Modeling a first interaction with a client, Mann writes, "I told her every thought I had about her when I saw her, and then I apologized for myself and every other Black woman who had assumed that they knew her and what she needed." How beautiful is that, Mann's humility, her understanding of historical trauma. Mann wisely helps us see that same-race pairings are at least as complex as cross race pairings; both require sustained willingness to look beyond stereotype and fear to a place of deep recognition and listening.

The collection includes chapters steeped in race-conscious research alongside writing by clinicians who offer personal wisdom from their own healing strategies and what their clients have taught them. It is marvelous to see both sources of knowledge in a single volume; that the book allowed the authors to remain embodied as they wrote about the dynamics of embodiment they see as possible for their clients. This is an illustrative example of how by enhancing our understanding of Black women and eating problems, the volume is changing the face of the research. This book shows that it is possible to be both a clinician specializing in eating problems and a woman who has healed from them at the same time. Jennifer Ashby-Bullock and Joyce Woodson both do this beautifully in their chapters. They understand that being an esteemed professional does not mean having to cut yourselves off from your own lived experience. All parts of us are welcome in this dance of healing.

This collection comes from a long line of forward-thinking, brave writing dedicated to seeing Black women as leaders and healers. They come from a tradition that recognizes that when you make the world truly welcome for Black women, everyone else will be welcomed as well. From Sojourner Truth to Angela Davis and Wilma Mankiller, from Ida B. Wells to the Combahee River Collective, from Kimberlé Crenshaw's legal definition of intersectional feminism to Tarana Burke's naming #MeToo, Black and Native women are the original feminists in the US. What a Black feminist framework means for research on eating problems is that when the barriers for comprehensive treatment that African American women experience are dismantled, the walls that have gotten in the way of Caribbean women receiving comprehensive care may come down too.

Once we take seriously the relationship between food insecurity and binging among Black women, the barriers that White working-class women face to skilled and compassionate care will be identified as well. Once Black queer women are considered central to discussions of eating problems and recovery, room will emerge for understanding queer lives across race and class as worthy of considered attention. This is the power of an inclusive framework, one carefully and ethically offered in this long-awaited book.

While this collection is unflinching in its willingness to name the mundane, extreme acts of racism that Black women cope with, there are moments of hope sprinkled throughout the book as well. In her important chapter that explores embodiment techniques for Black queer women, Anisha Cooper writes how when she referred to her belly as having stretch marks, her daughter whispered, "Mommy, your belly made room for me." Cooper continues, "I stood there before her astonished, observing how quickly my daughter consoled me with her compassion for my body stretching beyond capacity to carry a life—her life." As we know we must think about seven generations to heal the planet, so too we know that a Black feminist ethic of care is rooted in listening to the young ones, creating practices so that they do not have to fight to live comfortably and with ease in their bodies.

Introduction

Charlynn Small

To show why this book is needed, allow me to introduce you to Jasmine. Jasmine is a 22-year-old Black female graduate student at a very large, predominantly White college (PWC) on the Northeast coast. She is a first-generation college student, and she attended this school for both undergrad and graduate school. During fall semester of her junior year, Jasmine came to the realization that she has bulimia.

In high school, Jasmine sang in the choir and joined a few clubs. She never felt special or attractive. But she never felt particularly unattractive, either. Establishing relationships always seemed difficult for her, and she experienced a sense of disconnection from her family and from herself, although she could never fully clarify what she meant by feeling disconnected from herself. Her identity development impacted her self-esteem and self-confidence. At college, she had hoped to find a supportive group of others. Instead, she felt unwelcome and on the periphery of groups, as she attempted to navigate two different worlds simultaneously. Her dual identity was conflicting as she found she was seen as "too White" for her peers of color, yet not "White enough" for her White peers.

Jasmine is from a middle-class family living in Brooklyn, New York. Her father is a policeman, and her mother is an administrative assistant at a major accounting firm. Both of her parents are from small, Southern towns in North Carolina, where "thicc" women are considered desirable. Her mother is of average height, with wide hips and voluptuous thighs (two of the main things that attracted Jasmine's father to her mother). Her mother also has very fair skin and long wavy hair (her father valued these things also). Her father is tall, with a fairly slim build, very dark skin, and short, tightly curled hair. Jasmine's resemblance to him is uncanny, except that she has her mother's height and figure. Jasmine has two older sisters. They both have their mom's fair skin and wavy hair. They both have a slimmer build. Jasmine always felt that her parents favored her sisters over her and that things were always easier for them. Neither ever cared much about earning good grades and chose not to attend college. However, they each married well and appear to be happy. Jasmine was closest to their younger brother, who also noticed their parents' favoritism.

As an undergrad, Jasmine struggled to find a niche and others with whom she could identify. Although the university boasted a racially diverse student body with 25 percent people of color (e.g., Blacks, Asians, Latinx, and other international students), there were fewer than 4 percent Black students on campus. There were no places for Black students to gather and socialize. In addition, there were few professors who looked like Jasmine. She found it even more difficult than usual to manage interpersonal connections.

Determined to be a successful accountant, Jasmine decided that social interactions were not all that important. Accordingly, she resolved to focus all of her efforts into being an A student. Slowly, Jasmine became aware that she felt a certain pressure to represent all Black people positively, and thus, good grades were not optional. It was what she believed she needed to do. Still, she always felt a sense from others that while she was somehow granted acceptance to this elite school, she hadn't really earned the right to be there. And while it often seemed that Jasmine was looked upon to speak on behalf of all Black people everywhere, at the same time, she felt her input was devalued. Experiencing the climate as hostile, Jasmine grew more and more resentful.

When Jasmine was taking courses in her accounting major, she began binging and purging almost daily after classes. At first, she felt a strange relief afterward. Engaging in the behaviors gave her a certain comfort. Still, while not fully insightful about all that was happening, she had the sense that she shouldn't have been binging and purging. Jasmine sometimes didn't eat at all, hopeful that this would prevent her from throwing up. But approximately one year later, she realized that she couldn't stop restricting, binging, or purging. She also found herself in awe about the relative ease with which she became able to purge.

She finally sought help at the university's counseling center. Still, she was initially reluctant to go there because there were no counselors on staff who looked like her. For this reason, she figured none of them would understand what was happening with her. And she was, frankly, a little too embarrassed to share anything about which she felt hurt or unhappy. The thought of anyone asking her about feeling like an outsider on campus or about her family dynamics seemed too personal and made her uncomfortable. She prayed that no one would ask her about her deepest feelings. Her sole objective was to get help to stop restricting, binging, and purging.

Jasmine is a composite of many people I, a Black female certified eating disorders specialist and iaedp™-approved supervisor (CEDS-S), have worked with over the years. The challenges she faced are shared by many Black women. Jasmine never felt the security of an adequate support network among family or friends, rarely felt good about herself, and felt devalued as a person. If she came to you for help, how would you treat her? Would you know what questions to ask to facilitate processing her concerns? Would you feel comfortable asking them?

Black Women: In the Shadows of Eating Disorders

My co-author, Mazella Fuller, CED-S, and I met a few Novembers ago at one of the premier conferences for the treatment of persons with eating disorders

(EDs). It seemed we were put together at that place and time on purpose. We found that we had much in common, including that we were both in attendance at the same historically Black college or university (HBCU) at the same time, though our paths didn't cross during that time. We are both employed in the Counseling and Psychological Services (CAPS) at our respective predominantly White colleges (PWC). However, the most salient knowledge we acquired at the conference was that many non-Black therapists were surprised by the number of young Black women who struggle with EDs, body-image issues, or both. Hence, we decided we had an obligation to help get Black women out of the shadows of eating disorders and bring much-needed attention to their concerns. This book is one of our contributions toward ensuring that Black women's stories reach a wider audience of practitioners who can help those women address their concerns in culturally sensitive contexts.

Recent literature concerning Black women and body image more frequently addresses the misconception that Black women are well protected from eating disorders. Even so, for a number of reasons, many health care providers fail to recognize eating disturbances in Black women. One of the most important reasons for this failure is many practitioners fear asking questions that often concern racial differences and identity issues. These questions can be instrumental in helping practitioners recognize potentially mediating factors in the development of EDs.

Our book presents many of the unique challenges and needs of Black women that make them vulnerable to developing EDs, beginning with the misconception that they are somehow well protected from them.

One reason for this mistaken idea is sociocultural models of eating pathology (Shaw, Ramirez, Trost, Randall, & Stice, 2004). These models predict that women of color have a lower risk for eating disorders because they experience less cultural pressure to be thin and because they embrace larger, more attainable body ideals (Shaw et al., 2004; Gordon, Castro, Sitnikov, & Holm-Denoma, 2010; Hesse-Biber, Livinstone, Ramirez, Barko, & Johnson, 2010; Kelch-Oliver & Ancis, 2011; Taylor et al., 2013). Lore suggests that Black men typically prefer fuller, more voluptuous figures, which theoretically reduces the pressure to conform to a thinner appearance ideal (Gordon et al., 2010).

Other factors contributing to the misconception that Black women like Jasmine are protected from eating disorders include clinical approaches to classification (NEDA, 2005; Taylor et al., 2013), conflicting research results (Shaw et al., 2004), and the extant measures for assessing symptoms and risk factors (Kelly, Mitchell et al., 2012). The result of relying upon these evaluation procedures without considering additional data at the same time is that clinicians don't always recognize EDs in Black women (Becker, Franko, Speck, & Herzog, 2003; Cachelin, Rebeck, Veisel, & Striegel-Moore, 2001).

Similar to the way current DSM criteria are based on White populations (Taylor et al., 2013), most of the existing measures were developed and validated in samples that did not include Black women (Grabe & Hyde, 2006). However, Black women have been included in studies employing these measures (Kelly, Mitchell et al., 2012). Various research studies have shown mixed results when comparing Black and White women with ED symptoms using these measures, further fueling the myth. As such, they may not be useful in identifying Black women with eating disorders because they may not meet criteria, perhaps due to cultural differences (Taylor et al., 2013). For example, Black women tend to report lower rates of body dissatisfaction (Hesse-Biber et al., 2010; Gillen & Lefkowitz, 2012; Taylor et al., 2013) and lower rates of restrictive eating disorder symptomology than White women (Taylor et al., 2013; Kelly, Mitchell et al., 2012) when responding on these measures. Yet among the range of issues with eating and weight, Black women appear to be more vulnerable to binge eating (Taylor et al., 2013) and obesity. If body dissatisfaction and restrictive eating are the two variables a chosen instrument measures, and Black women score low on it, the implication is that they may not have EDs, when in fact they may. Furthermore, these measures don't always capture the myriad of complex issues affecting them that contribute to their vulnerability to EDs.

Initiatives such as the National Eating Disorders Screening Program (D'Sousa, Forman, & Austin, 2005; Becker et al., 2003) have employed these types of measures (i.e., Eating Attitudes Test; EAT-26; Garner, Olmsted, Bohr, & Garfinkel, 1982) in their research. Certain mental health facilities (such as university counseling centers) have included items from similar instruments (i.e., Eating Disorder Examination Questionnaire, EDE-Q; Kelly, Cotter et al., 2012) on their websites to help facilitate respondents' self-assessments of their eating patterns and behaviors (Kelly, Cotter et al., 2012). Many of these assessment items focus on internalizing a thin appearance ideal and thus may not be relevant for Black women, whose disordered eating may be more likely to take the form of binging or overeating. Respondents might score higher (and thus perhaps be recognized as having EDs) if an instrument included more items designed to measure binging and overeating variables.

While practitioners and researchers do not intentionally design misleading measures, the skewed results have important ramifications. Specifically, clinicians do not always recognize EDs in Black women based upon these results—results that make Black women less likely to receive referrals for further treatment or make them seek treatment on their own (Kelly, Cotter et al., 2012). Additionally, because these scores are often used in part to inform recommendations for further treatment, it is important that clinicians ask whether these measures are psychometrically adequate for use with Black women (Kelly, Cotter et al., 2012; Bardone-Cone & Boyd, 2007).

Still, arguably, one of the most important reasons practitioners fail to recognize eating disorders in these groups is because they fear asking (or have some other reason for not asking) the pertinent questions during assessment (Sanchez-Hucles, 2001) that will help them to recognize potentially mediating factors in the development of eating disorders. Often these questions are difficult, concerning racial differences and identity issues. The reluctance of practitioners to broach these sensitive concerns with Black clients is not limited to White practitioners. Black mental health care professionals have also reported difficulty raising these concerns with their clients of color (see Chapter 3, "A Gap in the Research").

Mediating Factors in the Development of Eating Disorders

What factors mediate the development of disordered eating in Black women? What are their unique vulnerabilities, and what predisposing factors do they share with White women?

Black Women Are Not Monolithic

To answer the question of what some instruments are not capturing, we first have to clarify and underscore that Black women are not the same on any measure. There are many differences among them; thus, they are multidimensional. Moreover, Black women continually grapple with important issues among their own group members. Consider the case of Jasmine, whose parents favored her sisters with their slim builds, fair skin, and long, wavy hair over her. These are the kinds of issues that are largely unaccounted for by the extant measures and clinical classification codes. Finally, these issues are often easily overlooked during a typical initial assessment process. We offer evidence of such in the beginning section of this book.

One such important issue is style, texture, and length of hair. Should it be worn naturally curly (for example, in Afros, locks, or braids) or straight? Skin color is another issue that has been the seed of perhaps some of our deepest pain. Despite our extraordinary range of shades and hues, so many of us continue to hold firm to the notion that a fair complexion is prettier or somehow better than a rich, dark, chocolaty complexion. Because of these beliefs, Black women often treat each other accordingly. The size and shape of Black women's bodies and body parts are the source of additional problems. Some of these women have been indoctrinated to believe that if they possess ample bosoms, voluptuous hips, and full lips, they are more desirable than a Black woman who is less well endowed.

Historically, such issues have often been the source of intense debates and hurt feelings among these groups. Some theorists agree that intergroup processes such as colorism are remnants of slavery and contribute significantly to intergenerational trauma (Halloran, 2018) and to explaining why Black women continue to grapple with these concerns.

Acculturative Stress

Traumatizing acculturative stress events can also serve as mediating factors in the development of eating disorders. Black women often experience acculturative stress events like racism and bigotry. These events are at times blatant while quite subtle at other times. Often, these events can be so subtle that one may not be aware that anything has actually occurred. This kind of uncertainty can be particularly distressing. Studies (e.g., Merritt, Bennett, Williams, Edwards, & Sollers, 2006) have shown that subtle racism is a psychosocial stressor that erodes the health of Black persons through chronically elevated cardiovascular responses. Some researchers believe that acculturative stress, rather than acculturation, is what predicts higher levels of bulimic symptoms among Black women (Gordon et al., 2010; NEDA, 2005), as they tend to be bulimic or binge eaters more than they restrict (Taylor et al., 2013). Again, these events are not always well accounted for during typical assessment processes. If clinicians don't know that these types of acculturative stress events are correlated with an increase in bulimic symptoms in Black women, then the experiences may be overlooked or dismissed as irrelevant when they are not.

Dr. Fuller and I have seen these issues playing out among students at different PWCs. A substantial body of research shows that Black college students in general continue to experience hostility on PWCs (Quinlan, 2016; Willie, 2003) and "microaggressive" indignities, such as racist attitudes and behaviors (Howard-Hamilton, 2003). Henry, Butler, and West (2011) state that many Black women college students report feeling isolated, marginalized, and misunderstood in their academic and social experiences on campus. At college and in the world beyond, facing these kinds of microaggressions can be detrimental to one's mental health, especially when experienced regularly over time. Kempa and Thomas (2000) found that grappling with discrimination experienced while immersed in a culture different from one's own and membership in groups considered subordinate are among the factors that can increase the risk for eating disorder development. Jasmine began restricting, binging, and purging to seek relief from feeling devalued as she attempted to navigate different cultures at the same time.

Black women attending PWCs must often negotiate dual identities or code switching as they attempt to navigate different cultures at the same time, which can be quite conflicting. Some clinicians have learned that while it may be assumed that Black women students feel good about their curvaceous figures, sometimes they don't. While few would suspect them of having body image issues and/or EDs, sometimes they do. And because they've been told that they should love their ample hips and thighs, they feel guilty when they don't. Thus, in addition to any acculturative stress or microaggressions experienced, some also experience isolation, feeling they don't fit in, and begin to wonder whether they belong at a PWC. For Black women, acculturative stress can amplify a vicious cycle: having an eating disorder when they are "not supposed to" makes them feel further isolated, and the sense of not fitting in feeds the painful emotions that contribute to disordered eating. Food is a source of comfort for many people, and disordered eating may arise when women engage in emotional eating to cope with continual stress and trauma.

History of Trauma Exposure

Eating disturbances are often associated with a history of exposure to trauma (Briere & Scott, 2007). Many kinds of traumatic events have been experienced by persons with eating disorders, with childhood sexual abuse or physical abuse being among the most common (Briere & Scott, 2007). When assessing

Black women for EDs, it is critical to consider the influence that race and ethnicity have on the relationship between identified childhood sexual abuse and obesity (Rohde et al., 2008), as Black children have nearly twice the risk of sexual trauma as White children (Sedlak et al., 2010). College-age women who were sexually abused as children are four times more likely than their nonabused peers to be diagnosed with eating disorders (Fuemmeler, Dedert, McClernon, & Beckham, 2009). Because Black women are more likely to engage in binge eating than in other ED behaviors, likely for comfort or to self-soothe, binge eating has been associated with an increase in obesity in this group (Taylor et al., 2013).

General Issues

In addition to issues specific to Black women and the acculturative stress events that disproportionately affect these groups, we are also affected by many of the general issues experienced by others. Some of the more general issues Black women experience that can yield vulnerability to EDs include biology, low food availability (including limited access to high-quality food), single motherhood, father–daughter relationship issues, and any number of other individual experiences that might be connected to disordered eating.

It is important to note that these precipitating experiences need not be major or traumatic. Disordered eating can arise simply from the realization that we can (to some extent) control the size and shape of our bodies. I myself recall a time 20 years ago when I had to take castor oil to prepare for a medical exam. The next morning, to my astonishment, I found that my stomach was as flat as a pancake! Three months later, I bought the perfect wedding dress. As the weeks went by, there were a number of dinners and other events to celebrate my doctorate degree and my upcoming wedding. Of course, because delectable, irresistible food was always the centerpiece of these events, it should come as no surprise that by the wedding date, I had gained a few extra pounds. What happened next should also come as no surprise. On the eve of my wedding, amid all the revelry, I paused for a minute to consider whether to drink some castor oil so that I could fit fabulously into that dress, as I had when I purchased it three months earlier. I didn't have a negative body image. I didn't think I was fat. There was no self-loathing, no internal whispers of "You shouldn't have gone to that last buffet." I simply considered that maybe if I did this thing, I'd have a flat stomach once again. This is one way eating disorders begin. There are many root causes that can yield problems with food. But it isn't always a mystery; disordered eating and related behaviors can occur simply after dieting or fasting.

Comorbid Conditions and Maintaining Factors

Black women also experience some of the same comorbid coping conditions and maintaining factors as other women with eating disorders, such as substance use, cutting, and purging. Black women also are affected by some of the newer trends that are defined below:

- Diabulimia: a condition affecting people with type I diabetes when they intentionally avoid taking their insulin in an attempt to stay or become thin (Moran & Wilkins, 2013)
- Drunkorexia: prevalent in college-aged binge drinkers who often starve during the day to offset calories consumed through alcohol in the evening (Moran & Wilkins, 2013)
- Pregorexia: anorexic or bulimic behaviors that occur during and after pregnancy (Moran & Wilkins, 2013)
- Orthorexia: fixation on only eating "healthy" or "pure" foods (Moran & Wilkins, 2013)

Other adverse health outcomes associated with eating disorders (binge eating in particular) that are also experienced by Black women include an increased risk of cardiovascular problems (i.e., high blood pressure, high cholesterol, and heart disease), type 2 diabetes, and gallbladder disease (NEDA, 2018).

What Readers Can Expect to Learn From This Book

Black women bring greatness and poise to the challenges of their eating disorders. *Treating Black Women* will provide an opportunity for readers to learn from the voices they have not heard—those of Black professionals treating Black women. This is the first guide of its kind dedicated to providing the most useful and culturally sensitive information for any practitioner's use when addressing the unique concerns of Black women with EDs. While there are several memoirs of Black women's struggles with eating disorders, this book is the first to offer a comprehensive approach to the treatment of Black women with EDs. The book reflects a variety of perspectives, including contributions from leading clinicians, physicians, educators, researchers, and practitioners in the field, each of whom has provided direct care to Black women with EDs.

From this book, readers can expect a mixture of current research, best practices in treatment trends, and clinical insight. In addition, clinicians will gain specific knowledge about the ravaging impact of the disorders on Black women's physical and emotional health and their resulting quality of life. This book is dedicated to women's interests. Because it offers an intersectional analysis, the book's content and style make it expressly feminist, which we fully embrace. And in addition to the focus on feminism, its editors' perspective is a holistic one—addressing the body, mind, and soul of Black women. What is particularly unique and compelling about our book is that it is an entire volume focused on the etiology, assessment, diagnosis, and best practices for treating EDs in this underrepresented population. Far too many books on disordered eating relegate issues of culture, race, and class to a single, brief chapter, if the topics are addressed at all.

This anthology provides a framework for education and training in the treatment of eating disorders in Black women. *Treating Black Women* includes 20 chapters addressing essential, culturally relevant concerns such as acculturative stress, media influences, LGTBQ perspectives, clinical implications, assessment, spiritual approaches to treatment, and nutritional needs. Accounts of Black women who have struggled with eating disorders are also included. The book provides hope for the Black women who are struggling with racism, class issues, and systemic oppression—factors that contribute to disordered eating.

References

Bardone-Cone, A. M., & Boyd, C. A. (2007). Psychometric properties of eating disorder instruments in Black and White young women: Internal consistency, temporal stability, and validity. *Psychological Assessment*, *19*(3), 356–362. https://doi.org/10.1037/1040-3590.19.3.356.

Becker, A. E., Franko, D. L., Speck, A., & Herzog, D. B. (2003). Ethnicity and differential access to care for eating disorder symptoms. *International Journal of Eating Disorders*, *33*, 205–212.

Briere, J., & Scott, C. (2007). Assessment of traumatic symptoms in eating-disordered populations. *Eating Disorders*, *15*, 347–358. https://doi.org/10.1080/10640260701454360.

Cachelin, F. M., Rebeck, R., Veisel, C., & Striegel-Moore, R. H. (2001). Barriers to treatment for eating disorders among ethnically diverse women. *International Journal of Eating Disorders*, *30*, 269–278.

D'Sousa, C. M., Forman, S. F., & Austin, S. B. (2005). Follow-up evaluation of a high school eating disorders screening program: Knowledge, awareness and self-referral. *Journal of Adolescent Health*, *36*, 208–213. https://doi.org/10.1016/j.jadohealth.2004.01.014.

Fuemmeler, B. F., Dedert, E., McClernon, F. J., & Beckham, J. C. (2009). Adverse childhood events are associated with obesity and disordered eating: Results from a U.S. population-based survey of young adults. *Journal of Traumatic Stress*, *22*, 329–333.

Garner, D. M., Olmsted, M. P., Bohr, Y., & Garfinkel, P. E. (1982). The eating attitudes test: Psychometric features and clinical correlates. *Psychological Medicine*, *12*, 871–878.

Gillen, M. M., & Lefkowitz, E. S. (2012). Gender and racial/ethnic differences in body image development among college students. *Body Image*, *9*, 126–130. https://doi.org/10.1016/j.bodyim.2011.09.004.

Gordon, K. H., Castro, Y., Sitnikov, L., & Holm-Denoma, J. M. (2010). Cultural body shape ideals and eating disorder symptoms among White, Latina, and Black college women. *Cultural Diversity and Ethnic Minority Psychology*, *16*(2), 135–143. https://doi.org/10.1037/a0018671.

Grabe, S., & Hyde, J. S. (2006). Ethnicity and body dissatisfaction among women in the United States: A meta-analysis. *Psychological Bulletin*, *132*, 622–640. https://doi.org/10.1037/0033-2909.132.4.622.

Halloran, M. J. (2018). African American health and posttraumatic slave syndrome: A terror management theory account. *Journal of Black Studies*, *50*(1), 45–65. https://doi.org/10.1177/0021934718803737.

Henry, W. J., Butler, D. M., & West, N. W. (2011). Things are not as rosy as they seem: Psychological issues of contemporary Black college women. *Journal of College Student Retention, 13*(2), 137–153.

Hesse-Biber, S., Livinstone, S., Ramirez, D., Barko, E. B., & Johnson, A. L. (2010). Racial identity and body image among Black female college students attending predominantly White colleges. *Sex Roles, 63,* 697–711. https://doi.org/10.1007/s11199-010-9862-7.

Howard-Hamilton, M. F. (2003). Theoretical frameworks for African-American women. In M. F. Howard-Hamilton (Ed.), *Meeting the needs of African American women: New directions for student services* (pp. 19–28). San Francisco, CA: Jossey-Bass.

Kelch-Oliver, K., & Ancis, J. R. (2011). Black women's body image: An analysis of culture-specific influences. *Women & Therapy, 34,* 345–358. https://doi.org/10.1080/02703149.

Kelly, N. R., Cotter, E. W., & Mazzeo, S. E. (2012). Eating Disorder Examination Questionnaire (EDE-Q): Norms for Black women. *Eating Behaviors, 13,* 429–432. https://doi.org/10.1016/j.eatbeh.2012.09.001.

Kelly, N. R., Mitchell, K. S., Gow, R. W., Trace, S. E., Lydecker, J. A., Blair, C. E., & Mazzeo, S. (2012). An evaluation of the reliability and construct validity of eating disorder measures in White and Black women. *Psychological Assessment, 24*(3), 608–618. https://doi.org/10.1037/a0026457.

Kempa, M. L., & Thomas, A. J. (2000). Culturally sensitive assessment and treatment of eating disorders. *Eating Disorders: The Journal of Treatment & Prevention, 8,* 17–30.

Merritt, M. M., Bennett, G. G., Williams, R. B., Edwards, C. L., & Sollers, J. J. (2006). Perceived racism and cardiovascular reactivity and recovery to personally relevant stress. *Health Psychology, 25*(3), 364–369.

Moran, M., & Wilkins, E. C. (2013). *Eating disorders: An epidemic.* Louisiana Ave, FL: Blue Horizon Eating Disorder Services, LLC.

National Eating Disorders Association. (2005). *Eating disorders in women of color: Explanations and implications.* Retrieved from www.nationaleatingdisorders.org.

National Eating Disorders Association. (2018). *Health consequences.* Retrieved from www.nationaleatingdisorders.org.

Quinlan, C. (2016). 5 things that make it hard to be a student at a mostly white college. *Think Process.*

Rohde, P., Ichikawa, L., Simon, G. E., Ludman, E. J., Linde, J. A., Jeffery, R. W., & Operskalski, B. H. (2008). Associations of child sexual and physical abuse with obesity and depression in middle-aged women. *Child Abuse & Neglect, 32,* 878–887.

Sanchez-Hucles, J. (2001). Staying the course: Psychotherapy in the African-American community. *Quest, 4*(2).

Sedlak, A. J., Mettenberg, J., Basena, M., Petta, I., McPherson, K., Greene, A., & Li, S. (2010). *Fourth national incidence study of child abuse and neglect (nis-4): Report to congress, executive summary.* Washington, DC: U.S. Department of Health and Human Services, Administration for Children and Families.

Shaw, H., Ramirez, L., Trost, A., Randall, P., & Stice, E. (2004). Body image and eating disturbances across ethnic groups: More similarities than differences. *Psychology of Addictive Behaviors, 18*(1), 12–18. https://doi.org/10.1037/0893-164X.18.1.12.

Taylor, J. Y., Caldwell, C. H., Baser, R. E., Matusko, N., Faison, J. S., & Jackson, J. S. (2013). Classification and correlates of eating disorders among Blacks: Findings from the National Survey of American Life. *Journal of Health Care and Underserved, 24*(1), 289–310. https://doi.org/10.1353/hpu2013.0027.

Willie, S. S. (2003). *Acting Black: College, identity, and the performance of race.* New York: Routledge.

Part I
Perspectives and Politics

1   Eating Because We're Hungry or Because Something's Eating Us?

Charlynn Small

Introduction

As stated in the introduction to this book, though more attention is directed at underrepresented groups who grapple with eating disorders, for several reasons, many health care providers still fail to recognize these disturbances in Black women. One important reason for this failure is many practitioners fear asking the difficult questions[1] concerning racial differences and identity issues that can be instrumental in helping them recognize and understand potentially mediating factors in the development of eating disorders in Black women. Eating disorders are not recognized in this group often enough, largely because health care providers are not talking about them.

Undeniably, these topics can be quite difficult to broach. However, having the conversations or not having them can potentially impact Black women's decisions to seek treatment or determine whether practitioners will properly diagnose Black women with eating disorders. In her autobiographical memoir, *Hunger*, Roxane Gay (2017, p. 201) wrote the following:

> It's hard for thin people to know how to talk to fat people about their bodies, whether their opinions are solicited or not. I get that, but it's insulting to pretend I am not fat or to deny my body and its reality. It's insulting to think I am somehow unaware of my physical appearance. And it's insulting to assume that I am ashamed of myself for being fat, no matter how close to the truth that might be.

Similar to how Gay conveys that it is hard for thin people to talk to fat people about their bodies, it is often hard for White and some other non-Black therapists to talk to Black women about their lived experiences as Black women. Consider, for example, the juxtaposition of Gay's quote and the following adaptation:

> It's hard for **White** people to know how to talk to **Black** people about their bodies, whether their opinions are solicited or not. I get that, but it's insulting to pretend I am not **Black** or to deny my **skin** and its reality. It's

insulting to think I am somehow unaware of my physical appearance. And it's insulting to assume that I am ashamed of myself for being **Black**, no matter how close to the truth that might be.

In the adaptation of Gay's affirmation, certain words are different, but the connotations and the context are similar. Gay's words were contextualized to accentuate the following dictum: To effectively treat Black women, health care providers must engage them in very difficult, often uncomfortable discussions about their bodies. As a Black woman and a licensed clinical psychologist who treats Black women with eating disorders, I am well aware that the hard questions must be asked of Black women, because often the answers are precursors to or are related to the development of their eating disorders. I must also note that the task of overcoming personal, racial, and systemic biases that act as barriers to effective work with Black women is not limited to White or non-Black professionals. Research suggests that Black clients can present unique challenges for Black practitioners (Goode-Cross & Grim, 2014; Goode-Cross, 2011). Similar physical appearances and other shared variables such as religious or social affiliations may facilitate or enhance the therapeutic alliance among same-race dyads (Goode-Cross & Grim, 2014). However, practitioners may differ from their clients in important ways (i.e., social class, country of origin, gender differences, political ideology, generational status, etc.) that could influence the dynamics of the therapeutic relationship in less favorable ways (Goode-Cross, 2011).

Colorism

Disordered eating and food rituals can result when emotional eating is habitually used to cope with macroaggressive and microaggressive events, colorism and its impact on Black women's bodies, acculturative stress, and other traumas. Research suggests that issues of colorism are remnants of the institution of slavery and contribute to the intergenerational trauma that began with the systematic dehumanization of African slaves (DeGruy, 2017). White slave holders perpetuated skin tone stratification when they created a skin tone hierarchy among Black people that determined the tasks they completed and where they completed them. The system of race hierarchy that was created and the tasks associated with the particular levels or tiers of skin color carried a relative status and advantages that remain as powerful in sculpting our current existence as they did centuries ago (DiAngelo, 2018; DeGruy, 2017). Issues of colorism and related traumas are sources of intense debate and hurt feelings for many Black women. Yet their relevance to a client's presenting concerns tends to frequently be overlooked by White therapists, and therefore are not processed. White therapists and other non-Black therapists who have limited exposure to persons from other races and cultures would not automatically be aware of the differences among Black women. Also, depending on some non-Black therapists' educational histories or other demographics, it is even more unlikely that they would have knowledge of the significance of skin color, hair differences, and body issues among Black women.

Are Black women eating because we're hungry or because something's eating us? So much of our lived experience is about colorism: rejection and mistreatment (Jackson-Lowman, 2013) and prejudice and discrimination against persons with dark skin by persons with fair skin—usually among people within the same racial or ethnic group (Hunter, 2007). Many Black people have the propensity to treat those with darker skin unjustly or less favorably than those with lighter skin. That is colorism at its core. This skin color stratification (Okazawa-Rey, Robinson, & Ward, 1987) is described as an expression of internalized racism (Association of Black Psychologists, 2013) and self-hate (Robinson, 2011). One example of how deep-rooted colorism operates is when Black people pose a question such as the following one: Is Vanessa Williams's fair complexion prettier or somehow better than Lupita Nyong'o's rich, dark-chocolate complexion? Many Black people firmly believe that the answer to this question is yes. While it is true that Vanessa Williams did win Miss America because she was indeed strikingly impressive, some Black people believe she won because she was strikingly impressive in a "White way," for she possesses fair skin, blondish hair, light-colored eyes, and at that time (1983), a petite frame.

Thus, in addition to societal racism and bigotry, for many of us, our lived experiences often include daily messages from our own groups that influence their members to deduce: "There's something wrong with me." These messages that are typically experienced from a very early age impact developing self-concepts and identity. Evidence of the negative impact of these messages on Black children's self-esteem and identity were demonstrated in the seminal Doll Test studies conducted by Kenneth and Mamie Clark during the 1940s. The Clarks found that as the result of "prejudice, discrimination, and segregation," these children experienced feelings of inferiority and a damaged sense of self-esteem (Clark & Clark, 1947). Low self-esteem has long been determined to be one of many significant underlying triggers involved in the development of disordered eating patterns.

Hair

Black women's hair has forever been controversial. It's been studied and examined from almost every conceivable perspective and within many different contexts, e.g., socially, culturally, and politically (Ashe, 2015). Hair texture and style have always elicited strong feelings and dialogue in Black communities. From the slave owners' derogatory insults of "burrhead" to Madam CJ Walker's improvement of the hot comb in the early 1900s to straighten our naturally curly tresses to the soulful pride and sophistication with which we donned our Afros, Black hair has always been an enormous deal. There have been as many statements made about Black hair as there have been statements made by Black hair. Black people of all ages have been barred, banned, prevented, or dismissed from public places, employment, and school because of the politics surrounding their hair. In a horrifying, mean-spirited act of what many have decried as racism and an abuse of power, New Jersey high school wrestler Andrew Johnson was forced to have his dreadlocks cut off during a match (NBC, 2019). There have been numerous occurrences of Black children being suspended from school or otherwise penalized because their natural hairstyles violated dress codes, as was the case with 12-year-old Florida student Vanessa VanDyke, whose "puffy" hair was deemed a distraction (Kim, 2013). Similarly, 16-year-old twins Mya and Deanna Cook were charged with violating their Boston area school's dress code because of their braided extensions (Lattimore, 2017), as was 11-year-old Faith Fennidy by her Terrytown, Louisiana school (Jacobs & Levin, 2018). These styles have often been called aggressive and unacceptable.[2] Such actions in the US school system perpetuate racial discrimination, education disparities, and trauma in Black communities. These types of experiences can adversely impact children's self-esteem and identity development, leaving them again to assume that "There's something wrong with me." These kinds of acculturative stressors have been linked to an increase in the prevalence of eating disorders in Black adolescents.

Black women's hair has always been a politicized issue that leaves them asking complex questions about their hair: Should we wear our hair naturally curly—the way it grew out of our heads and then coiffed into Afrocentric styles like Afros, braids, twists, and locks? Should it be worn chemically or heat-treated, or with bone-straight, fake hair weaved in, often at the risk of being accused by other Black persons of trying to be, look, or act White? As Black women continue to wrestle daily with identity and pressures to assimilate (Taylor et al., 2013), these issues become significant factors in the development of disordered eating.

Body

Another issue that generates strong emotion among Black women concerns the size and shape of their bodies and body parts, leaving them musing on other aspects of themselves. Do an ample bosom and voluptuous hips make some Black women more desirable than some less well-endowed Black women? Or vice versa? Sociocultural models of eating pathology predict lower risks for disorders in Black women because of their cultures' alleged embrace of voluptuous, more attainable body types, theoretically empowering Black women to resist the need to adopt or strive toward the goal of thinness (Gordon, Castro, Sitnikov, & Holm-Denoma, 2010). However, when fuller-figured, voluptuous Black women exist in environments outside of their Black communities, i.e., on predominantly White college campuses, they often find they are not cherished or desired. In other words, they often learn that a full figure is not the admired standard of beauty. Therefore, these women's risk of developing eating disorders increases as the result of trying to navigate spaces in which they feel devalued (Kempa & Thomas, 2000).

Acculturative Stress

Thompson (1994) found that eating problems evolved as survival strategies and ways women could cope with traumas such as racism. Aside from tensions arising from the myriad differences existing among Black women relating to body image, they face a range of innumerable difficulties affecting them in other ways as well. They continually experience anxiety from the invalidating, intimidating microaggressions (daily verbal or behavioral racial slights or indignities that can be intentional or unintentional; Sue, 2010) of acculturative stress. These assaults often come in the form of complementing our articulation and mastery of the dialect called standard American English, though those skills are not anomalous for Black people. These assaults also come in the form of White fright—when a White woman clutches her purse on an elevator after a Black person enters (Sue, 2010). The subtlety of some of these psychosocial stressors can be difficult to ascertain because of their ambiguity. The uncertainty of whether you have been the recipient of an act of subtle racism can be particularly distressing. Persistent exposure (Kempa & Thomas, 2000; Carter & Muchow, 2017) to these kinds of stressors or even one such surprising encounter can be intensely traumatizing, resulting in recurrent intrusive thoughts, anger, anxiety, depression (Carter & Muchow, 2017), and disordered eating (Taylor et al., 2013). A growing body of literature shows that these types of events can yield profoundly negative effects on the health of victims who are predominately Black. For example, Merritt, Bennett, Williams, Edwards, and Sollers (2006) found significant elevations in blood pressure and heart rate in response to subtle expressions of racial discrimination in a sample of Black men.

Black populations also struggle with the pressures and effects of macroaggressions (participation in or compliance with big systems of oppression) such as redlining and housing discrimination (Rothstein, 2017), school-to-prison pipelines (Seroczynski & Jobst, 2016), restriction of employment opportunities (Quillian, Pager, Hexel, & Midtboen, 2017), and police misconduct and human rights violations (Davis, 2017). Eating disorders can result from patterns of emotional eating to cope with these types of events.

Abuse, Neglect, and Other Trauma Exposure

A large body of research links disordered eating with a history of trauma exposure (Briere & Scott, 2007). This research shows that persons who have experienced abuse, neglect, or other traumas for long periods are particularly vulnerable to the damaging influences of eating disorders (Briere & Scott, 2007). Similarly, evidence shows that persons who report disordered eating symptomology have likely been victimized in some way as children, as adolescents, or as adults (Briere & Scott, 2007). Yet Black women grapple with the traumatizing effects of physical, sexual, and emotional abuse and neglect at alarmingly high rates compared with others. This may be related to findings from a number of studies on health outcomes, disease prevention, and intervention showing that Black children are disproportionately affected by adverse childhood experiences (i.e., sexual, physical, or emotional abuse, household dysfunction, neglect, etc.) more often than White and other non-Black children (Maguire-Jack, Font, & Dillard, 2019; Whiteside-Mansell, McKelvey, Saccente, & Selig, 2019; Coker Ross, 2019; Sacks & Murphey, 2018; Slopen et al., 2016). The clinical picture is quite complex when eating disorders are the result of childhood trauma. When abuse occurs early and continues over long periods, specific sequelae including sadness, anxiety, depression, distorted thinking, and nonsuicidal self-injury can be the result (Briere & Scott, 2007), and the survivor attempts to manage the distress in various ways (Briere & Spinazzola, 2005). When internal capacities for coping with negative emotions and images of trauma-related stimuli are depleted, survivors often rely on binging and purging to self-soothe (Briere & Scott, 2006) in the moment. Binging may numb painful thoughts and feelings (Felitti, 1985), while purging serves to relieve any shame, guilt, and bloating associated with binging (Briere & Scott, 2007). The behaviors occur in a cycle, reinforcing and maintaining the disorder (Briere & Scott, 2007). Often with children, only binging occurs without purging in an attempt to attain positive feelings—the opposite of pain and hurt. In many cases, this may lead to excessive weight gain and other associated health concerns. Shame, a distorted body image, self-criticism, and the need to be in control, perfect, and thin are also direct effects of abuse and are frequently associated with food restriction (Garner & Magana, 2006). These conditions underscore the importance of completing a thorough history that includes asking some very tough questions.

Violence and Injustice

Because of the intersectionality (e.g., wives, mothers, friends, employees, oppressed, underpaid, etc.) of Black women, we experience stress exponentially. As such, it is entirely plausible that our experience of eating disorders is also mediated by a number of other environmental stress factors such as abuse (NEDA, 2018) and violence that sometimes stem from police brutality. This appeared to be the case for Atatiana Jefferson, who was fatally shot by police during a reported welfare check while babysitting her 8-year-old nephew in her Fort Worth home (*The New York Post*, 2019). Similarly, Botham Jean was fatally wounded by police officer Amber Guyger, who reportedly confused his home with her own (*The Washington Post*, 2018). These factors increase Black women's vulnerability to eating disorders (NEDA, 2018).

A young White law professor facilitated a lecture about the laws that law-abiding citizens should know. The speaker began by asking, "How many of you believe the police can stop you whenever they want, for any reason they want?" Half of the members of the audience raised their hands. They were all Black. The professor explained to everyone, even to those who looked incredulous that the respondents reacted as they did, "because that's been their lived experience." Black people in the US do not feel safe.

While the law professor recognizes the traumatic lived experiences of Black people in America, some educators are still miseducating students about race relations in America. For instance, a non-Black instructor once told my daughter's driver education class that they did not need to fear police officers when they are stopped by them because officers would see them as their own children. My daughter and the other Black student in the class wondered whether they had misunderstood what their instructor had stated. Perhaps their responses did not reflect their own lived experience, but they witness police brutality in the media almost every day:

> In the digital age . . . images of police violence have never been as widespread. No longer confined to mainstream news coverage, these incidents are on our Facebook and Twitter feeds instantly and continually: police firing at Walter Scott as he bolts away; five-year-old Kodi Gaines telling his mother "They trying to kill us" moments before police shot and killed her and wounded him in their apartment; Eric Garner pleading "I can't breathe" as New York City officers gripped him in a chokehold. Yet because the images of police violence are so pervasive, they inflict a unique harm on viewers, particularly African Americans, who see themselves and those they love in these fatal encounters. This recognition becomes a form of violence in and of itself—and even more so when justice is denied.
>
> (Gregory, 2019)

The examples that Gregory (2019) points out in her article and my own interactions with police officers compel me to drill my children again and again on how to behave and how *not* to behave during any police encounter. My children are tall, dark-brown-skinned, Afro-wearing teenagers who fit the profile of Black children who are often stopped by police officers. I also instruct my children on how to interact with police officers just as my father who was a police officer did over 50 years ago when he taught my oldest brother how to respond if stopped by an officer. "Keep your hands in plain sight and make no sudden moves," he cautioned. A decade later, he provided the same instruction when he taught my other brother and me to drive.

This drilling, cautioning, and admonition is part of the impact of the same trauma experienced from one generation to another. These strategies and coping mechanisms are part of the adaptive ways we understand and cope with our existence, past and present. Equally important, for some women, if their children are not home when expected, they eat. Binge eating is often done to soothe, to allay, to assuage fears, and to reduce anxiety (Felitti, 1985). Yet many Black women are not treated or are not properly treated for eating disorders because clinicians do not ask the hard questions.

In a study examining the impact of client race on clinicians' detection of eating disorders, clinicians were presented with identical case studies demonstrating eating disorder symptoms in White, Latinx, and Black women. The clinicians were asked to identify whether the women's eating patterns were problematic. Forty-four percent identified the White women's behavior as problematic; 41% identified the Latinx women's behavior as problematic, and 17% identified the Black women's behavior as problematic (Gordon, Brattole, Wingate, & Joiner, 2006). Results of the study also showed that the clinicians were also less likely to recommend that the Black women should receive professional help (Gordon et al., 2006). This outcome was perhaps mediated in part by inadequate assessment.

Equity and Social Justice

Black women are hungry for equity in a pervasive manner. They continue to be among the lowest-paid groups across every sector of the US workforce, from academe to housekeeping, with pay averaging only 48 to 68 cents for every dollar paid to White, non-Latinx men (U.S. Census Bureau, 2018; AAUW, 2015). The National Center for Education Statistics (2019) reported that Black women held only 3% of the 1.5 million faculty positions in degree-granting postsecondary institutions, compared to 41% held by White men and 35% held by White women. In her Hechinger Report article (2016) detailing explanations for why colleges do not hire more faculty of color, Marybeth Gasman's short answer is that "We simply don't want them." The University of Pennsylvania professor offers some compelling evidence to support her assertion, including institutions' use of the words "low quality," which is usually code for "The candidate didn't obtain her PhD from an elite institution." In further unpacking this assumption, one is reminded that an adequate amount of social capital is required for matriculation at elite institutions (Gasman, 2016). This is a factor designed and driven in part by systemic racism that serves far too often as a barrier for people of color.

A related concern affecting Black women in academe is the notion of epistemic exclusion. Settles, Buchanan, and Dotson (2018) define epistemic exclusion as the perception of certain scholars and certain types of research as lacking value and legitimacy. It is often research that addresses issues affecting particular underrepresented groups (i.e., Black women) that is scrutinized in terms of its value and legitimacy. When scholars who attempt to advance the devalued research happen to be members of those groups, epistemic exclusion operates as another barrier that prohibits their participation in the academic process (Settles et al., 2018).

Bell (1997, p. 1) explains that the primary goal of social justice is "full and equal participation of all groups in a society that is mutually shaped to meet their needs," and she further states that it is one in which "the distribution of resources is equitable and all members are physically and psychologically safe and secure." Feminist scholars view the problem of eating disorders as one in which the real expression is the need for control in social positions of little power (Nasser, Katzman, & Gordon, 2001). Far too often, Black women find themselves in positions of little power. They endure the struggles associated with multiple intersectionalities (e.g., gender, race, class, and discrimination), increasing their risks and vulnerabilities to illnesses and conditions such as eating disorders.

Cultural Competence

In exploring the process of cultural competence, it is important to begin with what cultural competence is not. Cultural competence is not acknowledging that people are different. Nor is it taking a color-blind approach to assessment and treatment when working with people from different populations. Williams (2011) asserts, "A colorblind approach merely relieves the therapist of his or her obligation to address racial differences and difficulties" (2011). Brooks (2014) accentuates the problem that occurs when therapists do not see color: "By taking a colorblind approach, you end up rendering invisible and not meaningful, what actually is very important." This is particularly true when treating Black women with eating disorders, as the truly unique part of treating these women is in addressing race and identity issues, because identity really is at the heart of eating disorders (Brooks, 2014).

In my other life as an urban school psychologist, whenever I mentored newly graduated, idealistic young White persons who had joined our team, I would drive them around the community and show them the dwellings of some of the children we served. I would share about some of their daily lived experiences, because socially, they were worlds apart from those students. Thus, they needed some exposure to those students' backgrounds. In this way, they could gain an understanding of the qualitative manner in which some Black males obtained their quantitative scores on the WISC (Wechsler, 1949). Contrary to popular belief, Black males are not intellectually deficient in every case; hardly ever, in fact. Sometimes their responses are value laden, for they are often motivated by survival. That is, while their responses may not have been the ones deemed obviously correct, they may have been the ones that made the most sense to them in terms of securing their basic needs (i.e., safety, food, etc.). While the examiner is ethically obligated to report the obtained score, the psychoeducational assessment is more than just testing and measurement. Based on the results of the evaluation, the competent examiner will be able to provide an accurate assessment of students' intellectual ability and their ability to benefit from classroom instruction. Thus, my brief tours through the community were designed to provide some additional perspective and context, intended to aid in the process of linking assessment with intervention and to help prepare novice psychologists for the interactions they would have with Black students. What the new team members learned was that more often than not, their lives were vastly different from those of the students we served. They shared that their exposure in this way increased their sensitivity and appreciation for the potential ways in which culture and circumstances can impact one's life, whether positive or negative.

Engaging cultural competence, among other concepts, reflects a practitioner's decision to accept the responsibility of acknowledging and respecting the traditions and values of the persons she serves (Jongen, McCalman, & Bainbridge, 2018; U.S. Department of Health and Human Services, Office of Minority Health [HHS, OMH], 2013) and working to avoid stereotypes. Culturally sensitive practitioners appreciate the value in gaining new cultural experiences and demonstrate a willingness and the ability to engage within the different communities of persons they serve. My community engagement tours served as one of Havighurst's (1953) teachable moments to help facilitate this engagement. Culturally sensitive practitioners also understand that successful engagement with diverse clients requires improving their sensitivities to their own cultural values and biases. Without a commitment to learning more about their own individual cultures, health care providers can be influenced by both conscious and unconscious biases, yielding misdiagnoses and poor treatment outcomes (HHS, OMH, 2013). Additionally, providers may offend clients by unintentionally saying or doing something considered or interpreted by clients as culturally inappropriate or insensitive. An increase in awareness of self can yield new sensitivities that can help prevent misunderstandings or actions that would hinder or adversely affect the establishment of rapport and trust and that would increase provision of more culturally responsive assessments and treatment plans (HHS, OMH, 2013). Useful for aiding in the creation and maintenance of successful and effective therapeutic alliances, cultural competence is a purposeful, ever-changing developmental process that requires dedicated practitioners' responsibility and promise of continued learning (HHS, OMH, 2013). Two of the most important components in this process that can further encourage development of trusting, therapeutic alliances are linguistic competency and cultural humility.

Linguistic Competency

Linguistic competency is the ability of practitioners to productively and constructively work with clients, according to HHS, OMH (2013). To do so, clients must be able to easily participate in exchanges of information without apprehension. Plain language is the most easily understandable language. In cases in which clients may present different communication challenges including limited literacy skills, various disabilities, or languages that differ from practitioners' languages, practitioners must be prepared to present information through different modalities (Jongen et al., 2018; HHS, OMS, 2013). Failure to address cultural and linguistic differences can result in negative outcomes including miscommunication (Cass et al., 2002), mistrust, and confusion. Because health care facilities and practitioners should have policies (Cross et al., 1989), procedures, and dedicated resources in place (National Center for Cultural Competence [NCCC], 2006), ethical concerns may be raised with failure to address these concerns.

For effective communication in many cross-cultural situations, practitioners likely need only be proficient in applying previously acquired skills in different ways or to different groups (HHS, OMH, 2013). For example, it may be necessary for them to conduct additional research, to have additional consultations, to expand their referral lists, or to secure services from sign language interpreters (NCCC, 2006) or other translators (HHS, OMH, 2013). However, as the landscape continues to change for groups of underrepresented persons, it may become necessary for practitioners to make greater changes/additions, both qualitatively and quantitatively, including hiring a multilingual/multicultural staff and printing materials in easy-to-read, picture-and-symbol format, Braille, or enlarged print (NCCC, 2006). Cultural competence simply encourages practitioners to be mindful about useful opportunities for employing these cross-cultural skills and about using them with accuracy.

Cultural Humility

Cultural humility is an interactive approach toward understanding important aspects of one's cultural identity (Hook, Davis, Owen, Worthington, & Utsey, 2013; HHS, OMH, 2013). Cultural humility emphasizes practitioners' availability and efforts to learn about each client's individual background, development, and experiences as opposed to relying on practitioners' own precepts and conclusions. Also, it involves a commitment to continuous self-reflection on practitioners' own blind spots (Russell, Augustin, & Jones, 2017), assumptions, and practices. The quality or state of being humble in the client–practitioner relationship suggests a nullification of any prestige or power imbalance that might exist between the client and the practitioner (Hook et al., 2013). This kind of open-stance approach emphasizes an acceptance of being unfamiliar or previously uninformed about some of the cultural traditions, values, and ceremonial rites and rituals of other groups. This approach is made interactive by a flexibility to learn from and about others and incorporating this new knowledge into our existing frames of reference, and/or replacing long-held, inaccurate assumptions, beliefs, or stereotypes. However, despite this focus on seeking answers rather than making assumptions, underlying this approach remains the fact that "traditional behavioral health practices in the US are infused with Western, European and White-American male, heterosexual ideologies" (HHS, OMH, 2013). This point is underscored in the book *White Fragility* (2018) by Robin DiAngelo, who states that she can get through graduate school, law school, or a teacher-education program "without ever discussing racism" (p. 8). This is a point that begs the question, how then is a therapist so trained able to effectively provide, in this case, eating disorder treatment to persons whose lives have been so unfavorably impacted by that very thing – racism – that so greatly increases our risks for developing the disorder? DiAngelo (2018) also states that she "can be seen as qualified to lead a major or minor organization in this country with no understanding whatsoever of the perspectives or experiences of people of color, few if any relationships with people of color and virtually no ability to engage critically with the topic of race" (p. 8). It is because the particular ideological perspectives of the "traditional behavioral health practices in the US" do not give full consideration to aspects of its citizens' cultural identities that they themselves—in this case Black women—consider most important that an interactive approach to cultural humility is so vital to the health care of Black women.

Asking the Hard Questions

While diversity has been called the "new majority" in the US (Frey, 2015), with its various racial and ethnic groups combined (e.g., all Black, Latinx, Indian, and Asian groups) and comprising a very large portion of the total US population, they account for a significantly smaller proportion of all US mental health care providers (see Figure 1.1). Because of this imbalance, it is likely that persons from a particular minority group seeking mental health care will be treated by someone with a cultural or ethnic background different from their own. For this reason, it is critical that eating disorder treatment providers and trainers of treatment providers seek continued training experiences and opportunities for working with people from different ethnic and cultural groups.

Practitioners must be prepared to ask the hard questions when working with Black women with eating disorders. Racial differences cannot be ignored or dismissed for fear of being called racist or prejudiced, because as stated earlier, the unique part of treating Black women with eating disorders is in addressing race and identity issues (Brooks, 2014). Practitioners must develop lists of

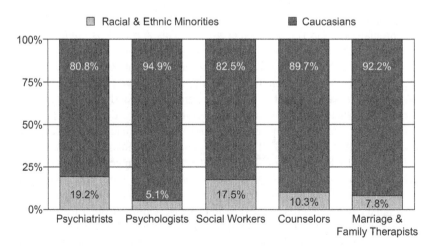

Figure 1.1 Percentage of Racial and Ethnic Minorities vs. White Behavioral Health Care Providers

Source: Substance Abuse and Mental Health Services Administration (2013).

questions or topics to facilitate processing these important issues with Black women and similar lists for their other culturally diverse clients, and they must work to become comfortable initiating them. Some of those questions[3] include:

- What is most important to you about your culture/ethnicity?
- What has it been like for you growing up in a culture of racism?
- What influence has your race/ethnicity played in shaping your body image and beauty standards?
- What influence has the region where you grew up and/or where you currently live played in shaping your body image and beauty standards?
- What influences have school or work settings played in shaping your body image and beauty standards?
- If you are spiritual or religious, what influence has your spirituality or religion played in shaping your body image and beauty standards?
- What influence has your socio-economic class played in shaping your body image and beauty standards?
- What influence has your gender and/or sexual orientation played in shaping your body image and beauty standards?
- What influence has hair (your own, that of others around you, or that of others you have observed) played in shaping your body image and beauty standards?
- What influence has body shape and weight (your own, that of others around you, or that of others you have observed) played in shaping your body image and beauty standards?

Practitioners should also consider some other general questions such as the following, adapted from measures of Daily Acculturative Stress Experiences (Williams, Yu, Jackson, & Anderson, 1997):

- Have you ever been told, "You're really pretty for a dark-skinned girl"?
- Have you ever been treated less courteously than others?
- Have you ever been treated with less respect than others?
- Have you ever received poor service at restaurants or in stores compared with others?
- Have you ever been treated by people as if they think you are unintelligent?
- Have you ever been asked, "Where did you ever find jeans that size?"
- Have you ever been treated by people as if they were afraid of you?
- Have you ever been treated by people as if they think you are dishonest?
- Have you ever been treated by people as if they think they are better than you are?
- Have you ever been called offensive names or been otherwise insulted?
- Have you ever been threatened or harassed?
- Have you ever been followed around in a store?
- Have you ever had someone clutch their purse or wallet when you enter an elevator or other enclosed space?

- Have you ever had someone move to the other side of the street when they see you approach?
- Have you ever noticed someone lock their car doors as you walked by?
- Have you ever been told, "You're so articulate?"
- Have you ever been told, "You speak very good English?"
- Have you ever been told, "I don't see you as Black?"
- Have you ever been asked, "No, you're White, aren't you?"
- Have you ever had your hair touched by someone without your permission?
- Have you ever been expected to speak for all Black people?
- Have you ever been told, "I just love Soul food," based on someone's perception of your ancestry?

Other general questions should also be considered, such as the following measures of macroaggressive experiences (adapted from Williams et al., 1997):

- Have you ever been fired from a job unjustly at any time in your life?
- Have you ever been refused a job for unjust reasons?
- Have you ever been unfairly denied a job promotion?
- Have you ever been stopped, searched, questioned, harassed, threatened, or physically abused by police without provocation?
- Have you ever been discouraged by a teacher, counselor, or advisor from continuing your education or pursuing study in a particular field or discipline?
- Have you ever been unjustly denied the opportunity to purchase or rent a house or apartment in a certain neighborhood by a landlord or realtor?
- Have you ever been denied home-loan funds or insurance because of where you live(d)?
- Have you ever been unjustly denied any type of bank loan?
- Have you ever received service for which you were expected to pay that was significantly substandard compared to what others received?
- Have you ever lived in a community with significantly substandard schools?
- Have you ever been unjustly denied any type of club, union, or professional membership?
- Have you ever lived in a community with food deserts?
- Have you ever lived in a community undergoing gentrification?
- Have you ever been unjustly affected by the "school-to-prison pipeline"?

Having these discussions with Black clients is vital to helping them heal. Race and ethnicity are significant parts of who they are. However, these conversations remain difficult and uncomfortable for many White or other non-Black practitioners for many different reasons (Duncan, 2005). System-level barriers to these discussions, for instance, include the very real fear of deportation by persons eligible for the Deferred Action for Childhood Arrivals (DACA) Program or other persons with undocumented citizenship status (Brindis et al.,

2014). Problems with communication and other difficulties negotiating health care organizations frequently serve as barriers to these discussions, leading or contributing to the cultural norm of delaying to seek care for physical and mental health issues for some (Brindis et al., 2014). Other barriers to these critical discussions include attempts to hide behind treatment specialties that may not relate to Black women's issues specifically and scheduling referrals to Black staff members (Duncan, 2005) or other practitioners because of fear or disinterest. However, as noted, it is very important to consider that part of the reluctance of some White practitioners to address the concerns of these groups is often related to their training in institutions that emphasize Eurocentric values that may be quite different from those of other cultures.

Ruptures in the Therapeutic Alliance

Successful treatment outcomes with Black women with eating disorders begins with a practitioner's willingness, comfort, and ability to initiate dialogue on these very sensitive issues (Cardemil & Battle, 2003; Sanchez-Hucles, 2001). However, in as much as these issues cannot be minimized or marginalized out of fear of saying something insensitive or offensive, care must be taken to raise these concerns within the proper timing and context (Duncan, 2005). Otherwise, there is the potential for misunderstandings that can lead to ruptures in the therapeutic alliance (Shahid, Finn, & Thompson, 2009). Safran, Muran, and Eubanks-Carter (2011) define such ruptures as episodes of tension or breakdown in the collaborative client–therapist relationship. These kinds of breaches can occur following a therapist's assumptions about a client's cultural, ethnic (Sanchez-Hucles, 2001), or gender identity; or if a therapist's nonverbal—or verbal—behaviors communicate their privilege, authority, control (Rodriguez, 2016) or other power differential; or if a practitioner is or seems dismissive of or demonstrates failure to understand or minimizes the impact of racism on their client. This kind of tension can result in premature termination or other withdrawal ruptures in the therapeutic alliance. Paramount at this point is that the practitioner acknowledges the client's feelings and then works actively with the client to repair the rupture. Rodriguez (2016) suggests that these moments should be viewed as a gift in treatment, because they offer opportunities to grow. If the practitioner has a good understanding of what was upsetting or offensive to the client, the practitioner will have a better perspective of the client's struggles in the world (Rodriguez, 2016) and will be better able to assist the client with problem solving.

An awareness and consideration of historical oppression, colorism, class, gender identity, religion, and the pain of past relationships—therapeutic or otherwise—are essential in the treatment of Black women with eating disorders. These complexities will enter the therapeutic space with these clients. A therapeutic approach emphasizing an understanding that each woman is different and acknowledging the importance of a comprehensive, culturally sensitive assessment are key to the effectiveness of treatment.

Notes

1. A list of potential questions that practitioners might ask Black women is discussed in this chapter.
2. For more information about the connection between Black children's hair and trauma, see "Black Girl Sent Home From School Over Hair Extensions" (2018) at www.nytimes.com/2018/08/21/us/black-student-extensions-louisiana.html, "When Black Hair Violates The Dress Code" (2017) at www.npr.org/sections/ed/2017/07/17/534448313/when-black-hair-violates-the-dress-code, and "Florida School Threatens to Expel Student Over 'Natural Hair'" (2013), http://www.msnbc.com/the-last-word-94
3. Some questions were adapted from Brooks (2014).

References

AAUW. (2015). *Baccalaureate and beyond longitudinal study (2008/12)*. U.S. Department of Education, Institute of Education Sciences, National Center for Education Statistics.

Ashe, B. (2015). *Twisted: My dreadlock chronicles*. Evanston, IL: Agate Bolden.

Association of Black Psychologists. (2013). *On dark girls*. Retrieved from http://static.oprah.com/pdf/dark-girls.pdf.

Bell, L. A. (1997). Theoretical foundations for social justice education. In M. Adams, L. A. Bell, & P. Griffin (Eds.), *Teaching for diversity and social justice: A sourcebook* (pp. 3–15). New York: Routledge.

Briere, J., & Scott, C. (2006). *Principles of trauma therapy: A guide to symptoms, evaluation, and treatment*. Thousand Oaks, CA: Sage Publications.

Briere, J., & Scott, C. (2007). Assessment of trauma symptoms in eating-disordered populations. *The Journal of Treatment & Prevention, 15*(4), 347–358. https://doi.org/0.1080/10640260701454360.

Briere, J., & Spinazzola, J. (2005). Phenomenology and psychological assessment of complex posttraumatic states. *Journal of Traumatic Stress, 18*(5), 401–412.

Brindis, C. D., Jacobs, K., Lucia, L., Pourat, N., Raymond-Flesch, M., Siemons, R., & Talamantes, E. (2014). *Realizing the Dream for Californians Eligible for Deferred Action for Childhood Arrivals (DACA): Health needs and access to health care*. Retrieved from http://laborcenter.berkeley.edu.

Brooks, G. (2014). *Multicultural perspectives . . . Why should I care?* The 24th Annual Renfrew Center Foundation Conference for Professionals—Feminist Relational Perspectives and Beyond: The "Practice" of Practice, Philadelphia, Pennsylvania.

Cardemil, E. V., & Battle, C. L. (2003). Guess who's coming to therapy? Getting comfortable with conversations about race and ethnicity in psychotherapy. *Professional Psychology: Research and Practice, 34*(3), 278–286.

Carter, R. T., & Muchow, C. (2017). Construct validity of the Race-Based Traumatic Stress Syndrome Scale and tests of measurement equivalence. *Psychological Trauma: Theory, Research, Practice and Policy, 9*(6), 688–695. http://doi.org/10.1037/tra0000256.

Cass, A., Lowell, A., Christie, M., Snelling, P. L., Flack, M., Marrnganyin, B., & Brown, I. (2002). Sharing the true stories: Improving communication between Aboriginal patients and healthcare workers. *Medical Journal of Australia, 176*(10), 466.

Clark, K. B., & Clark, M. K. (1947). The development of consciousness of the self and the emergence of racial identification in Negro children. *Journal of Social Psychology, 10*, 591–599.

Coker Ross, C. (2019). The impact of intergenerational or historical trauma on eating disorders in African Americans. *iaedp foundation Membership Spotlight.*

Cross, T. L., Bazron, B. J., & Dennis, K. W. (1989).

Toward a culturally competent system of care.

National Institute of Mental Health, Child and Adolescent Service Program (CASSP) Technical Assistance Center, Georgetown University Child Development Center.

Davis, A. J. (Ed.). (2017). *Policing the Black man.* New York: Pantheon Books.

DeGruy, J. A. (2017). *Post traumatic slave syndrome: America's legacy of enduring injury and healing.* Portland, OR: Joy DeGruy Publications.

DiAngelo, R. (2018). *White fragility.* Boston, MA: Beacon Press.

Duncan, L. E. (2005). Overcoming biases to effectively serve African-American college students: A call to the profession. *College Student Journal, 39*(4), 01463934.

Felitti, V. (1985). *Adverse childhood experience study.* San Diego, CA: Department of Preventive Medicine, Kaiser Permanente/Centers for Disease Control.

Frey, W. H. (2015). In the U.S., diversity is the new majority. *Los Angeles Times.* Retrieved from www.latimes.com/opinion/op-ed/la-oe-0310-frey-no-racial-majority-america-20150310-story.html.

Garner, D. M., & Magana, C. (2006). Cognitive vulnerability to anorexia nervosa. In L. B. Alloy & J. H. Riskind (Eds.), *Cognitive vulnerability to emotional disorders* (pp. 365–403). Mahwah, NJ: Lawrence Erlbaum Associates Publishers.

Gasman, M. (2016). *The five things no one will tell you about why colleges don't hire more faculty of color: It's time for higher ed to change its ways.* The Hechinger Report.

Gay, R. (2017). *Hunger.* New York: HarperCollins.

Goode-Cross, D. T. (2011). Same difference: Black therapists' experience of same-race therapeutic dyads. *Professional Psychology: Research and Practice, 42*(5), 368–374. https://doi.org/10.1037/a0025520.

Goode-Cross, D. T., & Grim, K. A. (2014). "An unspoken level of comfort": Black therapists' experiences working with Black clients. *Journal of Black Psychology, 42*(1), 29–53. https://doi.org/10.1177/0095798414552103.

Gordon, K. H., Brattole, M. M., Wingate, L. R., & Joiner, T. E. (2006). The impact of client race on clinician detection of eating disorders. *Behavior Therapy, 37*(4), 319–325. https://doi.org/10.1016/j.beth.2005.12.002.

Gordon, K. H., Castro, Y., Sitnikov, L., & Holm-Denoma, J. M. (2010). Cultural body shape ideals and eating disorder symptoms among White, Latina, and Black college women. *Cultural Diversity and Ethnic Minority Psychology, 16*(2), 135–143. https://doi.org/10.1037/a0018671.

Gregory, K. (2019). Killing us softly: How videos of police brutality traumatize African Americans and undermine the search for justice. *The New Republic.*

Havighurst, R. J. (1953). *Human development and education.* New York: McKay.

Hook, J. N., Davis, D. E., Owen, J., Worthington, E. L., Jr., & Utsey, S. O. (2013). Cultural humility: Measuring openness to culturally diverse clients. *Journal of Counseling Psychology, 60*(3), 353–366. https://doi.org/10.1037/a0032595.

Hunter, M. (2007). The persistent problem of colorism: Skin tone, status, and inequality. *Sociology Compass, 1*(1), 237–254.

Jackson-Lowman, H. (2013). An analysis of the impact of Eurocentric concepts of beauty on the lives of African American women. In H. Jackson-Lowman (Ed.) *African American women: Living at the crossroads of race, gender, class, and culture* (pp. 155–172). San Diego, CA: Cognella Academic Publishing.

Jacobs, J., & Levin, D. (2018). *Black girl sent home from school over hair extensions.* Retrieved from www.nytimes.com/2018/08/21/us/black-student-extensions-louisiana. html.

Jongen, C., McCalman, J., & Bainbridge, R. (2018). Health workforce cultural competency interventions: A systematic scoping review. *BMC Health Services Research, 18*(1), 232. https://doi.org/ 10.1186/s12913-018-3001-5.

Kempa, M. L., & Thomas, A. J. (2000). Culturally sensitive assessment and treatment of eating disorders. *Eating Disorders: Journal of Treatment & Prevention, 8,* 17–30.

Kim, C. (2013). *Florida school threatens to expel student over "natural hair."* Retrieved from http://www.msnbc.com/the-last-word-94.

Lattimore, K. (2017). *When Black hair violates the dress code.* Retrieved from www.npr. org/sections/ed/2017/07/17/534448313/when-black-hair-violates-the-dress-code.

Maguire-Jack, K., Font, S. A., & Dillard, R. (2019). Child protective services decision-making: The role of children's race and county factors. *American Journal of Orthopsychiatry.* Advance online publication. https://doi.org/10.1037/ort0000388.

Merritt, M. M., Bennett, G. G., Williams, R. B., Edwards, C. L., & Sollers, J. J. (2006). Perceived racism and cardiovascular reactivity and recovery to personally relevant stress. *Health Psychology, 25*(3), 364–369. https://doi.org/10.1037/0278-6133.25.3.364.

Nasser, M., Katzman, M. A., & Gordon, R. A. (Eds.). (2001). *Eating disorders and cultures in transition.* New York: Taylor & Francis.

National Center for Cultural Competence. (2006). Cultural and linguistic competence policy assessment. Georgetown University Center for Child and Human Development.

National Center for Education Statistics. (2019). *The condition of education: Characteristics of postsecondary faculty.* Retrieved from https://nces.ed.gov/programs/coe/ indicator_csc.asp.

National Eating Disorders Association. (2018). *People of color and eating disorders.* Retrieved from https://www.nationaleatingdisorders.org/people-color-and-eating-disorders.

NBC. (2019). *N.J. wrestler forced to cut dreadlocks still targeted over hair, lawyer says.* Retrieved from www.nbcnews.com/news/nbcblk/n-j-wrestler-forced-cut-dreadlocks-still-targeted-over-hair-n957116.

The New York Post. (2019, October 13). Woman killed by cop in own home was baby-sitting 8-year old nephew.

Okazawa-Rey, M., Robinson, T., & Ward, J. V. (1987). Black women and the politics of skin color and hair. *Women & Therapy, 6*(1–2), 89–102.

Quillian, L., Pager, D., Hexel, O., & Midtboen, A. H. (2017). Meta-analysis of field experiments shows no change in racial discrimination in hiring over time. *Proceedings of the National Academy of Sciences of the United States of America, 114,* 10870–10875. http://doi.org/10.1073/pnas.1706255114.

Robinson, C. (2011). Hair as race: Why "good hair" may be bad for black females. *Howard Journal of Communications, 22*(4), 358–376.

Rodriguez, A. (2016). Rupture and repair in the therapeutic relationship. *Psyched,* San Francisco.

Rothstein, R. (2017). *The color of law: A forgotten history of how our government segregated America.* New York: Liverlight.

Russell, C. T. S., Augustin, F., & Jones, P. (2017). Perspectives on the importance of integrating diversity into the healthcare administration curriculum: The role of cultural humility. *Journal of Health Administration Education, 34*(3), 371–393.

Sacks, V., & Murphey, D. (2018). *The prevalence of adverse childhood experiences, nationally, by state, and by race or ethnicity.* Retrieved from www.childtrends.org.

Safran, J. D., Muran, J. C., & Eubanks-Carter, C. (2011). Repairing alliance ruptures. *Psychotherapy, 48*(1), 80–87.

Sanchez-Hucles, J. (2001). Staying the course: Psychotherapy in the African-American community. *Quest, 4*(2).

Seroczynski, A. D., & Jobst, A. D. (2016). Latino youth and the school-to-prison pipeline: Addressing issues and achieving solutions. *Hispanic Journal of Behavioral Sciences, 38,* 423–445. https://doi.org/10.1177/0739986316663926.

Settles, I. H., Buchanan, N. T., & Dotson, K. (2018). Scrutinized but not recognized: (In)visibility and hypervisibility experiences of faculty of color. *Journal of Vocational Behavior, 113,* 62–74. https://doi.org/10.1016/j.jvb.2018.06.003.

Shahid, S., Finn, L., & Thompson, S. (2009). Barriers to participation of Aboriginal people in cancer care: Communication in the hospital setting. *Medical Journal of Australia, 190*(10), 574–579. https://doi.org/ 10.5694/j.1326-5377.2009.tb02569.x.

Slopen, N., Shonkoff, J. P., Albert, M. A., Yoshikawa, H., Jacobs, A., Stoltz, R., & Williams, D. R. (2016). Racial disparities in child adversity in the U.S.: Interactions with family immigration history and income. *American Journal of Preventative Medicine, 50*(1), 47–56. https://doi.org/10.1016/j.amepre.2015.06.013.

Substance Abuse and Mental Health Services Administration. (2013). *Report to Congress on the nation's substance abuse and mental health workforce issues.* Retrieved from https://store.samhsa.gov/shin/content/PEP13-RTC-BHWORK/PEP13-RTC-BHWORK.pdf.

Sue, D. W. (2010). *Racial microaggressions in everyday life: Race, gender, and sexual orientation.* Hoboken, NJ: Wiley & Sons.

Taylor, J. Y., Caldwell, C. H., Baser, R. E., Matusko, N., Faison, J. S., & Jackson, J. S. (2013). Classification and correlates of eating disorders among Blacks: Findings from the National Survey of American Life. *Journal of Health Care and Underserved, 24*(1), 289–310. https://doi.org/10.1353/hpu2013.0027.

Thompson, B. W. (1994). *A hunger so wide and so deep: A multiracial view of women's eating problems.* Minneapolis, MN: University of Minnesota Press.

U.S. Census Bureau. (2018). *Current Population Survey, Annual Social and Economic (ASEC) Supplement: Table PINC-05: Work experience in 2017—People 15 years old and over by total money earnings in 2017, age, race, Hispanic origin, sex, and disability status.* Retrieved March 19, 2019 from www.census.gov/data/tables/time-series/demo/income-poverty/cps-pinc/pinc-05.html (Unpublished calculation based on the median earnings for all women and men who worked full time, year-round in 2017; full time is defined as 35 hours a week or more.).

U.S. Department of Health and Human Services, Office of Minority Health (HHS OMH). (2013). National standards for culturally and linguistically appropriate services in health and health care: A blueprint for advancing and sustaining CLAS policy and practice. https://thinkculturalhealth.hhs.gov/pdfs/EnhancedCLASStandardsBlueprint.pdf.

The Washington Post. (2018, September 24). Dallas Police Dept. fires officer who killed Botham Jean in his apartment.https://www.washingtonpost.com/nation/2018/09/24/dallas-police-fire-officer-who-killed-botham-jean-his-apartment/.

Wechsler, D. (1949). *Wechsler Intelligence Scale for Children (WISC).* Pearson Assessments.

Whiteside-Mansell, L., McKelvey, L., Saccente, J., & Selig, J. P. (2019). Adverse childhood experiences of urban and rural preschool children in poverty. *International*

Journal of Environmental Research, Public Health, 16(14), 2623. https://doi.org/10.3390/ijerph16142623.

Williams, D. R., Yu, Y., Jackson, J. S., & Anderson, N. B. (1997). Racial differences in physical and mental health: Socioeconomic status, stress, and discrimination. *Journal of Health Psychology, 2*(3), 335–351. https://doi.org/10.1177/135910539700200305.

Williams, M. (2011). *African-American and psychotherapy: Why race is important.* Retrieved from www.monnicawilliams.com/black-therapist.php.

2 Black Women "Showing Up" for Therapeutic Healing

Mazella Fuller

A Complicated Past: Potential Causes of Disordered Eating in Black Women

Historically, Black women have had a complicated relationship with the US health care system. Yet, for the most part, health care providers have failed to recognize the harmful experiments that have been conducted on Black women by White men. Furthermore, research studies rarely consider how the legacy of slavery and structural racism negatively influence the present-day health outcomes of African American women. Black women's experiences in the health-care system are too numerous to identify within this narrow space of a chapter; however, a few egregious abuses of power on Black bodies are included here to demonstrate one reason fewer Black women seek treatment for eating disorders than White women (Thompson, 1994). The inhumane Tuskegee Study that was conducted on Black males from 1932–1972 and the unethical treatment of Henrietta Lacks in 1951 are examples of how Black women have been objectified in the health system and of how they, their progeny, and extended family members are exposed to long-term damaging health effects. Though worthy of discussion, these examples are not discussed in this chapter. One of the purposes of this chapter is to reveal unfamiliar or less familiar experiences about Black women's traumatic experiences that contribute to their disordered eating. The first example is J. Marion Sims, "the so-called father of modern gynecology" (Suite, Robert La Bril, Primm, & Harrison-Ross, 2007, p. 880), who "used three women slaves from Alabama to construct an operation to repair vesico vaginal fistulas." From 1845–1849, each one of "these women on whom Sims operated would each endure up to 30 painful operations" without anesthesia (Suite et al., 2007, p. 880). After exploiting Black women's bodies to hone his skills, Sims performed the surgeries "on white women (with anesthesia)" (Suite et al., 2007, p. 880).

Whether they are in health facilities or in the wider society, Black women struggle to protect their bodies. Davis (1971) argues that even in the posture of motherhood, Black women were not treated with compassion. She maintains that while the purity of White women could not be violated by the White male, they raped enslaved Black women to release their sexual urges. Similar "[a]cts of violence" on Black women's bodies "are illustrated in . . . sterilization abuses. 'Mississippi appendectomy' was a phrase created by White physicians from the South to denote the routine medical practice of sterilizing African-American women who were admitted to hospitals for other operations" (p. 11). Suite also reports that the sterilization procedures were performed until "the early 1970s" (Suite et al., 2007, p. 881).

Not only do Black women fight to protect their physical bodies, they also struggle to protect their mental health. For example, "cite an 1840 US Census Report that deliberately falsified the insanity rates among African Americans" (Suite et al., 2007, p. 881). The Report was altered to demonstrate "that the further north Blacks lived, the higher their rates of mental illness" (p. 881). Suite et al. (2007) go on to note that a 19th-century physician named Samuel A. Cartwright

> invented a mental disorder called "drapetomania," and it was character-
> ized by African slaves' uncontrollable urge to escape slavery, destroy
> property on plantation, be disobedient, talk back, fight with their masters
> and refuse to work.
>
> (p. 881)

Many Black persons who were enslaved in the US somehow survived the traumatic experiences that were afflicted upon them, but they did so with an unbreakable spirit.

A Complicated Present: Black Women Who *Show Up* for Therapeutic Healing

As a result of the inhumane and unethical treatment of Black persons, Black women are skeptical about the type of treatment they will receive in the health-care system, though they yearn for therapeutic healing. Black women with eating disorders, like all women with eating disorders, deserve equal access to treatment. For many Black women, eating becomes a survival strategy and a tool to cope with stress and trauma (Thompson & Thompson, 1992).

Thus, Black women are more likely to *show up* with the trauma of racism, sexism, and other forms of systemic oppression: eating disorders speak to the core identity of a Black woman. Additionally, Black women *show up* with higher levels of anxiety and depression, with severe medical challenges, and with somatic issues. They also *show up* with higher rates of diabetes and hypertension.

The source of many Black women's disordered eating is institutional racism that subtly manifests in *modern* society. For instance, though more Black women enter academic spaces as students and professionals, many of them are silenced in classrooms and in meetings and do not have a seat at the table where critical decisions are made about them. Their lack of voice or sense of agency in academia results in increased anxiety and depression. Nonetheless, more Black women are ready to lay down their emotional burdens and psychological scars of discrimination and structural racism, manifested through their eating disorders, and engage in conversations with therapists. As a result, in therapy sessions, they openly unpack the stress of their academic pursuits, of police violence on the bodies of people of color, and of driving while Black. The struggle is real for Black women—they show up with the wounds from navigating daily microaggressions and macroaggressions.

Moore and Madison-Colmore (2005) asks three poignant questions about Black women's lived experiences:

> What will it take to get rid of the burdens that lie heavily in the bosom of my heart? What will it take to look beyond the color of my skin, the texture of my hair, and the features of my body to see the beauty that lies beneath? What will it take to dispel the stereotypes and see the intellect that is rooted deeply in the cells of my brain?
>
> (p. 39)

Moore and Madison-Colmore (2005) focuses on the challenges Black women face in pursuing the same standard of care that White women are afforded. Moreover, scholars support the argument that discrimination and structural racism in present-day mental health settings further hinder Black women's journey toward healing, particularly when clinicians use measures of assessment validated only on White samples. Further, the lack of inclusive assessments, staff, treatment providers, and study and use of culturally adapted treatments impact Black women's personal growth and development.

In addition, in a 2018 interview, Mazella Fuller, a clinical social worker, and Karla Mosley, an American actress and singer, discussed and highlighted the challenges in eating disorder symptomatology and accessing treatment. Referring to her own experience with eating disorders, Mosely affirms that inpatient treatment can be isolating and that at times, she felt alone on her journey to recovery. She recalls that her experiences were alienating because she was "the only brown face in the room" (5:07), having no practitioners who looked like her. She also states that the lack of providers who looked like her and who could not share her cultural experiences created a barrier to her recovery. Because she had a name for what she was struggling with, she eventually navigated the clinical setting with providers who shared her cultural and lived experiences. Mosley's experience proves that clinicians must offer "safe spaces" to their clients and must demonstrate "interest in providing [quality care] for each person on an individual level," according to Mosley (2019, 37:31). The diversity of thought and values offers a more welcoming healing space for Black women. Evidence shows that when clinicians lack cultural competence and when they use measures of assessment validated only on White samples, they create barriers to their clients' recovery processes.

In "White Privilege in a White Coat: How Racism Shaped My Medical Education," Romano (2017) writes:

> While white Americans often think of "racism" as a social construct primarily affecting people of color, "racism" is a system of both racial disadvantage as well as reciprocal racial advantage. Medical professionals are

increasingly aware of how social determinants of health lead to important health disparities, however white physicians seldom ask how their own racial privilege reinforces a white supremacist culture and what effects this may have on our patients' health.

(p. 261)

When his article was published, Romano, a White family medicine physician, worked at Johns Hopkins Bloomberg School of Public Health. Romano acknowledges that the health system

is structured to individually and systemically favor white physicians and patients in ways that white people are trained to ignore. Most white doctors do not think race affects them or their clinical decisions and are taught to ignore their own racial privilege in favor of a meritocratic social myth. However, multiple studies reinforce the existence of racial bias among physicians and its negative implications for patient care. . . . Failure to confront racism within the medical profession has implications for the patients we serve: infants of color continue to die at higher rates, children of color get less needed care, and adults of color receive poorer quality care than their white counterparts, and the trends are not improving.

(p. 262)

Romano affirms that racism is pervasive in the health system, and thus in some way, it adversely shapes the physical and mental health of African American women (Prather et al., 2018).

A Positive Future: Properly Treating Black Women Who *Show Up* for Therapeutic Healing

Black women have emerged from the shadows with an unbreakable spirit, and they are *showing up*. What should clinicians do to treat Black women with eating disorders when they *show up*?

- Clinicians should be prepared to understand and act upon the impact of historical trauma and White supremacy on Black women.
- The culturally competent clinician should be aware of their bias and implicit bias when treating Black women with eating disorders.
- The clinician should respect the lived experiences of Black women and join them in treatment for successful healing to occur.
- The clinician should take the time to understand the client's experience with racism, sexism, and gender identity issues. This transformative experience will empower Black women to begin to heal from the psychological wounds of oppression and structural racism.

The therapeutic healing space is a place where Black women are overcoming the challenges of race, class, and gender, so they are cultivating a strong sense of self. In that space, they are also connected to their feelings and sense of self, so that outside that space, they can use their voices to elevate their community through activism and through speaking truth to power. Black women are embracing a strong Black identity with intrinsic cultural values and healing from eating disorders. They are using the therapeutic space to work through their transference issues in the healing space. They recognize that Black therapists are able to manage both the transference and countertransference in the therapeutic relationship. Black women *show up* with an awareness that their food issues are connected to their feelings, and they are ready to jump over the hurdles of structural racism, colonialism, and sexism. The transformative experience of the therapeutic space prepares the Black woman to aim high. Finally, they are focusing on holistic wellness and connecting their physical, emotional, and spiritual health to eliminate eating disorders and build resiliency.

This chapter was written to provide a platform for a practicing Black clinician to teach other clinicians how to help Black women in treatment heal from the wounds of structural racism and the historical wounds of trauma. I have been a practicing clinician for more than 25 years, and I have had the privilege of witnessing Black women's strength and resiliency in overcoming their eating disorders. I have witnessed and understand the coping skills needed to negotiate two worlds Black women occupy: the duality of navigating a Black world and a White world. It is essential to understand the strengths and resilience of Black women. We show up with a strong ethnic pride and a higher level of enculturation. We embrace our history and understand the impact of stereotypes on our core identity. To provide a therapeutic space focusing on empowerment and a strong foundation for Black women to recover and heal is to engage social justice and equality. The therapeutic healing space is critical in the development of self-compassion, self-efficacy, and healing. Good therapy allows a Black woman to live her best life. The therapeutic healing space is a place to value the Black woman as a unique individual, as a member of an oppressed group, and as a citizen of the world.

References

Davis, A. (1971). The Black woman's role in the community of slaves. *The Black Scholar, 3*, 2–15.

Moore, J. L., & Madison-Colmore, O. (2005). Using H.E.R.S model in counseling African American women. *Journal of African American Studies, 9*, 39–50.

Mosley, K. (2019). NEDA Hope Interview with Dr. Mazella Fuller, Claire Mysko, and Karla Mosley. Retrieved from https://youtu.be/5vUBKm7JAnQ.

Prather, C., Fuller, T. R., Jefferies, W. L., Marshal, K. J., Vyann Howell, A., Belyue-Umole, A., & King, W. (2018). Racism, African American women, and their sexual and reproductive health: A review of historical and contemporary evidence and implications for health equity. *Health Equity, 2*(1), 249–259. https://doi.org/10.1089/heq.2017.0045.

Romano, J. M. (2017). White privilege in a white coat: How racism shaped my medical education. *Annals of Family Medicine, 16*(3), 261–263.

Suite, D. H., Robert La Bril, R., Primm, A., & Harrison-Ross, P. (2007). Beyond mis-diagnosis, misunderstanding and mistrust: Relevance of the historical perspective in the medical and mental health treatment of people of color. *Journal of the National Medical Association, 99*(8), 879–885.

Thompson, B. W. (1994). *A hunger so wide and deep: A multicultural view of women's eating problems*. Minneapolis, MN: University of Minnesota Press.

Thompson, B., & Thompson, W. (1992). "A way outa no way" eating problems among African-American, Latina and White women. *Gender and Society, 6*(4), 546–561.

3 A Gap in the Research

Race-Specific Issues and Difficult Questions

Eulena Jonsson

Introduction

This chapter exacts the essence of the book and posits that a gap exists in the investigation of issues specific to Black women with eating disorders. I present evidence that Black clinicians and practitioners who treat Black women with eating disorders assess for, examine, and analyze critical issues that non-Black professionals do not typically assess for. The issues that Black practitioners examine can be prominent and meaningful in the assessment, diagnosis, and treatment of Black women with eating disorders. This chapter details relevant research and presents recent findings on Black women with eating disorders. While most of the clinician and practitioner respondents do not avoid discussing topics uncomfortable to them or their clients, there are differences in avoidance itself and topics avoided by the race of the practitioner. Consequently, this chapter offers topics of self-reflection and professional development for eating disorder practitioners as they engage with Black female students. Additionally, I suggest future action steps for eating disorder researchers. With practices further informed by filling the findings gap, practitioners as a whole move closer toward providing optimal experiences for Black women with eating disorders.

Overview

A clear dearth of literature exists on the challenges faced by practitioners who treat Black women with eating disorders. Traditionally, the narrative of individuals with eating disorders was built on a White female base, and the research conducted reflected similar cultural blind spots. More recently and positively, dialogue and research around eating disorders on college campuses has expanded. Researchers have found that while the race and ethnicity of female-identified students do not impact the manifestation of eating disorders, race and ethnicity can, however, impact students' identification and care. When investigating minority female-identified students, including the population of interest, Black women, researchers identified a mismatch between higher self-reported eating disorders and lower treatment numbers. Digging deeper into the mismatch, researcher' focus has been on the students themselves and on variables such as type of eating disorder, age of onset, and cultural stereotypes. More recent research has shifted the focus from minority student variables to practitioner variables, seeking to shine light on the part that practitioners themselves play in how dissimilar treatment experiences may emerge. However, there is little research about Black professionals who provide treatment for eating disorders and ways to support their engagement and advancement in the field. The narrative has not stretched fully to encompass the differences in critical issues discussed by Black and non-Black practitioners and the impact that it can have when such issues are included or omitted from treatment. Another research question yet incompletely answered is whether non-Black practitioners face identical challenges when providing care for Black women dealing with eating disorders, especially on predominantly White college campuses. If challenges exist and are disparate, how do the differences present? This chapter presents findings from an initial foray into filling this information gap. It offers a snapshot of issues that surface for Black eating disorder professionals and their non-Black colleagues in practice when working with Black women, and it offers recommendations for how this necessary and valuable research should continue. While the chapter focuses on college-age women and the practitioners who treat them, the issues and findings discussed within likely apply more broadly.

Context

According to the National Institute of Mental Health, eating disorders are "serious medical illnesses marked by severe disturbances to a person's eating behaviors" that may have indicators such as "[o]bsessions with food, body weight, and shape" (National Institute of Mental Health, 2018, p. 2). "Feeding and eating disorders" are defined in the American Psychiatric Association's *Diagnostic and Statistical Manual of Mental Disorders* as "[being] characterized by a persistent disturbance of eating or eating-related behavior that results in the altered consumption or absorption of food and that significantly impairs physical health or psychosocial functioning" (American Psychiatric Association & American Psychiatric Association. DSM-5 Task Force, 2013, p. 329). Anorexia nervosa, bulimia nervosa, and binge eating disorder are some potential diagnoses. Other feeding and eating disorders include pica, rumination disorder, and avoidant/restrictive food intake disorder, as well as designations included in the categories "other specified feeding or eating disorder" and "unspecified feeding or eating disorder." The literature reviewed for this chapter focused on the first three categories of eating disorder: anorexia nervosa, bulimia nervosa, and binge eating disorder.

Eating disorders have historically been associated with non-Black girls and women. Media representation of individuals with eating disorder symptoms, including terms such as the "waifs" and "Golden Girls," has centered on young White females, especially non-Black females, and continues to do so (Gordon, Perez, & Joiner, 2002; Lague, 1993, para. 5; Striegel-Moore & Smolak, 2001a;

Yarrow, 2018). In a clinical context, the mental connection between eating disorders and non-Black clients can lead to missed diagnoses. In a 2006 study, mental health practitioners were asked to read fictional vignettes describing a 16-year-old female "Mary" character. Participating clinicians were significantly less likely to recognize an eating disorder syndrome when "Mary" was described as African American than when she was described as White or Hispanic (Gordon, Brattole, Wingate, & Joiner, 2006). Even though the vignettes differed only in the race of the main character, 44.4% recognized that "Mary" had an eating disorder when she was White, versus 40.5% when she was identified as Hispanic and 16.7% when identified as African American. Interestingly, the race of the potential patient "Mary" did not affect clinicians' identification of individual eating disorder symptoms or the ratings of anxiety and depression. Even so, "Mary's" assigned race did impact the overall identification of the character's eating disorder.

Is the deep-rooted association between eating disorders and White females truly a misconception, or is it based on fact? Earlier literature tended to conclude that women of Color in the United States were buffered from key risk factors of eating disorders by different body ideal norms (Gluck & Geliebter, 2002; Gordon, Castro, Sitnikov, & Holm-Denoma, 2010; Striegel-Moore & Smolak, 2001b). Cultural buffering was given as rationale behind why women of color were less likely to seek out treatment for eating disorders (Cachelin & Striegel-Moore, 2006; Striegel-Moore & Bulik, 2007; Wilfley, Pike, Dohm, Striegel-Moore, & Fairburn, 2001). Current research paints a more complex picture, and suggests that the belief that eating disorders are confined to White females is archaic and inaccurate. According to the National Eating Disorders Association (National Eating Disorders Association, 2018), non-White ethnicities are affected by eating disorders at similar or even higher rates than Whites relating to attempted weight loss (Kilpatrick, Ohannessian, & Bartholomew, 1999), bulimic behavior (Goeree, Ham, & Iorio, 2011), and binge eating (Swanson et al., 2012). Eating disorders are represented across age (Lucas, Beard, O'Fallon, & Kurland, 1991; Mangweth-Matzek et al., 2013; Mangweth-Matzek et al., 2006), gender (Striegel-Moore et al., 2009), and race identity variables (Grabe & Hyde, 2006; Roberts, Cash, Feingold, & Johnson, 2006; Schaefer et al., 2018; Striegel-Moore, Wilfley, Pike, Dohm, & Fairburn, 2000).

While the current literature would suggest that people of color need treatment for eating disorders in comparable numbers to their White counterparts, help-seeking behavior does not seem to match expected demand. Specific to eating disorders, primarily binge eating disorders, ethnic/racial minorities were less likely to seek treatment. Non-Hispanic Blacks also reported a later age of first seeking help for bulimia nervosa relative to non-Hispanic Whites (Coffino, Udo, & Grilo, 2019). Looking more broadly, statistics from the National Alliance on Mental Illness show a mismatch between prevalence of adult mental illness in Black adults, an estimated 18.6%, and use of mental health services, 10.3% for Black females. The difference in need and treatment seeking is much more extreme than that for White adults (National Alliance on Mental Illness, 2015). Data on eating disorder prevalence as compared to lifetime mental health service utilization statistics reflects a similar finding (Marques et al., 2011). Researchers, using data from the NIMH Collaborative Psychiatric Epidemiological Studies, found that lifetime mental health service utilization was lower among Latinos, Asians, and African Americans than their non-Latino White counterparts. Lower utilization occurred even though the prevalence of some types of eating disorders, for example binge eating, was more prevalent across all three minority groups covered than non-Latino White respondents.

Why does a mismatch exist between self-identified eating disorder needs and actual eating disorder treatment for non-White women? One possibility is that Black women are seeking help but not being diagnosed as having an eating disorder. Symptoms for Black women may present differently to those of White women, with practitioners not taking potential eating disorder symptom differences into account. For example, Black women with eating disorders are more likely to binge eat, which is linked to higher levels of excess weight (Striegel-Moore et al., 2000; Talleyrand, 2006) and older ages of onset (Taylor, Caldwell, Baser, Faison, & Jackson, 2007). A 2003 study found that people of color with self-reported eating disorders were significantly less likely than White participants to have been asked by a practitioner about eating disorder symptoms (Becker, Franko, Speck, & Herzog, 2003).

From the eating disorders literature, Black practitioners may be more likely than non-Black practitioners to recognize and create dialogue around culturally relevant topics shown to be connected to eating disorder incidence (Small & Fuller, 2016b). Topics include ethnocultural transference and countertransference (Satir, Thompson-Brenner, Boisseau, & Crisafulli, 2009), level of identification with racial identity (Talleyrand, 2006, 2012), and acculturation (George & Franko, 2010; Rodgers, Berry, & Franko, 2018; Rogers Wood & Petrie, 2010); all shown to be positively correlated with eating disorder prevalence. What implications do differences in eating disorder identification in Black women have for client/practitioner race/ethnicity matches? In a meta-analysis of 52 studies examining participants' preferences for therapist race/ethnicity and associated outcomes, African American participants were most affected by a race/ethnicity match. African American clients' perception of their therapist was strongly linked to the therapist's race/ethnicity, and outcomes such as retention in treatment and satisfaction with provider were mildly positively impacted (Cabral & Smith, 2011). Nonetheless, the problem is more complex than a simple solution of matching provider to potential client. The American Psychological Association (APA) reports that in 2016, only 4% of psychologist members identified as Black (American Psychological Association, 2017), meaning that the likelihood of a Black female college student with an eating disorder being matched with a Black eating disorder practitioner are low. The odds are that Black women in need of eating disorder identification and treatment will be matched with a non-Black practitioner. Non-Black practitioners therefore need to possess cultural competence knowledge regarding specific issues that may be critical to the care of Black women. Recent research findings present a promising case for a nuanced relationship between race and the experience of mental health care. Ethnic minority clients felt that it was important that the practitioner be knowledgeable about their ethnic/racial group's history of prejudice and discriminations. Provider knowledge of topics related to race and culture by practitioners was related to positive client perceptions of accessibility of treatment, quality of care, and general satisfaction (Meyer & Zane, 2013).

Accordingly, the goal of this chapter is to detail initial data obtained about the experiences of professionals who serve Black women with eating disorders. The focus of the research is the potentially unique experiences of White and non-White providers with clients and characteristics of such interactions.

Background to Research

The research that is described in this chapter emerged following the formation of the African American Eating Disorders Professional (AAEDP) committee in June 2016. The AAEDP committee, part of the International Association of Eating Disorders Professionals (iaedp), came about to address the underrepresentation of Black practitioners providing care for eating disorders and related issues and to increase Black membership in the iaedp (iaedp, 2019). Additionally, part of the mission of the AAEDP is to "conduct research focused on the unique societal challenges impacting eating behavior and the barriers to the professional advancement of African-American women and men in the field" (Small & Fuller, 2016a, p. 5).

Current Study

Eating disorder practitioners were invited to complete the "Engaging African-American Eating Disorders Professional Survey." The survey's goals were twofold: to describe the experience of practitioners treating Black women with eating disorders, particularly from the Black practitioner's perspective, and to engage Black eating disorders treatment professionals in the field. Participants were recruited from iaedp membership in two waves, the first inviting specifically Black eating disorder professionals to participate in the survey. AAEDP co-chairs Dr. Small and Dr. Fuller sent out an email invitation that stated:

> As with many areas of health care, there appears to be an under-representation of Black professionals who provide treatment for eating disorders and related concerns. To address these concerns, we are researching patterns and levels of engagement among Black therapists and Black college students with eating disorders and body image concerns. Please assist us by completing the enclosed brief, 10-item survey.

Ten survey questions consisted of the following: demographic questions about race, gender, years as an eating disorder professional, treatment modality, and therapeutic orientation; class as an impediment to treatment; the practitioner's own body image or concept of beauty standards as an impediment to treating Black women with eating disorders; and an exploration of practitioners' potential avoidance of or difficulty in broaching specific culturally-related topics. Forty-two Black eating disorder professionals responded to the survey between 8/6/2016 and 11/20/2016. Approximately one year later, White eating disorder professionals were invited to complete the survey as well to allow for comparison data. Twenty-four White eating disorder professionals participated in the survey between 8/21/17 and 10/9/2017.

Relevant Findings

The data collected in the survey are all categorical or grouping variables, so Pearson's chi-square test, a test that detects whether there is a significant association between two categorical variables (Field, 2013), was calculated where appropriate. The Pearson's chi-square test compares the frequencies observed to the variables expected by chance. Patterns of responses were examined in the responses collected.

Respondent Demographics

Of the 66 total respondents, most were female (83%), Black mental health professionals (64%) who had been providing eating disorder/body image issues treatment for more than 10 years (48%). More than half provided individual treatment (65%), and the majority described themselves as generalists (64%). Practitioners who were not generalists used descriptors ranging from family systems and relational to multicultural, Rogerian, and "depending on client needs."

Barriers to Treatment

Just under half of respondents, 47.5%, indicated that class or socioeconomic status was a barrier to their treatment of Black college-age students with eating disorders. Years as a mental health professional providing eating disorders treatment did cross significantly with class as a barrier. More than half of respondents who had served for more than 10 years (57%) saw class as a barrier to the course of treatment, while only 25% of those who had served 0 to 5 years did, $X^2(2, N = 56) = 5.82, p = .05$. Most Black eating disorder practitioners, 61%, indicated that class was not an impediment to treatment, with a smaller-than-expected proportion of non-Black practitioners indicating the same, 39%, although this difference was not significant.

About 20% of respondents provided specific ways in which class or socioeconomic status presented as a barrier, with financial/affording treatment and insurance coverage emerging as the top themes: "Some students did not have the financial means to obtain treatment outside of the university services where I was treating them." Other ways included access/referral, "limited access to a higher level of care," and minority status, "clients were hesitant to come into treatment due to being either the only, or one of the few, non White participants."

Few respondents overall, 8%, responded affirmatively to the question "Has your own body image and concept of beauty standards ever impacted your ability to treat Black women with eating disorders or body image concerns?" Just over half of respondents responded to this specific question.

Challenging Issues to Address

Eating disorder practitioners were asked to identify issues that they may have found difficult to address as a therapist with Black college-age clients. Race of the practitioner impacted the top issues identified. White practitioners were more likely to select as the issues "Family relationships," "Body part size, shape (i.e., thin or petite vs. voluptuous, full-figured)," and "Hair (i.e., texture, style, length)" tied with "Skin (i.e., dark vs. light complexion)." For Black practitioners, the top issues were "Skin (i.e., dark vs. light complexion)," followed by "Family relationships" and "Body part size, shape (i.e., thin or petite vs. voluptuous, full-figured)." Issues specified in the "Other" category in descending order of frequency were:

- None: Respondents used the space to state that none of the items have been difficult to address, e.g., "No problem addressing these issues. If you are working with Black college age clients, these are relevant issues to address at some point in treatment"; "None of these items have been difficult."
- Ethnic comparisons and perceived power differentials based on ethnicity, e.g., I have struggled with discussing hair, skin, and body size as it is hard to address projections onto your identity when (a) you may not know they are happening or (b) when you do address but the client still believes you hold an advantageous position (e.g., being light-skinned, petite/ curvy, etc.).

A majority of respondents overall, 65%, stated that they did not avoid discussing topics that were uncomfortable for them or their client. Of those that did state that they avoided discussing at some point, White practitioners self-reported higher proportions of avoiding topics (29%) than expected as compared to Black practitioners (8%), although the difference was not significant.

Practitioner's descriptions of the issues that caused discomfort or perceptions of uncomfortable topics altogether fell into the following categories, categorized by race of practitioner.

Black Practitioners

- Uncomfortable topics can be difficult but important, not avoided:

    Some eating disorder practitioners stated that they did not avoid issues, as they thought them to be necessary to address at an appropriate time, e.g., "Not avoided but looked at the timing of the inquiry. Building the relationship with the client makes it easier for the client to respond to these areas"; "Students initiate conversation regarding challenging topics and I am fine with this."

- Skin color:

    "Uncomfortable for client because I was lighter skinned"; "The client wanted to discuss inter-racial dating which was fine with me. I then learned that she feels more attractive and valuable if she can get a White man to date her. She then asked about the race of my partner and I did not reveal his race for many reasons including that he is White."

- Not remembered:

    "I don't remember actually, but most probably this has been true more than once. Not specifically about ED though."

White Practitioners

- Uncomfortable topics can be difficult but important, not avoided:

    This theme was echoed, and timing mentioned too, e.g., "Racism can sometimes be difficult to discuss directly but is so important. It hasn't limited me, it's just uncomfortable to hear the experiences"; "Clients are uncomfortable at times with all the listed items so pacing is critical in treatment."

- Not thought of before:

    "I do not think I considered them part of the discussion up until you brought it up."

Most respondents did not see issues, including the example given of being a different gender from their client, as being difficult to broach with clients, with 81% responding that no issues were difficult to broach. Specific examples given by those who did see their treatment impacted included body size, feeling that anger was displaced to White provider ("How to address a client's anger towards White people when I am White. And how to give space to how I do not know from my own experience what it's like to be a minority"), and insufficient rapport. Note that there was a significant difference in expected percentages, where White practitioners were more likely to, and indeed were the only practitioners who indicated having had issues that were difficult to broach for particular reasons, $X^2(2, N = 56) = 14.14, p < .001$.

Recommendations for the Future

The survey detailed is a rich source of information that can be expanded on and drilled down into further in the future. It is notable that most practitioners who shared their experiences, despite discomfort, do report tackling difficult topics, with timing being a very important part of the practitioner–client experience. Class emerged as a demographic that practitioners viewed as being a potential barrier with Black female clients. How does this particular impediment and perception of class differences play out at a predominantly White college? Is this feeling of a barrier being present based on reality or based in processes such as countertransference and practitioners' assumptions? Further research is recommended to dig into this variable and reasons provider participants perceive it as impacting their treatment of Black women.

Other key findings include differences between Black and non-Black practitioners on trends of avoiding uncomfortable cultural topics and the specific types of topics that are avoided. Does the finding that "Family relationships" are first for White practitioners signal potentially fruitful cultural dialogue opportunities that are being missed? How does Black practitioners' top theme being "Skin (i.e., dark vs. light complexion)" speak to the impact of colorism and acculturalism on treatment strategies and the practitioner–client relationship?

This chapter presented findings that are just a foray into an area that invites further exploration. Initial goals included furthering the narrative on professional development areas for practitioners working with Black women with eating disorders. By illuminating some characteristics of interactions between Black or White providers and Black women with eating disorders, we provided context for dialogue and increased research. Recommendations for subsequent investigation include recruitment of more practitioners and more intensive qualitative data collection processes, such as interviews that would allow for elaboration on responses. For example, "Have you ever avoided discussing any issue with a client because it was uncomfortable for you, or because it seemed uncomfortable or embarrassing for your client?" yielded valuable insight. Moving forward, this would be a very appropriate question to target to gain information about how practitioners field the topics themselves. Additionally, it would be of great interest to link the more involved responses on practitioner discomfort with Black women clients' outcomes.

References

American Psychiatric Association & American Psychiatric Association. DSM-5 Task Force. (2013). *Diagnostic and statistical manual of mental disorders: DSM-5* (5th ed.). Washington, DC: American Psychiatric Association.

American Psychological Association. (2017). *Demographics of the U.S. psychology workforce*. Retrieved from www.apa.org/workforce/data-tools/demographics. aspx.

Becker, A. E., Franko, D. L., Speck, A., & Herzog, D. B. (2003). Ethnicity and differential access to care for eating disorder symptoms. *International Journal of Eating Disorders, 33*(2), 205–212. https://doi.org/10.1002/eat.10129.

Cabral, R. R., & Smith, T. B. (2011). Racial/ethnic matching of clients and therapists in mental health services: A meta-analytic review of preferences, perceptions, and outcomes. *Journal of Counseling Psychology, 58*(4), 537–554. https://doi.org/10.1037/a0025266.

Cachelin, F. M., & Striegel-Moore, R. H. (2006). Help seeking and barriers to treatment in a community sample of Mexican American and European American women with eating disorders. *International Journal of Eating Disorders, 39*(2), 154–161. https://doi.org/10.1002/eat.20213.

Coffino, J. A., Udo, T., & Grilo, C. M. (2019). Rates of help-seeking in US adults with lifetime DSM-5 eating disorders: Prevalence across diagnoses and differences by sex and ethnicity/race. *Mayo Clinic Proceedings, 94*(8), 1415–1426. https://doi.org/10.1016/j.mayocp.2019.02.030.

Field, A. P. (2013). *Discovering statistics using IBM SPSS statistics: And sex and drugs and rock 'n' roll* (4th ed.). London: Sage.

George, J. B., & Franko, D. L. (2010). Cultural issues in eating pathology and body image among children and adolescents. *Journal of Pediatric Psychology, 35*(3), 231–242. https://doi.org/10.1093/jpepsy/jsp064.

Gluck, M. E., & Geliebter, A. (2002). Racial/ethnic differences in body image and eating behaviors. *Eating Behaviors, 3*(2), 143–151. https://doi.org/10.1016/s1471-0153(01)00052-6.

Goeree, M. S., Ham, J., & Iorio, D. (2011). Race, social class, and bulimia nervosa. *IZA Discussion Paper*. Retrieved from https://ssrn.com/abstract=1877636.

Gordon, K. H., Brattole, M. M., Wingate, L. R., & Joiner, T. E., Jr. (2006). The impact of client race on clinician detection of eating disorders. *Behavior Therapy, 37*(4), 319–325. https://doi.org/10.1016/j.beth.2005.12.002.

Gordon, K. H., Castro, Y., Sitnikov, L., & Holm-Denoma, J. M. (2010). Cultural body shape ideals and eating disorder symptoms among White, Latina, and Black college women. *Cultural Diversity and Ethnic Minority Psychology, 16*(2), 135–143. https://doi.org/10.1037/a0018671.

Gordon, K. H., Perez, M., & Joiner, T. E., Jr. (2002). The impact of racial stereotypes on eating disorder recognition. *International Journal of Eating Disorders, 32*(2), 219–224. https://doi.org/10.1002/eat.10070.

Grabe, S., & Hyde, J. S. (2006). Ethnicity and body dissatisfaction among women in the United States: A meta-analysis. *Psychological Bulletin, 132*(4), 622–640. https://doi.org/10.1037/0033-2909.132.4.622.

iaedp. (2019). *African American Eating Disorders Professionals (AAEDP) Committee: Message from Co-Chairs*. Retrieved from https://membershare.iaedp.com/introducing-the-iaedp-african-american-eating-disorders-professionals-aaedp-committee-people-of-color-poc-aaedp-subcommittee/.

Kilpatrick, M., Ohannessian, C., & Bartholomew, J. B. (1999). Adolescent weight management and perceptions: An analysis of the National Longitudinal Study of Adolescent Health. *Journal of School Health, 69*(4), 148–152.

Lague, L. (1993). How thin is too thin? *People, 40*.

Lucas, A. R., Beard, C. M., O'Fallon, W. M., & Kurland, L. T. (1991). 50-year trends in the incidence of anorexia nervosa in Rochester, Minn.: A population-based study. *American Journal of Psychiatry, 148*(7), 917–922. https://doi.org/10.1176/ajp.148. 7.917.

Mangweth-Matzek, B., Hoek, H. W., Rupp, C. I., Kemmler, G., Pope, H. G., Jr., & Kinzl, J. (2013). The menopausal transition: A possible window of vulnerability for eating pathology. *International Journal of Eating Disorders, 46*(6), 609–616. https://doi.org/10.1002/eat.22157.

Mangweth-Matzek, B., Rupp, C. I., Hausmann, A., Assmayr, K., Mariacher, E., Kemmler, G., . . . Biebl, W. (2006). Never too old for eating disorders or body dissatisfaction: A community study of elderly women. *International Journal of Eating Disorders, 39*(7), 583–586.

Marques, L., Alegria, M., Becker, A. E., Chen, C. N., Fang, A., Chosak, A., & Diniz, J. B. (2011). Comparative prevalence, correlates of impairment, and service utilization for eating disorders across US ethnic groups: Implications for reducing ethnic disparities in health care access for eating disorders. *International Journal of Eating Disorders, 44*(5), 412–420. https://doi.org/10.1002/eat.20787.

Meyer, O. L., & Zane, N. (2013). The influence of race and ethnicity in clients' experiences of mental health treatment. *Journal of Community Psychology, 41*(7), 884–901. https://doi.org/10.1002/jcop.21580.

National Alliance on Mental Illness. (2015). *Mental health facts; Multicultural.* Retrieved from https://www.nami.org/NAMI/media/NAMI-Media/Infographics/Infograph_multicultural_mhfacts.pdf.

National Eating Disorders Association. (2018). *People of color and eating disorders.* Retrieved from www.nationaleatingdisorders.org/people-color-and-eating-disorders.

National Institute of Mental Health. (2018). *Eating disorders: About more than food* (NIH Publication No. TR 17-4901). Retrieved from https://www.nimh.nih.gov/health/publications/eating-disorders/eatingdisorders_148810.pdf.

Roberts, A., Cash, T. F., Feingold, A., & Johnson, B. T. (2006). Are black-white differences in females' body dissatisfaction decreasing? A meta-analytic review. *Journal of Consulting and Clinical Psychology, 74*(6), 1121–1131. https://doi.org/10.1037/0022-006X.74.6.1121.

Rodgers, R. F., Berry, R., & Franko, D. L. (2018). Eating disorders in ethnic minorities: An update. *Current Psychiatry Reports, 20*(10), 90. https://doi.org/10.1007/s11920-018-0938-3.

Rogers Wood, N. A., & Petrie, T. A. (2010). Body dissatisfaction, ethnic identity, and disordered eating among African American women. *Journal of Counseling Psychology, 57*(2), 141–153. https://doi.org/10.1037/a0018922.

Satir, D. A., Thompson-Brenner, H., Boisseau, C. L., & Crisafulli, M. A. (2009). Countertransference reactions to adolescents with eating disorders: Relationships to clinician and patient factors. *International Journal of Eating Disorders, 42*(6), 511–521. https://doi.org/10.1002/eat.20650.

Schaefer, L. M., Burke, N. L., Calogero, R. M., Menzel, J. E., Krawczyk, R., & Thompson, J. K. (2018). Self-objectification, body shame, and disordered eating: Testing a core mediational model of objectification theory among White, Black, and Hispanic women. *Body Image, 24*, 5–12. https://doi.org/10.1016/j.bodyim.2017.10.005.

Small, C., & Fuller, M. B. (2016a). *African-American women on predominantly White college campuses: In the shadows in eating disorders.* Paper presented at the 2016 iaedp Symposium, Amelia Island, Florida.

Small, C., & Fuller, M. B. (2016b). *African-American women on predominantly White college campuses: In the shadows of eating disorders.* Retrieved from http://membershare.iaedp.com/african-american-women-on-predominantly-white-college-campuses-in-the-shadows-of-eating-disorders-2/.

Striegel-Moore, R. H., & Bulik, C. M. (2007). Risk factors for eating disorders. *American Psychologist, 62*(3), 181–198. https://doi.org/10.1037/0003-066X.62.3.181.

Striegel-Moore, R. H., Rosselli, F., Perrin, N., DeBar, L., Wilson, G. T., May, A., & Kraemer, H. C. (2009). Gender difference in the prevalence of eating disorder symptoms. *International Journal of Eating Disorders, 42*(5), 471–474. https://doi.org/10.1002/eat.20625.

Striegel-Moore, R. H., & Smolak, L. (2001a). Challenging the myth of the golden girl: Ethnicity and eating disorders. In *Eating disorders: Innovative directions for research and practice* (1st ed., pp. 111–132). Washington, DC: American Psychological Association.

Striegel-Moore, R. H., & Smolak, L. (2001b). *Eating disorders: Innovative directions for research and practice* (1st ed.). Washington, DC: American Psychological Association.

Striegel-Moore, R. H., Wilfley, D. E., Pike, K. M., Dohm, F. A., & Fairburn, C. G. (2000). Recurrent binge eating in black American women. *Archives of Family Medicine, 9*(1), 83–87.

Swanson, S. A., Saito, N., Borges, G., Benjet, C., Aguilar-Gaxiola, S., Medina-Mora, M. E., & Breslau, J. (2012). Change in binge eating and binge eating disorder associated with migration from Mexico to the U.S. *Journal of Psychiatric Research, 46*(1), 31–37. https://doi.org/10.1016/j.jpsychires.2011.10.008.

Talleyrand, R. M. (2006). Potential stressors contributing to eating disorder symptoms in African American Women: Implications for mental health counselors. *Journal of Mental Health Counseling, 28*(4), 338–352.

Talleyrand, R. M. (2012). Disordered eating in women of color: Some counseling considerations. *Journal of Counseling & Development, 90*(3), 271–280.

Taylor, J. Y., Caldwell, C. H., Baser, R. E., Faison, N., & Jackson, J. S. (2007). Prevalence of eating disorders among Blacks in the National Survey of American Life. *International Journal of Eating Disorders, 40*(Suppl. 3), S10–14. https://doi.org/10.1002/eat.20451.

Wilfley, D. E., Pike, K. M., Dohm, F. A., Striegel-Moore, R. H., & Fairburn, C. G. (2001). Bias in binge eating disorder: How representative are recruited clinic samples? *Journal of Consulting and Clinical Psychology, 69*(3), 383–388. https://doi.org/10.1037//0022-006x.69.3.383.

Yarrow, A. (2018, February 27). How eating disorders became a White women problem. *Huffington Post.* Retrieved from www.huffingtonpost.com/entry/opinion-yarrow-eating-disorders-white-women_us_5a945db3e4b0699553cb1d00.

4 Food for Thought, Mind, and Body

Exploring Embodiment Techniques for Black Queer Women

Anisha Cooper

Introduction

Black queer women are excluded from social norms intended for White cis, hetero folx. Hence, many Black queer women are writing their own code of conduct as I have done in this chapter about a neglected topic in the health profession. In this chapter, I define "queerness" as any identity outside of heteronormativity, and I center my own queerness as a Black sexual minority who identifies as a woman. Not only do I identify as a Black queer woman, I also identify as a Black queer woman with an eating disorder. Like most Black queer women with eating disorders, the relationship we create with our bodies constructs the relationship we create with food. If not for the unified "ayyyyes" from our girlfriends and the random "yaaaaas" from our peers, we would continue to navigate our worlds without affirmation and attunement mostly because of our limited access to treatment, limited access to trained professionals, and constant exposure to stigmas. Black women suffer from eating disorders, specifically binge eating behaviors, at higher rates than any other demographic; however, access to care and stigma prevent Black women from initiating and maintaining care (Brewster, Velez, Breslow, & Geiger, 2019). Accordingly, in this chapter, I explore guidelines for reaching and treating Black queer women.

I remember pinching the skin around my belly as I eyeballed little pigmented lines. They call these "stretch marks," I explained to my daughter, who wittingly responded in tears. My young empath found herself full of joy and whispered: "Mommy, your belly made room for me." I stood there before her astonished, observing how quickly my daughter consoled me with her compassion for my body stretching beyond capacity to carry a life—her life. Though my lived experience may not resonate with every reader of this chapter, it represents the disjointed relationship I had with my body—the body that created a life with a man but identified as lesbian—the body that birthed a child but strongly desired to hide any reminders of the work involved in conceiving my daughter. I often struggle with body dissatisfaction issues and wonder if I look "gay enough" or "feminine enough." I apprehensively admit these thoughts;

however, for the sake of liberating fellow queer Black women, I speak truth to the disenfranchising power struggle that manifests within my own home.

This power struggle births tension and dissension as social norms view the Black feminized body as an object (Moradi, Dirks, & Matteson, 2005). Somehow, quickly and ever so slowly, the beings who occupy Black queer feminized bodies externally observe their bodies. Similar to falling asleep, externalization occurs within a moment, without specificity. It occurs when social media debates which hair presentation is acceptable: natural hair, relaxed hair, or sew-ins. It appears when a celebrity identifies as queer and their specific aesthetic is now representative of a diverse and ever-changing group. Suddenly, the comparisons seep into ideas about worth and desirability, and the need to manipulate some part of the body increases as the media weighs in. This phenomenon is referred to as the objectification theory.

Objectification theory seeks to provide context for how these standards affect the body. More specifically, the theory posits that sociocultural standards of beauty increase body shame, surveillance, and eating disorder symptoms. Because Black women play consistent hypersexual, angry, and belligerent archetypes, it only makes sense that an increase in eating disorder symptoms exists among us. Nonetheless, when Black women present for treatment, only 17% of clinicians view their disordered eating behaviors as problematic, though eating disorders among queer Black women are equal to, if not more than those of heterosexual Black women (National Eating Disorder Association, 2018). Therefore, the first defense against eating disorders in Black women lies in an assessment.

The *Diagnostic and Statistical Manual of Mental Disorders* serves as the quintessential reference for eating disorder criteria in our profession. However, understanding the nuance of identity impacts the severity of symptoms. For example, solely using a screening tool that assesses attitudes toward food, appearance, and exercise may not capture clients in their fullness. For Black queer women, a sense of connectedness to the queer community shows a negative correlation with eating disorder behaviors (National Eating Disorders Association, 2018), yet Black people possess lower rates of acceptance for being a sexual minority, especially within religious communities (Human Rights Campaign, 2019). Assessing Black queer clients for connectedness and spiritual identity proves itself vital for disordered eating behaviors to remain subclinical. Thus, clients should define what is "normal" in their lives so clinicians can determine the effectiveness of their screening tools.

Furthermore, using the Objectification Consciousness Scale to screen for objectification aids the clinical intake process by identifying risk factors for treatment. The higher the objectification rates, the more likely body shame, surveillance, and discomfort exist for the client. Additionally, I encourage clinicians to examine how clients challenge these own ideas about themselves and whether they acknowledge how these ideas affect their relationship with food (McKinley & Hyde, 1996). To further emphasize this point, I will offer anecdotal evidence: Once after a White clinician asked me how I felt about food, I laughed my way through explaining how I loved it. I also emphasized my love of my curves, and I laughed at the notion of having any issues at all. A sense of rejecting White ideas of skinny and healthy presented itself as if I wanted to make her understand that I *couldn't* have an eating disorder; I'm Black. Never mind the ignorance of that comment, the truth is the misconception endures. Though I knew that I struggled to keep my curves and to maintain a flat stomach, I knew I had not achieved "slim thickness." To maintain my body ideal, I often skipped meals to reach this aesthetic marker while resenting every inch of my curves because my button-ups refused to fit over my wide hips and full chest. My idea of what "gay" looked like and how my body looked performing it haunted me. Subsequently, it loomed over my relationship with food. Again, I would be an ideal candidate for the Objectification Consciousness Scale, because it serves as a helpful tool in screening risk for Black queer women.

Another assessment tool includes screening for minority stressors such as ideas regarding racial and sexual discrimination, safety, and body awareness. As a young, queer Black woman residing in Atlanta during a time when Black women and girls are reported missing every other day, I would be remiss not to mention how much my safety feels compromised. Body surveillance increases due to social norms and thoughts regarding how Black women are viewed in the media become increasingly negative. Seeing that Black women's safety still isn't prioritized reinforces objectification. Our bodies are not regarded in the same light as others. For a clinician to not assess how current media affects the client's vision of themselves is a disservice to the client's mental health.

The relationship with the client develops before screening. Within your marketing and environment, Black queer women seek inclusivity. Notice how your website looks. Does it intentionally state that you have experience and interest in treating Black queer women? Does your environment and décor consider inclusivity? This attention to detail influences the relationship immediately. Clients spend little time on a therapist's webpage. Using media in this instance serves to attract black queer women as a demographic rather than deter them. Assess your efforts in reaching this demographic, but if they're already in the room with you, you're doing something right. Continue building rapport with the client by creating a nonjudgmental space that does not pathologize who they love. Some of you may argue that this is obvious; however, heteronormative questions assuming the gender of romantic partners or paperwork that only provides binary options are just some examples of rapport fractures.

Once thorough assessment and rapport building combine, you're set to start working through embodiment techniques rather than solely focusing on behaviors for eating. In conjunction with positively impacting your client's relationship with food, I hope this chapter encourages you to positively impact the relationship Black queer women have with their bodies. In doing so, you can encourage the client's experiences in the mental, physical, and social constructs and help the client increase awareness on perceptions of power and freedom in their minds, bodies, and social groups. Helping the client define embodiment after medical evaluation empowers the client. Without medical intervention, the client may not have any conceptualization of mindfulness or embodiment. When nutritional needs are met, the client and clinician work to reestablish body connection and comfort, agency and functionality, experience and expression of desire, attuned self-care, and inhabiting the body as a subjective site. Together, these dimensions define embodiment (Piran, 2017).

Embodiment for Black queer women starts with mindfulness techniques for the client. Bringing the client into current connection with how they view their body may seem triggering, but slowly introducing a depersonalized method of grounding can initiate this process (American Psychological Association, 2015). Encourage the client to notice the space and integrate senses to allow the client to create awareness of surroundings progressively. Introducing "safe space" in my own practice looks like focusing on intimacy. I like to refer to safe space as sacred space. I emphasize the importance of creating a space for the clients and their higher selves. In encouraging intimacy, body connection and safety are encouraged. The client creates a space for themselves, and this directly challenges how they navigate in a world that does not create those affirming spaces. This small step also encourages the client to reclaim power and agency. They're also listening to their own desires. The ability to hear and understand their desire allows clients to understand hunger, fullness, and pleasure cues later.

Essentially, Piran (2017) provides language for cocreating a new relationship with the body that reflects a subjective idea of aesthetic rather than a comparative, external one. Embodiment for the Black queer woman suggests she is allowed to take up space, she is allowed to heed her desires (e.g., food and pleasure), and she is allowed to take care of her body. This freedom liberates her from social constructs around body weight and Eurocentric views of beauty. Moreover, it decenters heterosexism and offers to affirm the client's sexual orientation. Narrative therapy suggests challenging how queer looks, moves, and operates. The therapist empowers the client to create definitions of queer identity and aesthetic.

Finding narratives that imply that one look is the norm or most appealing and ideas about how those narratives affect fueling the body open up opportunities for the client to increase agency and functionality once more. Now that the client is identifying your office as a space where they can explore how they see their body as well as how they move in their body, I suggest you reach out to other queer affirming colored spaces that also affirm your client's experience. Directly juxtaposing what the client experiences in the world inspires the client to expand and hold space in the room (Moradi & Grzanka, 2017). Some techniques to consider include stretching, grounding and deep breathing exercises, and body awareness. Body awareness statements should consider include the following:

- Where do you feel that? What color would the feeling be? What texture?
- Where do you feel discomfort/shame/guilt about your body? If you could love that part of your body, what would you say? How would you appreciate your body?
- Feel the rise and fall of your chest as you inhale and exhale. Feel the air on your upper lip as you breathe through your nose.
- Rest your tongue on the bottom of your mouth. Feel every tooth in your mouth, and as you breathe in, gently swallow and breathe through your throat.

Reassuring queer, Black women of their body experience, especially when they are recovering from an eating disorder, is vital in the recovery process. Notice their body language as they describe their relationship with food while directing their awareness to their body response. What happens when we discuss meal prepping? What happens when we discuss discomfort while eating? Allow your client to honor their body response; offering a few options helps to not overwhelm a person who is not accustomed to choices. One of the options needs to be *none of these options* or *nothing at all*. Slowly decreasing these options permits the client to develop their own response; however, use your clinical judgment to measure the client's comfort with their body before reducing the options (Piran, 2017).

Additionally, minorities in general hold tension within their body due to minority stress. As I mentioned, minority stress influences the Black queer experience and permits the person to activate their trauma response as they feel threatened. The traumatized brain reacts defensively, and clients may view their actions as "uncontrolled" or "natural." Increasing body attunement allows the brain to operate outside of trauma.

References

American Psychological Association. (2015). Guidelines for psychological practice with transgender and gender nonconforming people. *American Psychologist, 70,* 832–864.

Brewster, M. E., Velez, B. L., Breslow, A. S., & Geiger, E. F. (2019). Unpacking body image concerns and disordered eating for transgender women: The roles of sexual objectification and minority stress. *Journal of Counseling Psychology, 66*(2), 131–142. https://doi.org/10.1037/cou0000333.

Human Rights Campaign. (2019, November 17). Communities of color: Black & African American LGBTQ. Retrieved from https://www.hrc.org/.

McKinley, N. M., & Hyde, J. S. (1996). The objectified body consciousness scale: Development and validation. *Psychology of Women Quarterly, 20,* 181–215. http://doi.org/10.1111/j.1471-6402.1996.tb00467.x.

Moradi, B., Dirks, D., & Matteson, A. V. (2005). Roles of sexual objectification experiences and internalization of standards of beauty in eating disorder symptomatology: A test and extension of objectification theory. *Journal of Counseling Psychology, 52,* 420–428.

Moradi, B., & Grzanka, P. R. (2017). Using intersectionality responsibly: Toward critical epistemology, structural analysis, and social justice activism. *Journal of Counseling Psychology, 64*, 500–513.

National Eating Disorder Association. (2018). Statistics & research on eating disorders. Retrieved from https://www.nationaleatingdisorders.org/statistics-research-eating-disorders.

Piran, N. (2017). *Journeys of embodiment at the intersection of body and culture: The developmental theory of embodiment.* London, UK: Academic Press.

5 Social Desirability, Social Networking Sites, and Eating Disorders Among African American Women

Chantelle Bernard

Introduction

Understanding of the pervasiveness of Euro-centered ideals on African American women and its relationship to the rise of disordered eating among this demographic must be further researched. As a starting place, researchers must examine the historical representation of African American women and its relationship to early perspectives on desirability devised during slavery (Rogers-Wood & Petrie, 2010). Upon further examination, scholars may be able to establish a connection between early activities and treatment that took place during slavery, such as preferential treatment being given to slaves with lighter skin and eyes and straight hair versus those with darker skin and coarser hair (Rogers-Wood & Petrie, 2010). The residual effects of differential treatment based on skin color, hair texture, body shape, and size has evolved over the years; however, African American women still suffer the effects of early standards, as well as a sustained expectation to mold their body image into a narrower, euro-centered thin ideal (Nasser, 2009). In this way, early desirability standards have transcended through time and have directly influenced the current permutations of social desirability for African American women in modern day media (Rogers-Wood & Petrie, 2010; Ellis-Hervey, Doss, DeShae, Nicks, & Araiza, 2016). Giving strong consideration to this relationship will provide efficacy in the conceptualization of existing grooming activities, as well as the ongoing internalization of euro-centered standards within African American women, as well as in those who evaluate them (Nasser, 2009).

Researchers believe this European standard of beauty has so thoroughly permeated African American women's self-perception, body image, and feelings about social desirability that disordered eating behaviors among this demographic go largely unnoticed and undertreated (Rogers-Wood & Petrie, 2010; Ellis-Hervey et al., 2016). Every woman has her own standard of beauty; however, the euro-centered standards seemingly have permeated across social networking platforms and caused African American women to increase disordered eating behaviors to achieve a desired body shape and to meet society's standard of beauty (Ellis-Hervey et al., 2016). Researchers are beginning to consider the relationship between exposure to media and the prevalence of disordered eating among African American women, as well as the pressure felt by this demographic to conform to western beauty standards (Rogers-Wood & Petrie, 2010).

Social Desirability, Culture, and Body Image

Social desirability (SD) is defined as both a behavior and an achievement. Behaviorally, SD refers to an individual's tendency to provide culturally acceptable responses, images, or behaviors that mitigate unpleasant social reactions (i.e., comments, opinion, or rejection; Freitas, Oliveira, Correia, Pinh, & Poinhos, 2017). An example of achieved social desirability occurs when an individual perceives that he/she has met the criteria for a particular culture's standard of beauty and is deemed physically attractive or desirable by its majority (Freitas et al., 2017). Social cultural theorists believe a lack of social desirability can have a significant impact on an individual's psychological well-being, as well as beliefs about their own appearance, and how an individual interprets and internalizes negative feedback (Carriere & Kluck, 2014). Unfortunately, the connection between social desirability, body image, and eating behaviors has not been fully elucidated (Ellis-Hervey et al., 2016; Freitas et al., 2017). However, Rogers-Wood and Petrie (2010) believe social desirability aligns with a sociocultural model, where there is a transactional relationship between the internalization of societal beauty ideals, body dissatisfaction, and personal body image concerns.

According to Rucker and Cash (1992), body image has always been a difficult concept to deconstruct, particularly because body image is unidimensional, bears cultural considerations, is widely accepted, and embodies faulty assumptions that are held by diverse groups. Early studies on body image and eating disorders supported the notion of body dissatisfaction and lower body esteem as a concern among certain subcultural groups (i.e., Caucasian women, athletes, gymnasts, and models) (Nasser, 2009). However, Nasser (2009) suggests body image and body dissatisfaction is a global phenomenon and should not be narrowly defined by race, ethnicity, gender, or subgroup. Beyond the socio-cultural model, Rucker and Cash (1992) contend that body image should also be understood at the individual level and based upon a person's perceptual internalization (i.e., including body size, perceived distortions, and comparisons to idealized standards). Further, researchers suggest body image should be evaluated through an individual's attitudinal and psychological presentation (i.e., affect, cognitions, and behaviors; p. 291).

To this point,Rucker and Cash (1992) suggest the process of appearance appraisal is quite complex in women, and it begins to take shape in young girls as early as age seven. Studies have shown that many women are often groomed by subtle pressures from family members to lose weight, or to improve their body shape during important developmental periods, which often sets the stage for body dissatisfaction throughout adulthood (Greenwood & Dal Cin, 2012). Carriere and Kluck (2014) also contend that when women grow up with negative commentary about their appearance from family members, they are more prone to develop disordered eating behaviors.

Given the constant pressure to achieve a certain body image (i.e., "thin ideal") in the media, studies have shown that women have become highly susceptible to feelings of conformity and tend to accept negative commentary as opposed to feeling completely rejected in their relationships (Carriere & Kluck, 2014, Nasser, 2009). Carriere and Kluck (2014) suggest when an individual is socialized with negative comments about their body, they in turn modify their self-perception to sustain levels of trust in their relationships or environment. Carriere and Kluck (2014) also highlighted that being exposed to negative feedback from family members and peers extends beyond a sense of confirmation, social acceptance, or even body dissatisfaction; it is often tied to an acknowledgment of acceptance in close relationships (Carriere & Kluck, 2014).

Considering the way body ideals have taken shape in today's society and the way body satisfaction is shaped by societal norms, it is not surprising that body esteem can be so easily influenced by the internalization of social media commentary (Kim & Chock, 2015; Padgett & Biro, 2003; Greenwood & Dal Cin, 2012). In keeping with cultural consideration, Nasser (2009) also suggests changes in modernization, urbanization, and individualization have contributed to the way women perceive themselves, their bodies, and their relationship with food. The growth of online media, the diet industry, and consumerism has promoted the current thin body ideal and continued the perpetuation of thinness values (Freitas et al., 2017; Nasser, 2009).

In addition to changes in Western culture and the growth of technology, body image researchers suggest that disordered eating be examined from a cultural, subcultural, and intercultural framework. For example, in earlier studies, researchers reported that there are differences in the way Caucasian women experience body dissatisfaction as compared to African American women (Greenwood & Dal Cin, 2012; Padgett & Biro, 2003). Greenwood and Dal Cin (2012) suggested Caucasian women experience body dissatisfaction at a lower body mass index (BMI) than African American women, and Padgett and Biro (2003) suggest that when African American women reported body dissatisfaction, it was at a significantly higher BMI or when they were already overweight or obese (p. 351). This research highlights a noted misconception, as it alludes to African American women being less apt to internalize the "thin beauty" ideal, require a lower need for approval from others, and subscribe less to mainstream beauty norms (Padgett & Biro, 2003, p. 352; Greenwood & Dal Cin, 2012). Further, early literature suggested African American women were less likely to engage in disordered eating practices, as compared to Caucasian women (Rucker & Cash, 1992; Padgett & Biro, 2003). The earlier studies also suggested African American women maintain a lower prevalence of eating disorders, compared to other demographics (Perloff, 2014). However, newer studies have emerged and provided very different outcomes.

Today, studies have shown that African American women are participating in disordered eating, and the number is steadily increasing (Rogers-Wood & Petrie, 2010; Greenwood & Dal Cin, 2012). In addition, more recent studies suggest that there are fewer reported differences in body concerns across culture than once reported, and that the pre-occupation with thinness and eating is surprisingly not as dissimilar as researchers once believed (Greenwood & Dal Cin, 2012; Nasser, 2009). In fact, Rogers-Wood and Petrie (2010) suggest that African American women are actively participating in various forms of disordered eating, to include starving, fasting, restricting, and meal skipping.

Nasser (2009) believes the perpetuation of a Western, euro-centered "thin ideal" is not simply a biased perspective on physical presentation; it is a systemic problem that has significant implications for African American women's sense of authentic cultural identity. Sepúlveda and Calado (2012) suggest that the Western, euro-centered body ideals have also contributed to blind spots in treatment among cultural groups and diluted cultural specificity in clinical evaluation. Future examination of disordered eating behaviors from a multicultural framework will provide stronger efficacy in validating the impact of a standardized aesthetic ideal, as being contributory to the rise of psychological distress, eating disorders, and lowered body esteem in women from all cultures (Padgett & Biro, 2003). Nasser (2009) believes that with further examination, practitioners will be better apprised of the etiology and prevalence of eating disorders and may begin to factor in the influence of westernization, modernization, and urbanization as confounding variables for treatment of diverse groups (Nasser, 2009).

Influence of Social Networking Sites on Social Desirability in African American Women

Social networking sites (SNSs) have grown rapidly over the past two decades, serving as powerful transmitters of messages and images related to the ideal body image. SNSs have become popularized for their capacity to enhance self-promotion and provide immediate feedback regarding measures of social desirability in their users (Perloff, 2014). The recent growth of social networking sites has further cultivated beauty ideals established in the 20th century, and perpetuated an ideal body image (BI) for women around the world (Santarossa & Woodruff, 2017). Over time, exposure to ubiquitous messages and imagery has caused women to internalize societal standards and integrate their own beliefs into societies standard for beauty, attractiveness, and success (Rogers-Wood & Petrie, 2010; Ellis-Hervey et al., 2016).

Newer studies are emerging regarding the dependent use patterns of SNSs and the influence platforms (i.e., Facebook, Twitter, Instagram, and Pinterest) have on the development of eating disorders, anxiety, and feelings of depression (Santarossa & Woodruff, 2017). Researchers suggest that the increasing displays of slimmer figures in media have contributed largely to the declining well-being of women, and the increased prevalence of depressive symptoms and disordered eating practices (Cohen, 2006; Cohen, Newton-John, & Slater, 2018). Cohen (2006) contends that universal participation on social networking sites and other forms of online media has also contributed to decreased self-esteem and decreased feelings of social desirability in women and men

(Greenwood & Dal Cin, 2012; Perloff, 2014). Santarossa and Woodruff (2017) believe that since SNSs are primarily appearance mediated, the online environment has become a magnet for opportunities to establish negative thoughts about one's own social status, body image, and social acceptance (Santarossa & Woodruff, 2017). In a study of both African American and European American women, participants suggested they evaluated their bodies as lacking in terms of size and shape when confronted with the ubiquitous societal imagery (Ellis-Hervey et al., 2016). While both African American and Caucasian women reported being influenced by ubiquitous imagery on social networking sites (SNSs), most of the content displayed promoted a Euro-centered societal standard of a "thin beauty ideal" (Cohen et al., 2018; Santarossa & Woodruff, 2017). Rogers-Wood and Petrie (2010) suggested the pressure to "fit in," along with the continued exposure to SNSs and mainstream society's thinness values, has only increased the internalization of the thin ideal and body image concerns for all women, as well as contributed significantly to the prevalence of eating disorders among African American women (Rogers-Wood & Petrie, 2010).

Despite the growing influence of SNSs on African American women, researchers suggest the "thin ideal" is not actually a natural part of African American women's cultural value system. Ellis-Hervey et al. (2016) contend that the lack of consideration and representation of ethnic imagery in media has contributed significantly to many African American women believing they have to participate in acculturated euro-centered beauty ideals to be acceptable in a Western society (Rogers-Wood & Petrie, 2010; Ellis-Hervey et al., 2016). Rogers-Wood and Petrie (2010) also believe the mainstream "thinness values" have done more than contribute to increased body image concerns and eating disorders among African American women; but it has undermined opportunities for African American women to display authentic cultural expression.

With earlier reports in research suggesting that African American women maintained a lower body surveillance and a lower preoccupation with media personas, as compared to White women, there remains a gap in understanding the degree to which African American women are affected by the continued perpetuation of euro-centered standards (Dalleya et al., 2019; Rucker & Cash, 1992). In the past two decades, researchers have begun to highlight the growing prevalence of African American women as being susceptible to negative commentary, reporting higher degrees of body checking, dieting, and body dissatisfaction in response to the promotion of the Euro-centered thin ideal (Rogers-Wood & Petrie, 2010). Contrary to early studies, researchers Rogers-Wood and Petrie (2010) found that 59% of African American women surveyed in their study scored "at risk" for internalizing body image concerns and body dissatisfaction after exposure to online messages and images.

Given the constant evolution of social networking sites and other platforms (e.g., blogging, vlogging, Snapchat) to promote "thinness" from a Euro-centered perspective, African American women have a difficult task ahead to establish themselves as socially desirable in the United States (Perloff, 2014). Furthermore, with the persistent misrepresentation of African Americans in the media and literature, clinicians have found it difficult to consider the degree of psychological distress felt by African American women, who have been historically underrepresented, underevaluated, and undertreated for eating disorders (Greenwood & Dal Cin, 2012; Becker, Middlemass, Taylor, Johnson, & Gomez, 2017). Padgett and Biro (2003) contend that more research is warranted regarding the lack of cross-cultural representation in mass media and its impact on body dissatisfaction among African American women (Sepúlveda & Calado, 2012; Padgett & Biro, 2003). Continuing research from a multicultural framework will increase the understanding of the challenges African American women encounter, and it may further raise awareness regarding the influence and impact of societal beauty standards on psychological well-being (Rogers-Wood & Petrie, 2010). Finally, with newer research, clinicians will become more knowledgeable about internalized cultural beauty messaging and consider African American women as an at-risk demographic for body concerns and disordered eating behaviors (Rogers-Wood & Petrie, 2010).

Disordered Eating Behaviors, Food Insecurity, and Intermittent Fasting

Women, in general, tend to have a complex relationship with their bodies, and when there is constant pressure to achieve an idealized body image or a "thin ideal," studies have shown that restrictive dieting has become a well-adopted practice (Schaumberg, Anderson, Anderson, & Reilly, 2015). Research is growing regarding the direct relationship between internalization of societal beauty ideals and disordered eating. This poses a challenge for African American women, who have historically been advertised as full-figured, overweight, and out of shape, rendering their frame as ethically expected and acceptable (Nasser, 2009). Researchers believe the collective acceptance of this imagery over time has left some African American women in acceptance of this image, and others chasing the thin ideal, and in full participation of disordered eating to acquire some sense of social desirability (Rogers-Wood & Petrie, 2010). Recent studies have proven that African American women find themselves attempting to navigate a complex social climate, in which there is very little validation of their body image or brand of social desirability (Ellis-Hervey et al., 2016). While there have been significant strides made on social media to deliver more inclusive images that are representative of people of color, there is still a steady influence of euro-centered imagery portrayed through every platform (Ellis-Hervey et al., 2016). This has left a very narrow window for African American women to participate in self-promotion, and feel socially accepted and desirable in mainstream society (Nasser, 2009).

Alongside the influence of social media, African American women face contextual challenges when attempting to participate on the same nutritional playing field with other women. For example, the most prominent concern among African American women is gaining access to healthy foods to achieve their desired body frame (Schaumberg et al., 2015). In a study examining eating behaviors, with ethnic identity being moderated among the participants, Rogers-Wood and Petrie (2010) found there was a strong relationship between acculturation activities and restricted eating. To this point, Nasser (2009) suggested characteristics such as socioeconomic status, level of education, food security, and availability of fitness resources play a significant role in the types of decisions African American women make to manage their body image and body esteem. Nasser (2009) believes sociocultural influences have contributed to food insecurity, food deserts, lifestyle stressors, and lack of opportunities for exercise among African American women. Becker et al. (2017) suggested food insecurity has the potential to impact families more than two generations removed from the socioeconomic misfortune. In 2009, research suggested that one in seven households were food insecure, and the adults who suffered from food insecurity tended to have low nutritional intake, hypertension, diabetes, depression, and other mental health problems (Nasser, 2009).

Becker et al. (2017) identified generational, socioeconomic challenges, and personal lifestyle factors as the most significant contributors to African American women directly and indirectly participating in disordered eating behaviors. Becker et al. (2017) believe that food insecurity has some direct ties to the culturally accepted choices African American women make when intentionally or unintentionally participating in disordered eating. One might ask how do food insecurity and body image concerns coincide with disordered eating in African American women (Becker et al., 2017)? Research has determined that obesity, food insecurity, and body dissatisfaction are more prevalent among low-income populations (Becker et al., 2017). In fact, African American women were reported to be among the highest demographic with reported food insecurity in the United States (Becker et al., 2017). Nasser (2009) believes that the urbanization of cities, the evolution of eating patterns, cultural food preferences, and changes in mealtimes have also contributed to the increases in the rates of obesity and subsequent increases in weight consciousness, and disordered eating patterns among African American women. For this reason, there are three common disordered eating practices used among African American women: intermittent fasting, food restriction, and meal skipping (Becker et al., 2017).

In a study of African American women who were food insecure, more than 50% indicated that they unintentionally fasted, experienced poorer appetites (practiced restriction), and participated in meal-skipping practices despite having food available (Becker et al., 2017). Malinowski et al. (2019) highlighted that food-insecure adults tended to rely on low-cost, high-energy foods, leading to obesity, hypertension, diabetes, and other nutrition-related diseases. Nasser (2009) also suggests when there are insufficient resources to support well-being, women are bound to lose their appetites due to acculturative stress. Nasser (2009) also believes the associated stress contributes to maladaptive coping, where the body becomes a dominant means by which tension is manifested, as well as the platform of expression for disordered eating. This validates the primary rationale for African American women participating in restrictive and fasting types of dietary interventions.

Further, researchers have found that when examining the beliefs about obesity and eating disorders in African American women, one must also consider the interplay of religion, environment, and other multicontextual factors (e.g., stress, depression, physical illness, and mental illness) (Becker et al., 2017). Nasser (2009) suggests African American women can easily participate in restrictive types of disordered eating practices because the meal plan aligns well with cultural or faith teachings, which also coincides with their environment and the availability of resources (Nasser, 2009).

For example, the Intermittent Fasting (IF) diet is a newer form of time-restricted eating (typically 16 hours of fasting and 8 hours eating), which has gained popularity in recent years as a new paradigm and approach to weight loss or the reduction of inflammation (Malinowski et al., 2019). The IF diet has also been found to have a beneficial effect on lowering blood pressure and improving insulin uptake, which has significant health benefits for African American women with health-related risk factors (Malinowski et al., 2019). Intermittent fasting is also clinically indicated to manage culturally specific diseases, such as heart disease, diabetes, and hypertension, and is well-documented as a new effective dietetic solution aimed at reducing body mass index and body fats. Procedurally, the Intermittent Fasting (IF) diet involves the exchange of an individual's normal daily caloric intake with the use of intermittent, short-term caloric restriction (Malinowski et al., 2019). For example, those participating in an IF meal plan are encouraged to only consume food within a strictly defined time period or on a specific day of the week. The variants of timed eating restriction may include 16 or 24 hours a day of fasting without food intake to two days a week of calorie restriction and five days of a regular (normal) diet (Malinowski et al., 2019). The entire cycle is often conducted under medical supervision and is meant to be a temporary plan (Malinowski, et al., 2019).

While the IF plan is traditionally administered under the care of a medical provider, many choose to follow the plan on their own and experience success. However, despite the noted benefits of the IF meal plan, there are some disadvantages that are not without significance. One of the major drawbacks of intermittent fasting is that periods of fasting for even a few hours in the beginning can cause huge problems in emotional and psychological well-being. Malinowski et al. (2019) suggest the most common side effects of IF include bad breath, bad mood, fatigue, or dizziness due to the body using ketones instead of glucose for fuel. Further, the IF meal plan may not be sustainable for people with uncontrolled diabetes or reactive hypoglycemia (Malinowski et al., 2019). The IF diet is also difficult for those with certain psychological disorders, hormonal imbalances, and existing eating disorders (Malinowski et al., 2019). As discussed, when African American women participate in restrictive eating practices, it is not necessarily representative of a desire for control, as is often reported by their Caucasian counterparts (Padgett & Biro, 2003). For

African American women, restrictive eating has been found to be based upon a degree of starvation that is beyond a pre-occupation with the body and representative of a hunger in the mind (Padgett & Biro, 2003).

Whether the disordered eating behavior is intentional or accidental, further research is warranted on the relationship between social desirability, online imagery, and eating disorders among African American women. Considering the relative ease of participation and its relative low cost, it is believed that the IF diet and its varieties may continue to grow among African American women, regardless of its side effects or increased physical and emotional consequences. Without ongoing recognition and research, it is likely that restrictive eating practices and intermittent fasting behaviors will continue to become prevalent among all women, and African American women's disordered eating behaviors may continue to be overlooked (Dalleya et al., 2019; Schaumberg et al., 2015). As researchers continue to examine the movement of eating disorders from an individual neurosis to a cultural marker of distress, there may be greater interest in addressing the systemic forces that impact the psychological and physical well-being of African American women and women of color more broadly.

References

Becker, C. B., Middlemass, K., Taylor, B., Johnson, C., & Gomez, F. (2017). Food insecurity and eating disorder pathology. *International Journal of Eating Disorders*, *50*(9), 1031–1040.

Carriere, L. J., & Kluck, A. S. (2014). Appearance commentary from romantic partners: Evaluation of an adapted measure. *Body Image*, *11*, 137–145.

Cohen, R., Newton-John, T., & Slater, A. (2018). "Selfie"-objectification: The role of selfies in self-objectification and disordered eating in young women. *Computers in Human Behavior*, *79*, 68–74.

Cohen, S. (2006). Media exposure and the subsequent effects on body dissatisfaction, disordered eating, and drive for thinness: A review of the current research. *Mind Matters: The Wesleyan Journal of Psychology*, *1*, 57–57.

Dalleya, S. E., Vidalb, J., Buunka, A. P., Schmitta, S., Von Haugwitza, A. C., Kindsa, N.A., . . . Vlasmaa, A. (2019). Disentangling relations between the desirability of the thin-ideal, body checking, and worry on college women's weight-loss dieting: A self-regulation perspective. *Eating Behaviors*, *34*, 1–6.

Ellis-Hervey, N., Doss, A., DeShae, D., Nicks, R., & Araiza, P. (2016). African American personal presentation: Psychology of hair and self-perception. *Journal of Black Studies*, *47*(8), 869–882.

Freitas, D., Oliveira, B., Correia, F., Pinh, S., & Poinhos, R. (2017). Eating behaviour among nutrition students and social desirability as a confounder. *Appetite*, *113*, 187–192.

Greenwood, D. N., & Dal Cin, S. (2012). Ethnicity and body consciousness: Black and white American women's negotiation of media ideals and others' approval. *Psychology of Popular Media Culture*, *1*(4), 220–235.

Kim, J. W., & Chock, T. M. (2015). Body image 2.0: Associations between social grooming on Facebook and body image concerns. *Computers in Human Behavior*, *48*, 331–339.

Malinowski, B., Zalewska, K., Wesierska, A., Sokołowska, M. M., Socha, M., Liczner, G., . . . Wicinski, M. (2019). Intermittent fasting in cardiovascular disorders—An overview. *Nutrients, 11,* 1–18.

Nasser, M. (2009). Eating disorders across culture. *Psychiatry, 8*(9), 347–350.

Padgett, J., & Biro, F. M. (2003). Different shapes in different cultures: Body dissatisfaction, overweight, and obesity in African-American and Caucasian females. *Pediatric Adolescent Gynecology, 16,* 349–354.

Perloff, R. M. (2014). Social media effects on young women's body image concerns: Perspectives and an agenda for research. *Sex Roles, 71,* 363–377. https://doi.org/10.1007/s11199-014-0384-6.

Rogers-Wood, N. A., & Petrie, T. A. (2010). Body dissatisfaction, ethnic identity, and disordered eating among African American women. *Journal of Counseling Psychology, 57*(2), 141–153.

Rucker, C. E., & Cash, T. F. (1992). Body images, body size perceptions and eating behaviors among African-American and White College women. *International Journal of Eating Disorders, 12*(3), 291–299.

Santarossa, S., & Woodruff, S. J. (2017). #Social Media: Exploring the relationship of social networking sites on body image, self-esteem, and eating disorders. *Social Media Society,* 1–10.

Schaumberg, K., Anderson, D. A., Anderson, L. M., & Reilly, E. E. (2015). Does short-term fasting promote pathological eating patterns? *Eating Behaviors, 19,* 168–172.

Sepúlveda, R. A., & Calado, M. (2012). Westernization: The role of mass media on body image and eating disorders. In *Relevant topics in eating disorders* (pp. 47–64). Rijeka, Croatia: IntechOpen.

6   The Skin I'm In

Stereotypes and Body Image Development in Women of Color

Warrenetta Crawford Mann

Introduction

The moment our eyes met in the waiting area I knew I would have to work hard at building a positive relationship with this client. It was not until we both sat with our initial preconceptions that I fully understood why her face fell when she saw me. As an African American female therapist, I was accustomed to having to convince my clients that I was qualified to help them. From the time I was born I had heard over and over how people will discount my intellect, my femininity, and my work ethic. However, on this day, I saw a new look of trepidation, perhaps even disappointment, on the face of my new client. As she looked at me through big, brown eyes, caramel skin, and curly-kinky hair like mine, we both became keenly aware that in the space between us was a host of ethnic and cultural specters that we would have to overcome if we were to be successful in our work as client and clinician. These specters were rooted in the beliefs we held of ourselves and one another though we had never met before. While there was no indication of such in traditional evidence-based practice, disentangling these beliefs would prove to be a critical part of our work to free her, at least in part, from the history of poor body image and disordered eating that brought her in.

Stereotypes are powerful images that impact the way people see themselves and the world. The Oxford English Dictionary (2018) defines stereotype as "a widely held but fixed and oversimplified image or idea of a particular type of person or thing." For people of color, women, and gender and sexual minorities, these images are often the first ways in which people are known by those whose representation is accepted as dominant. Real, human, knowing relationships with people unlike themselves are often supplanted by what they come to believe they know about others through stereotypical images invoked by familial folklore or media images. As therapists, we are no exception. Despite the documented growth of people who identify as Black, brown, and multiracial in America, the racial and ethnic diversity of mental health professionals continues to considerably lag behind the wider American society (St. Louis, 2018). While the mental health professions have made a concerted effort to ensure multicultural competence is a standard part of the professions' educational and training curricula, it remains an exceptional occurrence for mental health professionals to have professors, supervisors, or peers of color who can help them contextualize perspectives on culture, racial politics, oppression, or power as they play out in mental health practice. Opportunities to gain advanced and intermediate practical training with populations of color are rare and often optional components of professional continuing education in the mental health professions. As a result, mental health practitioners find themselves bound by the same cultural encapsulation pervasive throughout American society. In their professional encounters with people of color, they enter the arena of a mental health clinic armed with the same knowledge base of racially, culturally, and ethnically skewed literature taught in standard graduate programs. To approach cultural competence, practitioners rely largely on their clients—those coming for help—to educate us about their experiences. When a therapist is relying on the client to contextualize their own experience of the world, there is an inherent challenge of teasing apart what represents true pathology in a clinical sense from the pathological representations of people and their cultures as expressed through the eyes of those who have the power to define them as "other."

Largely a view of the imaginations of the dominant group, stereotypes provide a uniquely oppressive perspective on who people are or are not (St. Jean & Feagin, 1998). As part of a more general system of oppression, stereotypes limit the subject to narrowly intense, one-dimensional, primarily one-down images that lack the subtlety, diversity, and nuance of the authentic human experience, particularly of women of color (Collins, 1990). The ability to know oneself and to be known by others is a foundational element of healthy relationship for anyone. For women who find themselves struggling to fully connect to their own body or sense of self through disordered relationships with food, this ability to be known becomes of particular importance. Therapists, regardless of their ethnic or racial backgrounds, are therefore at a veiled disadvantage when working with Black women. Before therapists can begin to be truly helpful to Black women, their first task is to understand how Black female clients may be imperceptibly dehumanized by stereotypes in therapists' minds and in their own lives.

We sat across from one another in what was for both of us a familiar dyadic pattern. She prepared to explain her history of body image problems as she had indicated on the obligatory prescreening questionnaire when my stereotypical Black Mamma, one of the better of the Black woman stereotypes, kicked in. This stereotype is capable of the kind of unconditional love and support that can nurture a Black child in a society that does everything in its power to destroy it.

"You looked disappointed when you saw me. Tell me about your relationships with Black women," I said.

Like any new client, she tried to dismiss and minimize her discomfort, but the powerful desire to be different that compels a young person into therapy took over, and she played along.

I told her every thought I had about her when I saw her, and then I apologized for myself and every other Black woman who had assumed that they knew her and what she needed. While the attributions that her mother, grandmother, aunts, and friends had of her were largely positive, those attributions were rooted in similarly narrow and one-dimensional definitions of who she might be. They dismissed her pain and assumed that she should be content with whatever bit of happiness or productivity occupied her life.

We both had to rethink who we were. Freedom from the power of these stereotypes emancipated both of us: her to move forward in a space of self-acceptance and affirmation and me to an improved understanding of how stereotypes impact how we see ourselves in our minds and in the mirror.

Stereotypes are barriers to the authentic process of relationship building that is paramount to a successful therapeutic relationship. They presumptuously move the client and therapist ahead of the process of discovery that is critical in the early stages of the work. The questions that should be asked may not be asked. And the speaking aloud of one's truths by the client is neglected. Stereotypes sit in a space in the therapeutic relationship that is better occupied with time spent engaging in dyadic discovery. Stereotypes, by definition, are false narratives and therefore offer no substance for people trying to regain their whole selves as part of the process. Moreover, for therapists, stereotypes serve as misleading shortcuts that hinder their ability to evaluate the client's ability to be known. For these reasons, stereotypes are particularly intrusive in relationships with women whose behavior may already be so fraught with secrecy. The stereotypes uniquely applied to Black women are therefore salient to understand due to the space they occupy when working with women whose body image and/or relationship with food is disturbed.

Mammy, Matriarch, Jezebel, and Sapphire are among the stereotypes commonly cited in the social science literature associated with Black women (Collins, 1990). These caricatures intended to represent the Black woman each encompass an aspect of physicality, selflessness, and relational orientation that, when applied, constricts the humanity and consciousness of any real woman. These limitations impact both the external and internal experience of a woman's self and, as such, are as present in the therapeutic space as all other psychological phenomena.

Mammy, the domestic servant, is the first of the stereotypes assigned to Black women. Physically, she is typically obese, dark skinned, and dressed for manual labor. Her hair is covered as if to insinuate that she either has not time for the vanities of self-care or seeks to shield it from the harshness of her reality as a domestic worker. Layers of hand-me-down quilted fabric cover her body to disguise any real shape. Instead, she is simply rendered round, an apron covering her entire front to obscure it from view. Her "self" is emotionless. She is neither happy nor sad, but dutiful. Her entire life is consumed with service to others. What those she is beholden to eat, wear, experience, and know becomes her work. She moves from one task to the next to satisfy the needs of those around her. Her relationships are utilitarian in nature. Her worth is derived from what she can do for others and the level of satisfaction they express with her productivity. She expresses no care for her own body, her own thoughts, her own talents or desires—her "self." As such the feedback of her masters becomes her mirror. To know how she is doing in life she, must simply wait for the random evaluation that comes her way at the whim of another— and adjust accordingly. This type of denial of the self is a manifestation of the complete neglect of one's own human needs that can sustain a mindset of abuse of the self.

Matriarch, the overbearing and harsh Black mother, is the remnant of the Mammy. When she has spent all that she has in subordinate service to the "others," she finds herself with precious little left for her own. She has no gentle kindness left for her partner or her children. No nuance in her speech or thought or behavior. She is raw, unrefined, and unfiltered in her expression, and those around her experience both fear and longing. She is laden with the responsibility of creating the appearance of success by ensuring that her family purports the best behavior at all times. As such, she becomes responsible for any offense of her children or her partner. It is her constant mission to create the appearance of perfection. Her body may take on the form of woman, but she lacks femininity and sexuality simply because as a Black woman, her worth is tied to her ability to provide direction and correction. Her thoughts and feelings have only the value to control those around her. Her relationships are controlling and transactional. Do what she says or feel the wrath. There is no comfort or solace to being with her because she lacks the ability to know or be known; she lives only to manage others' impressions. Simultaneously, due to her tenacity and grit, she is a great provider of the basic material sustenance of life. So those who have the unfortunate privilege of being connected to her learn to endure her in order to live another day. Her essence is strength, but in her unyielding strength, she lacks the capacity to tolerate true social and emotional vulnerability in herself and others.

Jezebel and Sapphire, the oversexualized Black stereotypes, are the antithesis to Mammy and Matriarch. Their physicality is made of the dreams and fantasies of those who would desire them. Flawless skin stretched over voluptuous curves and a cinched waist. Their sexuality is often intensified by notable amounts of eagerly applied makeup and clothing that reveals just enough of their secrets to pique almost uncontrollable curiosity. They may wear impractically high heels accompanied by sparkly baubles and beads. Their hair is bone straight and never betrays its natural kinky curl pattern. It is clear that neither of these types is valued for her intellect, and neither makes a very good mother.

On the one hand, Jezebel is busy fulfilling the carnal desires of any man that will have her. She is a direct threat to any wife because she has the ability to give without asking in return. On the other hand, Sapphire is mysteriously able to be sexually tantalizing but never actually available to men. Her value lies in the desire alone. She too is never the wife but always the "other" object and seems to be satisfied as such. Both lack the discipline or moral capacity to commit to anything but the most superficial of relationships. For these Black women, their bodies are the entirety of their worth, and their vanity and devotion to maintaining them to their partners' liking are their existence. They do not have time for motherhood, friendship, school, or commerce, only to attend to enhancing and arousing the ideals of masculine sexuality all around them. As women, they are loners who neither give nor receive from other women. The result is a hyperfocus on the physical attributes that catch the eye and tempt the senses; physical perfection is their only goal.

These stereotypes, along with a few lesser-known others, are commonly used to attempt to describe Black women from the perspective of one who has no real desire to know her as a human being that is both internally and externally impacted by the experiences that make up her existence. They neglect the capacity of a Black woman to think, to feel, to give and receive emotional connection or support. While these images are rarely represented in their original form, they are simply updated and refined into more modern versions of the depictions of the oppressor's imagination. These depictions, through media and expressive arts, have infiltrated the minds and hearts of us all (Harris-Perry, 2011). These depictions are manifested over and over in our cinematic obsession with stories of marginally competent members of the dominant culture who arise to greatness at the urging of some Black female spook who serves as the maid or secretary, caregiver or neighbor, a character who has little dimension to her own life but can so clearly help her dominant counterparts navigate theirs. And so we grapple with the ways in which these stereotypes further complicate the emancipation of Black women from the family of dysfunction known to us as eating and body image issues.

Images control what we think and do in ways so subtle and insidious that we have barely begun to understand them. At the advent of the #MeToo movement, Black women are left wondering if that movement really embraces "*me too.*" Violence and assault on our Black female bodies is so much a part of our history that it is difficult to separate that experience from who or what we are on any given day. When we find ourselves afflicted with any pain, whether physical or emotional, we readily assume it is simply a part of our burden to bear.

Stereotypes create barriers and boundaries that thwart the full expression of the unique personhood that we all have the potential to express. The negative stereotypes often applied to Black women limit their minds and bodies, keeping them trapped in patterns of behavior predetermined to minimize their humanity. Likewise, the positive stereotypes of the Strong Black Woman and Sister Christian dismiss the impact of the oppressive environments that nullify the complex existence often experienced by women who are both successful and depressed, disillusioned, or dissatisfied. To be authentically free of these false narratives, Black women benefit from the ability to examine the degree to which the women they have become, or want to become, are expressed in their physical beings, their selves, and their relationships. As a therapist, it is important to be able to acknowledge the impact that stereotypes have had on our personal and professional development. For White therapists, it may require the acknowledgment that it is only through these stereotypes that we have come to know Black women and that when we have struggled to connect or understand, these stereotypes have provided an escape from acknowledging the dehumanization associated with representation as a member of the oppressive group. Nonetheless, none of us escapes the power of stereotypes.

To the extent that stereotypes are limiting and constraining, they also provide us a place to begin. The concept of predestination is critical in reinforcing the powerlessness and oppression of people of color. When we as therapists begin to introduce the concept of choice into the therapy space related to any of our unconscious biases, our clients can then experiment with different ways of being. Any of us may have aspects of the Mammy, Matriarch, Jezebel, Sapphire, Black Mamma, or more modern iterations, but we are not limited to them. Our clients need to know that they have the power to choose how they show up in the world and that they do not have to show up the same way in every setting or every day. While the limitations of genetics are a more real and daunting influence on our bodies, they do not negate the impact of how we choose to nurture our skin and hair through nutrition and grooming. They do not relegate us to unhealthiness, and they cannot determine whether we exercise. Who we are is equally as spiritual as it is physical, and therefore the time we spend on ourselves understanding ourselves is not time idly spent. We should not be deemed lazy when we choose not to spend every waking moment in service to others, for we too are worthy of the powerful nurturance of our own thoughts and reflections. Moreover, if we choose to cater to the needs of our partners and our children, that too is a choice we have a right to make. We have the freedom to engage fully in relationship with those around us and to expect in return the reciprocal joy that is found in human connection when we allow others to know us and care for us. What we need most from our therapists is to be challenged to be as authentic in the world as we were created to be, not the manifestation of someone's imagination, but a genuine manifestation of body, mind, self and soul—no two exactly alike. We should not have to meet anyone's expectation of who we are, and we should not have to shed our Blackness to conform to an ideal generated from the needs of another to demonstrate their superiority. We can and will be healthy and whole when we can genuinely explore and celebrate who we truly are inside and out in all of its glorious complexity.

What White Therapists Can Do

1. Acknowledge that racism is real and that you have witnessed it. While it is not necessary to implicate yourself when doing so, it is important for the experiences of Black people to be validated in therapy. This means

acknowledging that you are aware of times when a Black woman's name, body, voice, or emotional expression has been used to characterize her as familiar even without knowing her. If you have ever observed even a subtle microaggression or experienced the slightest discomfort with something said about a person of color in your presence, use it as a tool to validate the hundreds of experiences that Black women have on a regular basis. This will allow you both to be more authentic.

2. Use your experiences to discuss the complexity of racially charged situations. If you can understand that O.J. probably did it but that the legal system was broken long before his verdict, this can go a long way in helping to shape a more deeply nuanced experience of intellectual and emotional experience. It is important for Black women to be free from having to agree or disagree with the dichotomous perspectives that lock us into all-or-nothing thinking.

3. Acknowledge that you do not know the experience of Black women, or people of color at all, and just listen. Resist the urge to minimize, justify, diminish, or reframe every emotionally destructive experience Black women have held on to. It makes it easier for us to let them go once we are heard. We, after all, need the same thing other human beings need.

4. Actively engage in understanding how race, culture, ethnicity, and oppression have been a part of your profession and the training and education provided to you. Work to undo any inappropriate beliefs that you have developed by seeking out formal and informal experiences that allow you to authentically engage in antiracist activity. It is difficult to effectively help Black women when you do not understand what they are attempting to recover from.

A Note for Black Female Therapists: It is important to be mindful that we too have taken in the dehumanizing images of stereotypes that constrict our ability to realize our full humanity. If we assume that we are impervious to the power of these stereotypes in our interaction with our clients, then we have wholly missed the point. It will be important to rework the images of ourselves as well as our clients in order to move forward an image of Black Women that is both broad and deep enough to be truly inclusive and healthy.

Traditional psychotherapy was born from the concept of the *tabula rasa*—the blank slate. Therapists of every ethnic and racial background have the opportunity to provide the wisdom of the blank slate to their clients. Black women are especially in need of spaces to shed the ideas that have constrained their genuine growth and development and build their identities from a new foundation free of preconceptions, choosing only what they want from what their experiences have taught them about themselves. In healing from eating concerns and body image issues, Black women need us to help them to see that they can choose life outside of that which has been defined for them internally and externally by whatever stereotype or preconceived notion exists to maintain their need to control and conform to unrealistic ideals. They need therapists, White and Black and other, who are not afraid to support what they may become once they are liberated.

References

Collins, P. H. (1990). *Black feminist thought: Knowledge, consciousness and the politics of empowerment*. New York: Routledge.

Harris-Perry, M. (2011). *Sister citizen: Shame, stereotypes and black women in America*. New Haven, CT: Yale University Press.

Oxford English Dictionary. (2018). Oxford: Oxford University Press.

St. Jean, Y., & Feagin, J. R. (1998). *Double burden: Black women and everyday racism*. Armonk, NY: Sharpe.

St. Louis, G. (2018). Leveling the mental health counseling racial playing field. *Psychology Today*. Retrieved from https://www.psychologytoday.com/us/blog/mind-matters/201802/leveling-the-mental-health-counseling-racial-playing-field.

Part II
Medical Management

7 "Father Hunger?" Engaging Fathers in the Eating Disorder Recovery Process

A Developing Country's Perspective

Caryl James Bateman and Abigail Harrison

Introduction

It has been well documented that eating disorders can have devastating effects on the lives of young women and men who have been diagnosed with them. Families are also affected and may feel helpless in the amount of support they can give and how best to offer this support, especially considering that the lives of their loved ones may be at risk. Eating disorders are abnormal eating behaviors and beliefs about eating and body shape, which profoundly affect biological, psychological, and social functioning (Grilo, 2014). Although they were once felt to be far more prevalent in developed countries, among the upper class, Caucasians, and females (Bruch, 1973), these stereotypes have been challenged as more recent findings indicate that eating disorders are not specific to a particular socio-economic group, ethnicity, gender, or age (Makino, Tsuboi, & Dennerstein, 2004; Mulders-Jones, Mitchison, Girosi, & Hay, 2017). Growing trends have been found in low- and middle-income countries of varied ethnicities, as evidenced by those identified in the Caribbean (Bhugra, Mastrogianni, Maharajh, & Harvey, 2003; Samms-Vaughan, 2002; White & Gardner, 2002; Walker, 2012; Sewell, Martin, & Abel, 2010), where the majority of the population is of African descent. It was not that long ago that eating disorders in Jamaica were felt by many to be rare, perhaps even nonexistent. Despite this, in 1998, two cases of anorexia nervosa were found, four years later, 11 cases of both anorexia and bulimia nervosa were described (White & Gardner, 2002), and 21 years later, more than 30 cases were seen privately (James & Harrison, 2014). Although these represent actual cases that exist in Jamaica, it is possible that the illness may have predated these reported cases. A study reporting on non-Caucasian cases of eating disorders in the United Kingdom between 1981 and 1983 made mention of a Jamaican who was treated for bulimia nervosa along with two other cases of anorexia nervosa that had Jamaican and Barbadian parental lineage (Thomas & Szmukler, 1985). The possibility also exists that there may have been other missed cases in Jamaica, as in reviewing past hospital records, its Caribbean counterpart Curacao found that there were cases that may have met the criteria for anorexia nervosa (Hoek et al., 2005). Other studies also noted that the focus on shape and weight may have resulted in missed opportunities to identify disordered eating behaviors such as self-induced vomiting (Burk, 2015).

More recent studies present cause for concern as the rates of disordered eating behaviors, the precursor to the full-blown eating disorder, continue to grow, which would increase the likelihood that Jamaican professionals will have more cases to contend with. One recent study indicates that one in five Jamaican adolescents is at risk for developing an eating disorder (Harrison et al., 2019), with an increase in prevalence of disordered eating behaviors such as use of laxatives and purging compared to previous reports (Fox & Gordon-Strachan, 2007). Many explanations have been offered as to why the prevalence of disordered eating and eating disorders continues to grow, some of which include the media, globalization, and tourism (Anderson-Fye, 2004; Ichinohe et al., 2004).

Despite the evidence, the myths about eating disorder stereotypes still continue to loom over the island and may continue to play a significant role in the prevention of identifying and providing treatment for persons suffering from the illness. Notwithstanding this, there are cases such as this case of Margaret, which provide detailed information of the psychological and physical complications that come with having an eating disorder, as well as that of the struggles faced by her parents in saving her life. The effects of an eating disorder are the same irrespective of the ethnicity and the country of origin (Hillege, Beale, & Macmaster, 2006; Ma, 2007; Mumford, 1993).

The treatment of eating disorders takes a multidimensional approach of a team trained in the area; it includes a physician, dietitian, psychiatric nurses, psychiatrist, psychologist, and, in some instances, a social worker. In an ideal setting in which there are resources allocated to this, the individual is offered the support of a full team. However, in Jamaica, where there are limited resources and the stigma exists, many patients are seen privately. If seen privately, the individual is exposed to the treatment team, which comprises only two ED-trained specialists (a physician and a psychologist). The team has found that the most plausible approach and support in assisting with patients' recovery is the use of family-based therapy. Although research has shown the family environment is the child's first introduction to nurturance and is where its basic needs are met (Cooper, Whelan, Woolgar, Morrell, & Murray, 2004), by extension, research has shown that the family can have tremendous negative impact on the development of an eating disorder, and conversely, the family can also serve in preventing its development or can lead to successful recovery from an eating disorder.

A family-based approach, the Maudsley model, has proven to be effective in treating eating disorders such as anorexia nervosa (Lock, Le Grange, Agras, & Dare, 2001). This approach may prove to be ideal and perhaps adaptable in a setting in which the resources are limited. Application of the Maudsley approach in this matrifocal structured household setting unveiled some findings that are beneficial to recovery from anorexia nervosa. While the Maudsley approach indicates that parent involvement is critical, it fails to recognize parental gender variability in a Caribbean setting and the role that this might have in successful recovery. While there has been extensive research in Jamaica on contribution of mothers to the development of their children (Clarke, 1999; Burke, Kuczynski, & Perren, 2017), the research on the contributions of Jamaican fathers in the emotional and psychological well-being of their children has not been given equal attention. The lack of recognition of the positive roles that fathers play may be rooted in the historical events of slavery. Anderson and Daley (2015) and Anderson (2009) indicated that these historical events may have stereotyped Afro-Caribbean and Afro-Jamaican fathers as uninvolved and/or absent. More recently, these stereotypes have been challenged, as emerging research is indicating that Jamaican fathers do play a critical role in the emotional and psychological well-being of their children (Marshall Green, 2017; Anderson, 2009; Anderson & Daley, 2015).

Mothers Are Nurturers, So Where Does That Leave Fathers?

It has been well documented that mothers are nurturers, so much so that it can give the impression that fathers do not play as critical a role (Maine, 2004). While the role of the mother is emphasized, children are also born with an inner desire to have a close and loving relationship with their fathers. The nature of this relationship can act as a protective agent against eating pathology or may aid in its development (Brunton, Lacey, & Waller, 2005; Jones, Leung, & Harris, 2006). The same can be said about the nature of the relationship between mother and father (Zerbe, 1993).

While these relationships are key in identifying at-risk cases, research has not underscored the value of gender differences in effecting outcomes. We have found that the longstanding emotional desire for a connection with father, a term referred to as "father hunger" (Herzog, 1980, 2001), can serve as motivation in working through the discomfort one faces in recovery from an ED. Additionally, a more pragmatic approach as taken by a father can propel the rate at which recovery progresses. This holds implications for a society that has been indoctrinated in a culture in which mothers were expected to stay at home and take care of the children, while fathers serve as the breadwinners with little to do with child rearing (Wilson, 1969). This perspective persists as the society continues to assign sole responsibility for nurturance to the mother while negating the influence of the father in the Jamaican culture (Anderson, 2009; Anderson & Daley, 2015). This case study takes into account the culture of Jamaican society and its implications for patient and family recovery from anorexia nervosa. More specifically, it explores the father's role in influencing the therapeutic modality and gains in recovery of a patient suffering from anorexia nervosa.

Case Summary

Margaret is a 19-year-old biracial female who was diagnosed with generalized anxiety disorder and anorexia nervosa restrictive type. She had been suffering from anorexia nervosa for approximately 10 years, during which she sought treatment overseas. She, however, had not been responsive to the interventions made and decided to try treatment locally with the return of recently ED-trained professionals. Upon presentation to a local eating disorder team, the illness had already had significant physical and psychological impact. Margaret's presenting concerns were the significant yellow discoloration of her skin, frequent episodes of chest tightness, chest pain and palpitations at night, with feelings of anxiety resulting in a two-hour delay in falling asleep.

She gave a history of significant dietary restriction of carbohydrates and fats for the past 10 years, with limited variety in foods eaten. She denied self-induced vomiting or use of medications to influence weight loss but reported exercising 30 to 45 minutes three times weekly with increased anxiety if this was interfered with. She had difficulty regulating body temperature, with cold intolerance, constipation, and dull, thinning hair with alopecia (hair loss). Margaret had experienced menarche at age 15 years (delayed in comparison to maternal menarche), but after having irregular cycles for two years had been amenorrheic thereafter for one year up to presentation to the local team. Margaret had been diagnosed with generalized anxiety disorder two years prior and had been adherent with fluoxetine 20 mg once daily since then. The family history was significant for a cousin with an eating disorder.

Examination findings were significant for generalized reduced bulk, body mass index (BMI) of 17.0 kg/m^2 (< 5th percentile), facial lanugo hair, acrocyanosis (blue discoloration of digits), and generalized carotenoid pigmentation of her skin. Vitals revealed bradycardia with low normal blood pressure and no postural changes. Review of her growth parameters over time revealed decreased weight velocity as compared with expected growth based on measurements of early and middle childhood. Margaret's body fat on bioimpedance assessment was 16.5%, and her weight was assessed at 84.2% of target weight. Investigations revealed sinus bradycardia on electrocardiogram (ECG), hypoestrogenic state (low estrogen), hypocholesterolemia (low total cholesterol), and leucopenia (low white blood cell count) and low normal bone mineral density.

Margaret was started on multivitamins and calcium supplements but was poorly adherent. Nutritional rehabilitation had to be guided by the physician, as referral to the dietitian was refused, compounded by there being no ED-trained dietitian locally available. Margaret persisted in restricting nutritional intake and refused to follow meal plans provided. Intake changed minimally, adding one small snack per day. Margaret regularly complained of stomach-aches and bloating and increased her exercise to one hour daily to "overcome the anxiety of eating more" despite being told not to engage in any exercise. There was fluctuation of weight with overall weight loss during the first two months of follow-up with the physician and a general psychiatrist. Olanzapine was commenced at 2.5 mg once daily and was gradually increased to 5 mg daily. Attempts were made at psychoeducation of parents and Margaret regarding the illness, but little change in insight was achieved, with father once describing Margaret using the physician and psychiatrist as "props to hold her up." At the close of month 2, there had been a decrease in weight to 83% of target weight, persistent failed adherence with meal plans, and there was now noted increase in difficulty concentrating with schoolwork. At this point, an eating disorder–trained psychologist became available locally and joined the ED physician, forming the first local team of ED specialists.

Psychological assessment at this point revealed Margaret was experiencing difficulties in recognizing as well as tolerating her emotions—numbing her emotions. She expressed unhappiness, had become less engaged, had intermittent angry outbursts, and her focus was primarily on the fear of losing control, overeating, and weight. She demonstrated paralyzing anxiety surrounding food and a lack of desire to live. Cognitively, there was impairment in her ability to think, with impaired concentration and problem-solving skills. Behaviorally, she was hiding food, was noncompliant with having variety in her meals, and displayed interpersonal issues such as keeping herself isolated from family and friends.

Review of Progress

We will now delineate Margaret's progress, starting at the point of formation of the ED team—specialist-trained psychologist and physician.

The ED team engaged Margaret in a treatment regime of weekly visits to the physician, twice-weekly individual sessions with the psychologist, and family sessions alternate weeks. The ED team (physician and psychologist) met at least biweekly to review the patient's progress and adjust the management plan where necessary. Monthly team meetings were held with Margaret, her parents, and the ED team to review progress as well as challenges and to adjust management accordingly.

Month 1: Family Dynamics—A Deliberate Intention to Keep Father Out of Decision Making

Margaret lives in a nuclear family with a history of enmeshment between mothers and daughters spanning two generations. Margaret expressed grave concerns about her relationship with her mother and believed that her illness was perpetuated by mother's involvement, as mother had always been in charge of her meals and decision making. Her mother, on the other hand, said she felt helpless seeing her daughter not eating and felt that at least she provided her with "something to eat, even though it was 'low-calorie options." Both Margaret and mother felt a strain in their relationship as mother often played the role of "a nurse" rather than a mother figure, with her decision making often going beyond meals and extending into Margaret's social life. Despite her mother's efforts to help her daughter, this had resulted in facilitating the illness—supplying low-calorie foods reinforced the eating disorder, while intervening in Margaret's social life increased frustration, resulting in her relying even more on the illness to cope with these stressors.

Dad generally played an active role in the family but was disengaged with the illness, largely because of the negative reactions received when he tried to intervene in the enmeshed mother–daughter relationship. Margaret had always maintained a firm stance of not wanting father involved in her treatment to spare the similar negative impact this had with her relationship with mother. In various encounters with the family, it became clear that mother and father were opposites in how they dealt with the illness—father seemed more practical and somewhat firm in his approach, while mother seemed more emotional and was careful not to upset her daughter. The family's response to the illness was to blame, revisit past mistakes, and avoid conflict.

When the treatment team first met Margaret and her mother, attempts were made to get her father involved in treatment. This was met by many excuses from the mother–daughter dyad—including father being busy with work and not having time to be involved. After one month of working with Margaret and her mother, no progress had been made, with continued restriction and minimal improvements in variety of foods eaten. Vital signs remained stable but without weight gain and unchanged psychological and cognitive function.

Months 2 and 3: Breaking the Cycle, Getting Dad Involved

Margaret's progress to this point was that there had been no weight gain. Exercise had been discontinued, with slow increase in variety of foods eaten. Restriction persisted, with failure to adhere with the meal plan and increased anxiety and thought disturbance around food. Mother tried to sustain her daughter's life by continuing to purchase "diet" foods. Though understandable, her actions only served to further enable the illness.

During month 2, the ED team was finally able to have father attend his first team meeting, facilitating updates and observation of family dynamics. Our initial approach was to offer psychoeducation about the illness, highlighting the proposed treatment regimen based on our training background and offering opportunities for their feedback. Parental response to the illness differed— father was of the opinion that mother facilitated "the illness" and in fact was not convinced this was an illness but that his daughter was spoiled and "simply needed to eat." Mother continued to respond to Margaret at an emotional level and father in a pragmatic manner.

In month 3, inpatient nutritional rehabilitation was recommended but was refused by the family. In lieu of this, we attempted to mirror aspects of inpatient treatment—mother was taught meal support. She, however, had challenges in implementing this appropriately, so Margaret started outpatient meal support with the ED psychologist twice per week. Mother was invited so that she could learn how to support her daughter during meals. The ED team decided to also involve father in meal support. The need for a team approach between parents was heavily emphasized.

Month 4: Father Becomes More Involved

Weight restoration finally resumed, with an increase to 85% of target weight. Both Margaret and mother opted at this point to discontinue Olanzapine, stating a fear of side effects and that it had not helped. Father increased his level of involvement with meal support. However, it was still predominantly done by mother. Meal support was increasingly difficult for mom, as it was hard to see her daughter become upset, and to appease her, mother would at times acquiesce to disordered eating requests from Margaret. During this time, however, Margaret increasingly acknowledged the enabling role mother played despite continuing to bargain with her and the illness.

Months 5 and 6: Father Initiates More Challenges and Goal Setting

Weight gain again halted, and father suggested setting firm goal-oriented rules with consequences for failure to weight restore. This created tension within the family, as both mother and Margaret were not in agreement with father's recommendation, and this again threatened the parental team approach. We saw evidence of the illness's strain on mother, as she at times expressed her doubt as to whether her daughter was capable of recovery. We could see evidence of how taxing the illness was for mom.

Month 7

Previously, team emails were sent to mother, the primary communicant with the team from the outset, with the understanding that she would update father. As it became clear there was not always full disclosure to father, the management team decided to include father individually in all emails. Father again introduced weight-attainment goals with rewards that were meaningful to the patient, with significant consequences within his singular control if not achieved. Persistent stepwise weight gain was achieved, with Margaret attaining 88% of target weight and significant improvement in variety of foods eaten.

Month 8

A period of static weight gain occurred again, and father decided to again push the envelope and set new goals for client's restoration. Previously, all goals were not being achieved; consequences were inconsistently reinforced, as he had not always been involved with follow-up, and mother faced difficulty following through with the consequences. At team meeting, consequences were reviewed, with an assurance from father he would follow through. Immediate resumption of weight gain was noted, and the goal of 90% target weight was achieved within two months.

Months 12–15: The Last Stretch

Dad continued to set time-sensitive goals with reinforcement of consequences. Margaret showed continued progress, attaining 95% of target weight in month 14 and resumption of menses in month 15 at 96% of target weight. There was a total weight gain of 9.2 kg, all hematological and biochemical results returned to normal, and there was no significant change in bone mineral density.

Margaret had also shown significant progress psychologically and emotionally. There was notable reduction in disordered eating behaviors and attitudes. She was able to concentrate in sessions and began reconnecting with her peers and exploring the roots of her eating disorder. Margaret had a better handle on her emotions and was able to regulate, no longer experiencing constant irritability and being able to embrace emotions with tolerance. Her relationship with her mother began to change, and mother's role shifted from being her nurse toward a more united mother–daughter relationship. Her relationship with father remained healthy.

Discussion

This case was particularly challenging in the context of a developing country but serves as clear evidence of the existence of severe eating disorders in this context and corroborates previous findings regarding the illness's impact on the individual, both psychologically and physically (Gard & Freeman, 1996), as well as on the family. It is imperative that we inform widely about patient care and intervention in a developing country where specialized care for eating disorders has not yet evolved but is already making significant impact. While not disputing the psychological and medical interventions, we wish to highlight the involvement of fathers and the benefits of involving them in promoting recovery of their daughters (or sons) from eating disorders.

Research has explored the effects of the father–daughter relationship and its impact on the evolution of the eating disorder. However, very little has been done previously on the role fathers can and should play in recovery. While extensive research has been done on the role of mothers on the psychological and emotional development of their children, fathers have not been given the same attention. First-world countries have begun to bridge this gap by extending the research on fathers in this area. Unfortunately, for other less developed countries such as Jamaica, this research is comparatively sparse and may have been further prevented because of the stereotypical notions that the country has towards fathers' involvement in the emotional well-being of their children (Anderson, 2009; Anderson & Daley, 2015).

This case study serves to further acknowledge the importance of understanding that the illness goes beyond the shallow, superficial notion of beauty that society often portrays. It seeks to emphasize that despite ethnicity and country of origin, eating disorders do exist in Jamaica, and like for any other sufferer of anorexia nervosa, these can have serious psychological and medical consequences which can be taxing not only for the sufferer but for family members as well. It demonstrates that a key ingredient to a daughter's recovery seems to be based on the yearning for a father who can withstand the emotional upheavals, stand firm, and make goals in the refeeding and recovery of his child. It requires him being present to follow up on her accomplishments and consistently follow through with rewards and consequences. This case study challenges the local cultural belief that a father's role in the family should be as financial provider and mother as the nurturer. It seems as though Margaret herself was also subscribing to this culture by keeping her father at a distance when it came to seeking support from him. She later learned that her father's involvement was essential for her recovery.

The medical interventions, individual psychotherapy, family sessions, and team meetings were the ingredients to facilitate father's involvement in treatment. We learned that when given the opportunity, the "voice" of the father can enable significant improvement. We do not dispute that there is a role for mother; in fact, Margaret's mother was there for her meltdowns and shared in the difficulties of her illness and prevented her from succumbing to it, but she needed the support of her partner to take her daughter and, by extension, the family through the process of weight restoration. We endorse a team approach that includes patient and parents, along with a specialized group of professionals working closely together, to help guide individuals through this difficult disease. While this serves as a case study, we see these salient themes as a springboard to further investigations on a larger scale.

References

Anderson, P. (2009). *The changing roles of fathers in Jamaican family life*. Kingston, Jamaica: Planning Institute of Jamaica Policy Research Unit.

Anderson, P., & Daley, C. (2015). African-Caribbean fathers: The conflict between masculinity and fathering. In J. Roopnarine (Ed.), *Fathers across cultures: The importance, roles, and diverse practices of dads* (pp. 13–38). Santa Barbara, CA: Praeger.

Anderson-Fye, E. P. (2004). A "Coca-Cola" shape: Cultural change, body image, and eating disorders in San Andrés, Belize. *Culture, Medicine and Psychiatry, 28*(4), 561–595. https://doi.org/10.1007/s11013-004-1068-4.

Bhugra, D., Mastrogianni, A., Maharajh, H., & Harvey, S. (2003). Prevalence of bulimic behaviours and eating attitudes in schoolgirls from Trinidad and Barbados. *Transcultural psychiatry, 40*(3), 409–428. https://doi.org/10.1177/13634615030403005.

Bruch, H. (1973). *Evolution of a psychotherapeutic approach to eating disorders: Obesity, anorexia nervosa, and the person within*. New York: Basic Books Inc.

Brunton, N. J., Lacey, H. J., & Waller, G. (2005). Eating psychopathology in young non-clinical adults: A pilot study of the impact of parental personality. *European Eating Disorders Review, 13*, 406–410. https://doi.org/10.1002/erv.625.

Burk, B. N. (2015). Black girls' perceptions of health and ideal body types. *Journal of Gender Studies, 24*(5), 496–511. https://doi.org/10.1080/09589236.2013.856750.

Burke, T., Kuczynski, L., & Perren, S. (2017). An exploration of Jamaican mothers' perceptions of closeness and intimacy in the mother–child relationship during middle childhood. *Frontiers in Psychology, 8,* 2148. https://doi.org/10.3389/fpsyg. 2017.02148.

Clarke, E. (1999). *My mother who fathered me: A study of the families in three selected communities of Jamaica.* Mona, Kingston: University of West Indies Press.

Cooper, P. J., Whelan, E., Woolgar, M., Morrell, J., & Murray, L. (2004). Association between childhood feeding problems and maternal eating disorder: Role of the family environment. *British Journal of Psychiatry, 184*(3), 210–215. https://doi.org/10.1192/bjp.184.3.210.

Fox, K., & Gordon-Strachan, G. (2007). *Jamaican Youth Risk and Resiliency Behaviour Survey 2005.* School-based Survey on Risk and Resiliency Behaviours.

Gard, M. C. E., & Freeman, C. P. (1996). The dismantling of a myth: A review of eating disorders and socioeconomic status. *International Journal of Eating Disorder, 20*(1), 1–12. https://doi.org/10.1002/(SICI)1098-108X(199607)20:1<1::AID-EAT1> 3.0.CO;2-M.

Grilo, C. M. (2014). *Eating and weight disorders.* New York: Psychology Press.

Harrison, A., James Bateman, C., Younger-Coleman, N., Williams, M., Roke, K., ClatoDay-Scarlett, S., & Chang, S. (2019). Disordered eating behaviours and attitudes among adolescents in a middle-income country. *Eating and Weight Disorders-Studies on Anorexia, Bulimia and Obesity.* https://doi.org/10.1007/s40519-019-00814-5.

Herzog, J. M. (1980). Sleep disturbance and father hunger in 18- to 28-Month-old boys. The Erlkönig syndrome. *The Psychoanalytic Study of the Child, 35*(1), 219–233. https://doi.org/10.1080/00797308.1980.11823111.

Herzog, J. M. (2001). *Father hunger: Exploration with adults and children.* Hillsdale, NJ: The Psychoanalytic Press Inc.

Hillege, S., Beale, B., & McMaster, R. (2006). Impact of eating disorders on family life: Individual parents' stories. *Journal of Clinical Nursing, 15*(8), 1016–1022. https://doi.org/10.1111/j.1365-2702.2006.01367.x.

Hoek, H. W., van Harten, P. N., Hermans, K. M., Katzman, M. A., Matroos, G. E., & Susser, E. S. (2005). The incidence of anorexia nervosa on Curacao. *American Journal of Psychiatry, 162*(4), 748–752. https://doi.org/10.1176/appi.ajp.162.4.748.

Ichinohe, M., Mita, R., Saito, K., Shinkawa, H., Nakaji, S., Coombs, M., & Fuller, E. (2004). Obesity and lifestyle in Jamaica. *International Collaboration in Community Health, 1267,* 39–50. https://doi.org/10.1016/j.ics.2004.01.070.

James, C., & Harrison, A. (2014). *Eating disorders in the Caribbean The Jamaican experience.* Conference Proceedings, "Dying to be Beautiful? Body Image, Eating Behaviours and Health in the Caribbean," Biennial Conference, University of the West Indies, Mona.

Jones, J. C., Leung, N., & Harris, G. (2006). Father–daughter relationship and eating psychopathology: The mediating role of core beliefs. *The British Journal of Psychiatry, 45,* 319–330. https://doi.org/10.1348/014466505x53489.

Lock, J., Le Grange, D Agras, W. S., & Dare, C. (2001). *Treatment manual for anorexia nervosa: A family-based approach.* New York: Guilford Publications.

Ma, L. C. J. (2007). Meanings of eating disorders discerned from family treatment and its implications for family education: The case of Shenzhen. *Child & Family Social Work, 12,* 409–416. https://doi.org/10.1111/j.1365-2206.2007.00496.x.

Maine, M. (2004). *Father hunger: Fathers, daughters and the pursuit of thinness* (2nd ed.). Carlsbad, CA: Gurze Books.

Makino, M., Tsuboi, K., & Dennerstein, L. (2004). Prevalence of eating disorders: A comparison of Western and non-Western countries. *Medscape General Medicine, 6*(3).

Marshall Green, A. (2017). *A generative perspective of Afro-Jamaican fathers' socialization of values for their children in middle childhood.* Doctoral dissertation.

Mulders-Jones, B., Mitchison, D., Girosi, F., & Hay, P. (2017). Socioeconomic correlates of eating disorder symptoms in an Australian population-based sample. *PloS ONE, 12*(1), e0170603. https://doi.org/10.1371/journal.pone.0170603.

Mumford, D. B. (1993). Eating disorders in different cultures. *International Review of Psychiatry, 5*(1), 109–114. https://doi.org/10.3109/09540269309028299.

Samms-Vaughan, M. (2002). Eating disorders. What's new? *West Indian Medical Journal, 51*(1), 1–3.

Sewell, C. A., Martin, J. S., & Abel, W. D. (2010). Eating disorders: An emerging pathology. *West Indian Medical Journal, 59*(6), 589–590.

Thomas, J. P., & Szmukler, G. I. (1985). Anorexia nervosa in patients of Afro-Caribbean extraction. *The British Journal of Psychiatry, 146*(6), 653–656. https://doi.org/10.1192/bjp.146.6.653.

Walker, S. N. A. B. (2012). An analysis and treatment of eating disorders in Jamaican adolescents. *International Journal of Humanities and Social Science, 2*(5), 60.

White, V. O., & Gardner, J. M. (2002). Presence of anorexia nervosa and bulimia nervosa in Jamaica. *West Indian Medical Journal, 51*(1), 32–39.

Wilson, P. J. (1969). Reputation and respectability: A suggestion for Caribbean ethnology. *Man, 4*(1), 70–84.

Zerbe, J. K. (1993). *The body betrayed: Women, eating disorders, and treatment.* Washington, DC: American Psychiatric Press Inc.

8 An Integrative Approach to Understanding and Treating Disordered Eating in African American Women

Carolyn Coker Ross

Introduction

Black[1] women are sometimes assumed to be less susceptible to body dissatisfaction based on the notion that African American culture embraces larger or curvier body types than the dominant culture does. Eating disorders are becoming a major health concern for Black women. While some research suggests that anorexia nervosa is less common in Black women than in White women (Striegel-Moore et al., 2003), recurrent binge eating occurs at higher rates in Black women than in White women (Striegel-Moore, 2000). How can clinicians do a better job of detecting and treating eating disorders in Black women? Improving care for Black women starts with conceptualizing disordered eating not solely as a preoccupation with appearance but also as a strategy for coping with stress, depression, and trauma (Thompson, 1992).

Stress, trauma, and insecure attachment contribute to the development of eating disorders in African American women (Cortés-García, Takkouche, Seoane, & Senra, 2019; Tasca & Balfour, 2014). These early adversities exert their effects through their impact on brain development, architecture of the brain, and gene expression and are more intersected in African American communities. Early adversity has been linked to later impairments in learning, behavior, and both physical and mental well-being. Newer research on the impact of childhood maltreatment on adult health is challenging us to move beyond the notion of "genetic predispositions" to understand the influence of environment and early experiences and how, when, and to what degree different genes are activated. Understanding this interaction can explain the mechanism through which gene–environment interaction or epigenetics affects lifelong behavior, development, and health (Bagot & Meaney, 2010) and may also explain the transmission of these effects from generation to generation. The effects of stress, attachment disorders, and trauma in childhood can persist into adulthood, putting individuals at higher risk for depression, obesity, and eating disorders. Once a child has been maltreated, the trajectory of their long-term potential may be highjacked, putting them at risk for lifelong consequences in the areas of educational achievement, economic productivity, health status, and longevity (Shonkoff et al., 2011). Because early adversities, stress, and insecure attachment are more prevalent in African Americans (as will be discussed in what follows) (Slopen et al., 2016), these factors should be evaluated when treating African American clients who present with eating disorders.

Stress

Problematic eating patterns in African American women may develop in response to stress, and existing eating disorders may be worsened by stress. In order to understand the underlying causes of eating disorders in African American women, it's important to understand the effect of stress on children and adults. Stress can begin before birth through exposure to maternal stress. Both prenatal stress and early life stress can increase the risk of developing an eating disorder, addiction, and obesity (Su et al., 2016; Thomas, Hu, Lee, Bhatnagar, & Becker, 2009). Exposure to early life stress can result in more difficulty managing stress and regulating emotions throughout life, as well as a predisposition to mood disorders, impulsive and compulsive disorders such as eating disorders, attention deficit hyperactivity disorder, and addictions (Enoch, 2010; Warren et al., 2014). The relationship between childhood adversity and eating disorders is mediated by emotional dysregulation (Trottier & MacDonald, 2017).

Both animal and human studies have shown that fetal exposure to maternal stress can affect responsiveness to stress in later life. This effect has been shown in animals to be passed down through subsequent generations. Prolonged stress after birth without the buffering protection of supportive adult relationships is called toxic stress. Toxic stress in childhood includes events studied in the Adverse Childhood Experiences Study and includes abuse, neglect, exposure to violence, and having a parent with mental illness or a substance use disorder (McEwen, 2005)

Childhood experiences stimulate neurodevelopment. Having a range of experiences stimulates different parts of the brain, leading to balanced brain development. Noted child trauma researcher Perry (2002) has stated:

> The simple and unavoidable conclusion of these neurodevelopmental principles is that the organizing, sensitive brain of an infant or young child is more malleable to experience than a mature brain. While experience may alter the behavior of an adult, experience literally provides the organizing framework for an infant and child. Because the brain is most plastic (receptive to environmental input) in early childhood, the child is most vulnerable to variance of experience during this time.
>
> (p. 88)

A young child's brain is like a sponge—taking in and using experiences that are helpful to the growing brain and also ones that are not. This spongelike quality of the young child explains why chronic or severe stress can be so toxic to the brain. Chronic severe stress (toxic stress) causes the release of stress hormones that shape and mold the developing brain, which is very sensitive to the chemical influence of stress hormones. Chronic stress results in increased size and function of the emotional parts of the brain (the amygdala and orbitofrontal cortex) and decrease in size and function of the prefrontal cortex and hippocampus, which govern memory, executive, function and learning (Slopen et al., 2016). Early traumatic experiences can lead to hyperactivity of the stress response. Depending on the severity of the trauma or on the type of trauma, there can be a significant dysregulation of the stress response. Physical or sexual abuse before age five has a more significant impact on children (Cicchetti, Rogosch, Gunnar, & Toth, 2010) than it does on those who were older at the time of their abuse or on children who were victims of emotional abuse or neglect.

Some stress is normal, and it helps children learn to react to future challenges. However, when a child is exposed to repeated experiences of abuse and neglect, those experiences can lead to toxic stress and can disrupt the child's brain development. Further, other parts of the brain may be weakened by early traumatic experiences (i.e., the parts of the brain having to do with emotional self-regulation, impulse control, judgment, social interactions, and abstract thinking; "Preventing Adverse Childhood Experiences | VetoViolence," 2019).

Because of the hyperactivity of the stress response system, survivors of trauma are typically hypervigilant, always on the lookout for the next threat. This continual feeling of tension is uncomfortable, so trauma survivors often engage in adaptive behaviors in response to the discomfort. Binge eating, emotional overeating, and eating addiction are common reactions, particularly among Black women. Some African American women with past or present trauma may have used food as the only reliable source of pleasure or comfort in their lives.

Socioeconomic factors can also be a source of stress. Black women are more likely than their White counterparts to experience poverty ("Poverty in the U.S. | Poverty Solutions," 2019), a major, pervasive source of stress. African American women are also confronted with the stressors of racism and microaggressions—a form of covert racism. Microaggressions can be defined as "brief, everyday exchanges that send denigrating messages to people of color because they belong to a racial minority group" (Sue et al., 2007, p. 273).

In a study of Black undergraduates, 63 percent reported experiencing at least one episode of overt racism in the previous year, and 96 percent experienced several episodes of microaggressions. Both were also predictive of depressive symptoms (Donovan, Galban, Grace, Bennett, & Felicié, 2012). Black women are greatly affected by discrimination and sexual harassment in the workplace, and they may have limited avenues for effective recourse. While reports of sexual harassment of White women have declined overall (from the 1990s to the 2010s), harassment of Black women has stayed at basically the same level for more than 20 years. Black women are 3.8 times more likely to report sexual harassment as White women (Cassino & Besen-Cassino, 2019; Krieger et al., 2006).

These results show that the lived experience of Black women is vastly different than that of their White counterparts. The race, class, and gender inequities that these studies report is illustrative of the ways in which treating Black women with eating disorders is different than treating White women with eating disorders.

Independent of other factors, children exposed to toxic stress in childhood are more likely to have behavioral problems, to struggle academically, and to have health problems. The hair-trigger response or state of being on constant red alert that accompanies childhood exposure to stress may make some children appear overly reactive to even mild stressors and less able to cope with future stresses. In adulthood, the adoption of unhealthy or risky behaviors can be seen as a coping mechanism that may explain why exposure to childhood adversities and toxic stress is associated with tobacco use, substance use disorders, obesity, and eating disorders in adults ("Persistent Fear and Anxiety Can Affect Young Children," 2019; Gunnar & Quevedo, 2007).

Beyond childhood, toxic stress causes wear and tear on the body that lasts into adulthood and is associated with medical conditions including heart disease, diabetes, lowered immune function, autoimmune diseases, poor wound healing, and depression (Cohen et al., 2012). Black women and children have greater exposure to stress both prenatally and during their lifetime that comes from numerous environmental sources including racism, microaggressions, and other unique cultural factors. Culturally competent care must include an understanding of the significant physical and mental disorders that result from stress.

Individual Trauma

The Adverse Childhood Experiences (ACE) Study has catalogued the impact of trauma that occurs before age 18. The ACE study was started by Kaiser Permanente in San Diego; now it is jointly run with the Centers for Disease Control. This study of more than 17,000 participants looked at abuse (physical, emotional, or sexual), neglect (emotional and physical), and household challenges (witnessing domestic violence, household substance abuse, mental illness in the household, parental separation or divorce, and having a family member who is incarcerated). The ACE study is groundbreaking because it is the first of its kind to explore and validate the link between adverse childhood experiences and the development in adulthood of physical and mental health disorders (Child Abuse and Neglect Prevention | Violence Prevention | Injury Center | CDC, 2019).

The essence of the impact of trauma—whether it is from abuse, neglect, loss, or violence—is a loss of an essential part of ourselves—a sense of safety, trust, or security. A history of trauma is particularly important to ascertain in African Americans who present for treatment of eating disorders. Across all racial groups, Black and Hispanic children have been exposed to more adversities than White children. Nine percent of African Americans have been diagnosed with PTSD (vs. 6.8% of Whites; Alim et al., 2006; Slopen et al., 2016).

Lifetime prevalence of PTSD after trauma was 51% in a study of African American patients in primary care offices, and it was higher in females than in males (Alim, Charney, & Mellman, 2006).

Socioeconomic status is another contributing factor to the exposure to trauma. Children from low-income families have an even higher risk of exposure to frightening or threatening experiences than do other children. Low-income children, of whom Black children are disproportionately high, were 18% more likely than children from higher-income families to have been exposed to one adversity, 15% more likely to experience two adverse experiences, and 74% more likely to have three or more exposures. When looked at through the lens of race, Black children were 45% more likely than White children to have two adverse exposures and 21% more likely to have three or more. These statistics reflect the intersection of race and income; more children in low-income homes are African American, and children from these homes are more likely to experience trauma ("Toxic stress and children's outcomes: African American children growing up poor are at greater risk of disrupted physiological functioning and depressed academic achievement"; Morsy & Rothstein, 2019).

The ACE study has found that two-thirds of all American households have at least 1 ACE, and one in five have three or more ACEs. This is significant, because clinicians now know that ACEs are common. There is also a strong dose–response relationship between the number of adverse events before the age of 18 and social, mental, and behavioral outcomes. ACEs affect all types of families, all races, all communities, and all socio-economic levels. Finally, the study found that a history of more than one early-life adversity is associated with a higher risk for eating disorders, substance use disorders, and depression, and it is also associated with more than 40 other disorders including heart disease, stroke, and diabetes.

Historic or Intergenerational Trauma

Trauma ultimately can define our behaviors, actions, and sense of self. Beyond childhood trauma, research shows the destructive effects of trauma being passed down from generation to generation in the expression of our DNA and in our cultural nurturing. Intergenerational trauma was initially studied in the children and grandchildren of Holocaust survivors in the 1960s. Offspring of Holocaust survivors showed a variety of trauma response pathology and experienced themselves as "different or damaged" by their parents' experiences (Sotero, 2006, p. 96). Studies on families of Holocaust survivors show an association between eating disorders and Holocaust exposure (Zohar, Giladi, & Givati, 2006), and they show the transmission of trauma coping pathology and insecure attachment through three generations (Bar-On et al., 1998).

More recent studies involving historical trauma have focused on American Indian/Alaska Native (AIAN) populations. Brave Heart describes historical trauma as "the cumulative emotional and psychological wounding over one's lifetime and from generation to generation following loss of lives, land and vital aspects of culture" (Sotero, 2006, p. 96; Brave Heart & DeBruyn, 2001). Brave Heart also developed a lexicon of terminology to describe the AIAN experience, including "historical unresolved grief," to describe how the losses they suffered had never been mourned, and the "survivor's-child complex" to describe the similar dynamics among children of survivors and their descendants.

This definition of historical or intergenerational trauma fits African Americans who were taken to North America from Africa and the Caribbean. They lost their cultures; many lost their lives in the Middle Passage and later on slave plantations. Additionally, they were separated from their families, children, and spouses by slaveowners and experienced innumerable traumatic experiences that have continued through racial oppression, family separation, and mass incarceration of Black men. In his 1952 semiautobiographical novel *Go Tell It On the Mountain*, the esteemed African American author James Baldwin asked the question: "Could a curse come down so many ages? Did it live in time, or in the moment?" (Halloran, 2018, p. 46).

Baldwin's reference to intergenerational trauma is echoed in research through discussions on the long-term impact of slavery on African Americans. For instance, DeGruy (2017) articulated a condition called posttraumatic slave syndrome (PTSS) to reflect a condition that exists as a consequence of centuries of chattel slavery followed by institutionalized racism and oppression. Chattel slavery was based on the belief that Black persons are inherently and genetically inferior to Whites. The systemized trauma of slavery, racism, and oppression is a cultural process that became part of the collective identity of African Americans (Eyerman, 2004). Generations after slavery was abolished, children were witness to their parents' or grandparents' daily degradation at the hands of the dominant culture. For example, while Black Americans may have been granted the right to vote, they often did not have the freedom to vote and many times were turned away at the polls because of gerrymandering and other obstructive political practices. For many, the legacy of slavery has led to feelings of inferiority that are passed from generation to generation and that keep individuals from reaching their full potential. Other examples of systematic oppression include the ongoing deaths of Black men at the hands of the police and the excessive incarceration of Black men, which has continued the fragmentation of the Black family that began during slavery. There are also deprecating accounts of African Americans in the media, disrespect in the school system, and daily microaggressions.

DeGruy described three outcomes of the trauma of slavery: low self-esteem, ever-present anger (or sensitivity to disrespect, also called "shame-proneness"), and racist socialization. She goes on to explain intergenerational trauma transmission as being a result of parental modeling. Racist socialization can show up in the belief that light-skinned Black persons are superior to darker-skinned individuals or that straight hair is better than kinky hair. This can contribute to body image issues in Black women with eating disorders. Low self-esteem and depression also found in Black women with eating disorders is further evidence of the long-term impact of living as a Black woman in America. Many use food as a way to deal with the stress and emotions associated with the Black experience.

The injuries from slavery have led to individual and collective injury that shows up in low self-esteem, self-destructive behaviors, interpersonal conflict within the home and community, and often maladaptive beliefs and behaviors (Gump, 2000). The trauma can also become a family legacy, whether survivors talked about it or kept it silent, even to children who were born after the trauma.

Posttraumatic slave syndrome, then, begins with the ways in which individuals and the Black community have coped over many generations. Some of them were positive, such as resilience demonstrated by the strong Black woman syndrome (SBWS). African American women learned from their mothers and grandmothers to be strong, suppress emotions, and hide vulnerability. The SBWS also involves a determination to succeed even with limited resources. Within the SBWS was also the obligation to help others. While the SBWS is evidence of great resiliency, it can come at the cost of strained interpersonal relationships, health consequences due to the delay in seeking self-care, and stress disorders such as anxiety, depression, obesity, and adverse maternal health outcomes. The SBWS may also explain the reticence in the Black community to seek care for mental health problems, including eating disorders (Woods-Giscombé, 2010).

Many Black women identify with the SBWS, not out of choice but because they have had to be strong. They may be raising their children as single parents; some are even raising their grandchildren at the same time they are working full time and volunteering at their church. The stress involved can lead to overeating and other eating disorder behaviors as survival behaviors, or they may have started using food to deal with childhood or adult traumas for which they may never have received treatment. While White individuals with eating disorders may have experienced trauma in their past, or even intergenerational trauma, it is important to recognize that past traumas are compounded with the stressors in everyday life of being Black. Stress and trauma (past, present, or intergenerational), along with insecure attachment, which will be discussed next, all present differently in Black women with eating disorders and work in concert to make it even more difficult for Black women to give up survival behaviors that have provided a source of comfort and security when the world around them may feel unsafe and insecure simply because they are Black.

Attachment

When a child's interactions with their caregiver are inconsistent, unreliable, or insensitive, this interferes with the development of a secure and stable mental foundation. While there are few studies that explore race and attachment styles, one study (Bakermans-Kranenburg, Ijzendoorn, & Kroonenberg, 2004) shows that in almost all ways, Black families are different than White families. For example, Black mothers in this study tended to be almost four years younger than their White counterparts, and income was almost half that of White families. These differences might explain why Black mothers tended to be more stressed and why Black children were already showing attachment difficulties by the age of two. As well, a distinct relationship has been found in research between childhood trauma and insecure attachment in African American women. Research shows that a history of emotional abuse can lead to more insecure attachment styles in African American women (Gaskin-Wasson et al., 2016).

Other unique cultural factors may also influence the development of attachment bonds in African American children. For example, living in a dangerous neighborhood, as is the case for some Black women who may present for treatment, can be related to greater psychological distress and poorer long-term adjustment. When evaluating adults with eating disorders who may have insecure attachment and depression, it is important to be aware that they may also have higher rates of childhood physical, psychological, or sexual abuse. The interaction between attachment insecurity and psychopathology is also fostered by stressful life events and poverty (Mikulincer & Shaver, 2012).

One of the deficits in studying attachment in African Americans is that the mother is usually used as the attachment figure. However, in Black culture, it is not uncommon for extended family members to provide or share the care of children in the family, and there may be more than one attachment relationship. These strong kinship ties can provide resiliency and security when a primary caregiver (mother or father) is not able due to illness, mental health issues, or addiction. Despite changes in the family structure in the United States, extended African American families are still resources of strength, resilience, and survival (Hall, 2007).

Therefore, when assessing attachment styles, it is important for clinicians to look beyond just a primary caregiver to caregivers in the extended family such as grandparents or aunts when evaluating African Americans who present with an eating disorder.

Connecting the Dots

The most significant impact of life experiences is on the brain. As mentioned, trauma can be exacerbated by prenatal or postnatal toxic stress and by attachment insecurity. This stress leads to dysregulation of brain neurotransmitters such as serotonin and dopamine, and the brain reward circuits are also affected.

The disruption in the brain's reward mechanism is just one of the mechanisms in which the brain is changed by life experiences in childhood that are carried over into adulthood.

Blum coined the term reward deficiency syndrome (RDS) to describe a failure in the brain's dopamine reward system (Blum & Badgaiyan, 2015). RDS is observable when a person has difficulty experiencing feelings of pleasure or satisfaction with normal pleasurable activities, including eating normally. Specifically, people with RDS have abnormally low levels of dopamine D_2 receptor activity, caused by genetics or early adverse life events. The brain thus has a harder time "hearing" the pleasure signal carried by dopamine, leading the person to want to "turn up the volume" by doing more of the pleasurable thing. Low D_2 receptor activity in the brain may make a person more prone to emotional eating and to binging. Stress is a major environmental factor contributing to changes in the brain that may lead to RDS.

Finally, attachment insecurity can compound the effects of trauma and stress, leading to emotional dysregulation, which is thought to mediate the development of eating disorders in people who have childhood maltreatment. Research since the 1960s in Holocaust survivor families, families of Vietnam vets with PTSD, and others originally postulated that the effects on children had to do with the difficulties of living with a parent or parents who had been traumatized. Newer studies during the "age of the brain" in research have looked at the impact of trauma on the brain's development—the number of nerve cells and neurocircuitry of the brain.

Studies in the 1980s identified potentially hereditable changes in the expression of genes that can be triggered by life experiences. It is known that when the brain has been affected by trauma, stress, and attachment insecurity, the DNA does not change. If the genetic code does not change, how can trauma, attachment insecurity, or stress be passed from generation to generation? A new field of study called epigenetics helps answer that question. Epigenetic changes are changes in the *expression* of a gene. For example, not everyone who has the genetic predisposition to addiction or eating disorders will develop an addiction or an eating disorder. The expression of the gene for an eating disorder, for example, may be turned on by trauma, early child maltreatment, prenatal stress, and toxic childhood stress. Now that this gene has been "turned on," it may also be passed from generation to generation. More studies are needed to validate the mechanism of epigenetic changes, but there is no doubt that trauma psychopathology as well as resilience can be passed intergenerationally.

Summary

Disordered eating and eating disorders are not really about food at all. They are about how food is used to tamp down or amp up emotions, to numb negative emotions, or to distract from the pain of past experiences. African American women may adopt cultural values that put them at higher risk for emotional eating and that make it more difficult for them to seek and accept help for the problem. In particular, they may hold themselves to the "strong Black woman" standard. In a study of a demographically diverse sample of African American women, researchers found that participants reported reluctance in expressing their emotions, felt a responsibility to meet everyone else's needs before their own, and hesitated in seeking assistance from others (Woods-Giscombé,

2010). Like a beach ball held under water, emotions that are repressed may resurface with a vengeance, often in another form. Many participants in this study reported stress-related compulsive behaviors such as emotional eating and smoking.

Parents who have experienced trauma not uncommonly have children who experience trauma. As well, a child's response or adaptation to the original trauma may make them even more vulnerable to future traumatic experiences. African American children living in urban environments are at high risk for repeated trauma exposures. They are more likely to live in poverty, to experience interactions with the police and the justice system, to be placed in foster or substitute care, to be exposed to family and community violence, or to become homeless. In addition to individual trauma experiences, African American children have to cope with the legacy of historical trauma of slavery and the intergenerational effects of racism and continued racial disparities. Research is now confirming that the direct experience of racism or microaggressions and other race-based stressors is predictive of emotional distress, psychiatric symptoms, and the development of PTSD ("Complex Trauma: In Urban African-American Children, Youth, and Families," 2019).

Though slavery was abolished in 1865, its intergenerational effects persist. While African American clients who present with eating disorders are the same in many ways as other patients we treat, they are also different. Being open to learning about these differences is important in healing current and past trauma and ensuring a more stable recovery from an eating disorder. The Centers for Disease Control (CDC) has identified the promotion of safe, stable, nurturing relationships (SSNRs) as a key strategy for the public health approach to child maltreatment prevention. Establishing therapeutic relationships and helping patients improve other relationships in their lives that model the CDC guidelines can also go a long way toward healing intergenerational trauma.

African American women are disproportionately affected by stressful and traumatic life experiences that increase their chances of developing an eating disorder, particularly binge eating, compulsive overeating, or disordered eating. Their struggles with food and eating may be overlooked by clinicians who think of eating disorders primarily in terms of anorexia, perfectionism, and preoccupation with beauty standards defined by extreme thinness. Clinicians should compassionately investigate experiences of stress, trauma, or depression that may contribute to their clients' disordered eating.

Treating the Whole Person Using Integrative Medicine

Integrative medicine has much to offer African American women when it comes to recovery from eating disorders. Problems such as eating addictions or compulsive overeating arise in a context of complex, interconnected factors, so it makes sense to take an integrative approach to their treatment. A client cannot change a difficult past, but she can change how she cares for herself in light of her experiences. Similarly, she cannot change her body, but she can transform her relationship to her body. Unlike other compulsive behaviors, eating is not something a person can be abstinent from. Consequently, African American women must establish a new, healthy relationship with food.

Healing from an eating disorder involves five levels of change:

1. Letting go of superficial behaviors such as dieting, restricting, and obsessing about food, because these behaviors do not solve the problem of out-of-control eating; they only function as a distraction from the underlying emotional issues.
2. Learning new ways to effectively cope with stress and beginning to acknowledge and express the painful emotions that may have been driving the eating disorder.
3. Developing body awareness, reconnecting with sensations, and learning to see the body as a source of wisdom rather than as a recalcitrant adversary that has to be "whipped into shape" or "kept in line."
4. Letting go of core beliefs (such as "It's not safe to trust other people") that no longer serve a positive purpose and cultivating new beliefs that are accurate and functional in the present (such as "I can trust that certain people in my life truly want the best for me").
5. Discovering ways to satisfy the profound human need for authenticity and meaning, because these experiences are essential to a good life and also because they serve as natural positive reinforcers that help heal the brain's reward system.

Clinicians can help clients recover from disordered eating by guiding them through these five levels of healing.

While disordered eating is not fundamentally about food, diet and nutrition do matter. People with food sensitivities (intolerances) often have cravings for the very foods to which they are sensitive. Incomplete digestion of both gluten and dairy protein stimulates the production of opioid-like substances (casomorphins and gluteomorphins) that contribute to food cravings and addiction. Food sensitivities can be identified through an elimination diet, although this can be problematic for people with a history of food restriction, and for that reason, blood tests may be preferable.

Stress, food sensitivities, and a proinflammatory diet can all damage the intestinal lining and lead to intestinal permeability ("leaky gut syndrome"), allowing toxins into the bloodstream. They can also cause an imbalance in gut flora. Proper digestion of food and absorption of nutrients are key to good health. Healing the digestive system can improve both mental and physical symptoms, including cravings, binging, and obesity (Crawford, Cadogan, Richardson, & Watts, 2008).

When it comes to diet, one size does not fit all. Food intolerances may arise when a population changes its foodways more quickly than its genetic regulation of digestive enzymes can adapt. For instance, African Americans have high rates of lactose intolerance because their ancestors adopted dairy relatively late compared to Europeans. Thus, many African American women have found it helpful to model their dietary choices on the African ancestral diet. This involves prioritizing legumes, nuts, grains, vegetables (such as leafy greens, yams, and sweet potatoes), and healthy spices; it also means emphasizing fish and plant proteins over red meat and eggs. Such a diet may improve overall health and reduce the risk for obesity and depression.

Finally, it's important to consider the role of sleep. Sleep helps balance appetite by controlling the hormones ghrelin and leptin that regulate feelings of hunger and fullness ("More Sleep Would Make Most Americans Happier, Healthier and Safer," 2014).

Lack of sleep is, by itself, associated with weight gain, emotional eating, and food cravings. Chronic sleep deprivation contributes to obesity, high blood pressure, diabetes, and addiction. Insufficient sleep may also cause fatigue that makes it difficult to burn off extra calories. Clients can be encouraged to practice good sleep hygiene and to seek help for insomnia or sleep disorders including sleep apnea. Sleep apnea can be both a cause and a result of weight gain.

There are still biases among clinicians who fail to recognize and diagnose eating disorders in African Americans. This can present an obvious barrier for African Americans being able to receive treatment. The second barrier to care is recognizing the significance of trauma as the root of both eating disorders and addictions and, therefore, the need for trauma treatment for individuals with eating disorders. Finally, for African Americans, it is important to understand the context of intergenerational trauma, racism, and systemized oppression as part and parcel of what may lead to the development of eating disorders. This complexity must be understood, however, in order to break the cycle of childhood maltreatment that is at its root. Helping families resolve traumas is imperative, where possible, in helping African American clients with eating disorders heal.

As clinicians, we are more effective in helping our clients when we take a holistic view of their lives. It is critically important that all clinicians work to understand the whole experience of their Black female clients, including their physical health and their emotional lives. Clinicians should also understand the many ways in which the stresses of racism, discrimination, poverty, trauma, family disruption, and adverse childhood experiences can contribute to disordered eating in African American women. In essence, it is imperative that we recognize the potential causes and symptoms of eating disorders in our African American clients so they do not suffer alone.

Note

1. Throughout this chapter, the terms "African American" and "Black" are used interchangeably to describe women of African ancestry.

References

Alim, T., Charney, D., & Mellman, T. (2006). An overview of posttraumatic stress disorder in African Americans. *Journal of Clinical Psychology, 62*(7), 801–813. https://doi.org/10.1002/jclp.20280.

Alim, T., Graves, E., Mellman, T., Aigbogun, N., Gray, E., Lawson, W., & Charney, D. (2006). Trauma exposure, posttraumatic stress disorder and depression in an African-American primary care population. *Journal of the National Medical Association, 98*(10), 1630–1636.

Bagot, R., & Meaney, M. (2010). Epigenetics and the biological basis of gene × environment interactions. *Journal of the American Academy of Child & Adolescent Psychiatry, 49*(8), 752–771. https://doi.org/10.1016/j.jaac.2010.06.001.

Bakermans-Kranenburg, M., IJzendoorn, M., & Kroonenberg, P. (2004). Differences in attachment security between African-American and white children: Ethnicity or socio-economic status? *Infant Behavior and Development, 27*(3), 417–433. https://doi.org/10.1016/j.infbeh.2004.02.002.

Bar-On, D., Eland, J., Kleber, R., Krell, R., Moore, Y., Sagi, A., . . . van IJzendoorn, M. H. (1998). Multigenerational perspectives on coping with the holocaust experience: An attachment perspective for understanding the developmental sequelae of trauma across generations. *International Journal of Behavioral Development, 22*(2), 315–338. https://doi.org/10.1080/016502598384397.

Blum, K., & Badgaiyan, R. (2015). Reward Deficiency Syndrome (RDS): Entering the genomics and neuroscience era of addiction medicine. *Journal of Reward Deficiency Syndrome, 1*(1). https://doi.org/10.17756/jrds.2015-e001.

Brave Heart, M., & DeBruyn, L. (2001). *The American Indian holocaust: Healing historical unresolved grief.* Retrieved September 13, 2019 from www.ucdenver.edu/academics/colleges/PublicHealth/research/centers/CAIANH/journal/Documents/Volume%208/8(2)_YellowHorseBraveHeart_American_Indian_Holocaust_60-82.pdf.

Cassino, D., & Besen-Cassino, Y. (2019). Race, threat and workplace sexual harassment: The dynamics of harassment in the United States, 1997–2016. *Gender, Work & Organization, 26*(9), 1221–1240. https://doi.org/10.1111/gwao.12394.

Child Abuse and Neglect Prevention|Violence Prevention|Injury Center|CDC. (2019). Retrieved October 20, 2019 from www.cdc.gov/violenceprevention/childabuseandneglect/index.html.

Cicchetti, D., Rogosch, F., Gunnar, M., & Toth, S. (2010). The differential impacts of early physical and sexual abuse and internalizing problems on daytime cortisol rhythm in school-aged children. *Child Development, 81*(1), 252–269. https://doi.org/10.1111/j.1467-8624.2009.01393.x.

Cohen, S., Janicki-Deverts, D., Doyle, W., Miller, G., Frank, E., Rabin, B., & Turner, R. (2012). Chronic stress, glucocorticoid receptor resistance, inflammation, and disease risk. *Proceedings of the National Academy of Sciences, 109*(16), 5995–5999. https://doi.org/10.1073/pnas.1118355109.

Complex Trauma: In Urban African-American Children, Youth, and Families. (2019). Retrieved October 16, 2019 from www.nctsn.org/sites/default/files/resources/complex_trauma_facts_in_urban_african_american_children_youth_families.pdf.

Cortés-García, L., Takkouche, B., Seoane, G., & Senra, C. (2019). Mediators linking insecure attachment to eating symptoms: A systematic review and meta-analysis. *PLoS ONE, 14*(3), e0213099. https://doi.org/10.1371/journal.pone.0213099.

Crawford, M., Cadogan, O., Richardson, R., & Watts, M. (2008). *Nutrition and mental health: A handbook* [Ebook]. East Sussex: Pavilion Publishing and Media.

DeGruy, J. (2017). *Post traumatic slave syndrome.* Milwaukie, OR: Uptone Press.

Donovan, R., Galban, D., Grace, R., Bennett, J., & Felicié, S. (2012). Impact of racial macro- and microaggressions in Black women's lives. *Journal of Black Psychology, 39*(2), 185–196. https://doi.org/10.1177/0095798412443259.

Enoch, M. (2010). The role of early life stress as a predictor for alcohol and drug dependence. *Psychopharmacology, 214*(1), 17–31. https://doi.org/10.1007/s00213-010-1916-6.

Eyerman, R. (2004). The past in the present. *Acta Sociologica, 47*(2), 159–169. https://doi.org/10.1177/0001699304043853.

Gaskin-Wasson, A., Calamaras, M., LoParo, D., Goodnight, B., Remmert, B., Salami, T., . . . Kaslow, N. J. (2016). Childhood emotional abuse, self/other attachment, and hopelessness in African-American women. *Attachment & Human Development, 19*(1), 22–37. https://doi.org/10.1080/14616734.2016.1249895.

Gump, J. (2000). A White therapist, an African American patient—shame in the therapeutic dyad: Commentary on paper by Neil Altman. *Psychoanalytic Dialogues, 10*(4), 619–632. https://doi.org/10.1080/10481881009348571.

Gunnar, M., & Quevedo, K. (2007). The neurobiology of stress and development. *Annual Review of Psychology, 58*(1), 145–173. https://doi.org/10.1146/annurev.psych.58.110405.085605.

Hall, J. (2007). Kinship Ties: Attachment relationships that promote resilience in African American adult children of alcoholics. *Advances in Social Work, 8*(1), 130–140. https://doi.org/10.18060/136.

Halloran, M. (2018). African American Health and Posttraumatic Slave Syndrome: A terror management theory account. *Journal of Black Studies, 50*(1), 45–65. Retrieved September 13, 2019 from https://journals.sagepub.com/doi/abs/10.1177/0021934718803737.

Krieger, N., Waterman, P., Hartman, C., Bates, L., Stoddard, A., Quinn, M., . . . Barbeau, E. M. (2006). Social hazards on the job: Workplace abuse, sexual harassment, and racial discrimination—A study of Black, Latino, and White low-income women and men workers in the United States. *International Journal of Health Services, 36*(1), 51–85. https://doi.org/10.2190/3emb-ykrh-edj2-0h19.

McEwen, B. (2005). Stressed or stressed out? *Journal of Psychiatry & Neuroscience, 30*(5), 315–318.

Mikulincer, M., & Shaver, P. (2012). An attachment perspective on psychopathology. *World Psychiatry, 11*(1), 11–15. https://doi.org/10.1016/j.wpsyc.2012.01.003.

More Sleep Would Make Most Americans Happier, Healthier and Safer. (2014). Retrieved November 24, 2019 from www.apa.org/research/action/sleep-deprivation.

Morsy, L., & Rothstein, R. (2019). *Toxic stress and children's outcomes*. Washington, DC: Economic Policy Institute.

Perry, B. (2002). Childhood experience and the expression of genetic potential: What childhood neglect tells us about nature and nurture. *Brain and Mind, 3*, 79–100.

Persistent Fear and Anxiety Can Affect Young Children. (2019). Retrieved December 13, 2019 from https://developingchild.harvard.edu/resources/persistent-fear-and-anxiety-can-affect-young-childrens-learning-and-development/.

Poverty in the U.S.|Poverty Solutions. (2019). Retrieved December 13, 2019 from https://poverty.umich.edu/about/poverty-facts/us-poverty/.

Preventing Adverse Childhood Experiences|VetoViolence. (2019). Retrieved December 13, 2019 from https://vetoviolence.cdc.gov/apps/aces-training/#/#top.

Shonkoff, J., Garner, A., Siegel, B., Dobbins, M., Earls, M., Garner, A., & Wood, D. L. (2011). The lifelong effects of early childhood adversity and toxic stress. *Pediatrics, 129*(1), e232–e246. https://doi.org/10.1542/peds.2011-2663.

Slopen, N., Shonkoff, J., Albert, M., Yoshikawa, H., Jacobs, A., Stoltz, R., & Williams, D. (2016). Racial disparities in child adversity in the U.S. *American Journal of Preventive Medicine, 50*(1), 47–56. https://doi.org/10.1016/j.amepre.2015.06.013.

Sotero, M. (2006). *A conceptual model of historical trauma: Implications for public health practice and research.* Retrieved December 13, 2019 from www.ressources-actuarielles.net/EXT/ISFA/1226.nsf/0/bbd469e12b2d9eb2c12576000032b289/$FILE/Sotero_2006.pdf.

Striegel-Moore, R. (2000). Recurrent binge eating in Black American women. *Archives of Family Medicine, 9*(1), 83–87. https://doi.org/10.1001/archfami.9.1.83.

Striegel-Moore, R., Dohm, F., Kraemer, H., Taylor, C., Daniels, S., Crawford, P., & Schreiber, G. (2003). Eating disorders in White and Black women. *American Journal of Psychiatry, 160*(7), 1326–1331. https://doi.org/10.1176/appi.ajp.160.7.1326.

Su, X., Liang, H., Yuan, W., Olsen, J., Cnattingius, S., & Li, J. (2016). Prenatal and early life stress and risk of eating disorders in adolescent girls and young women. *European Child & Adolescent Psychiatry, 25*(11), 1245–1253. https://doi.org/10.1007/s00787-016-0848-z.

Sue, D., Capodilupo, C., Torino, G., Bucceri, J., Holder, A., Nadal, K., & Esquilin, M. (2007). Racial microaggressions in everyday life: Implications for clinical practice. *American Psychologist, 62*(4), 271–286. https://doi.org/10.1037/0003-066x.62.4.271.

Tasca, G., & Balfour, L. (2014). Attachment and eating disorders: A review of current research. *International Journal of Eating Disorders, 47*(7), 710–717. https://doi.org/10.1002/eat.22302.

Thomas, M., Hu, M., Lee, T., Bhatnagar, S., & Becker, J. (2009). Sex-specific susceptibility to cocaine in rats with a history of prenatal stress. *Physiology & Behavior, 97*(2), 270–277. https://doi.org/10.1016/j.physbeh.2009.02.025.

Thompson, B. (1992). A way outa no way. *Gender & Society, 6*(4), 546–561. https://doi.org/10.1177/089124392006004002.

Toxic stress and children's outcomes: African American children growing up poor are at greater risk of disrupted physiological functioning and depressed academic achievement. (2019). Retrieved December 13, 2019 from www.epi.org/publication/toxic-stress-and-childrens-outcomes-african-american-children-growing-up-poor-are-at-greater-risk-of-disrupted-physiological-functioning-and-depressed-academic-achievement/.

Trottier, K., & MacDonald, D. (2017). Update on psychological trauma, other severe adverse experiences and eating disorders: State of the research and future research directions. *Current Psychiatry Reports, 19*(8). https://doi.org/10.1007/s11920-017-0806-6.

Warren, B., Sial, O., Alcantara, L., Greenwood, M., Brewer, J., Rozofsky, J., . . . Bolaños-Guzmán, C. A. (2014). Altered gene expression and spine density in nucleus accumbens of adolescent and adult male mice exposed to emotional and physical stress. *Developmental Neuroscience, 36*(3–4), 250–260. https://doi.org/10.1159/000362875.

Woods-Giscombé, C. (2010). Superwoman schema: African American women's views on stress, strength, and health. *Qualitative Health Research, 20*(5), 668–683. https://doi.org/10.1177/1049732310361892.

Zohar, A., Giladi, L., & Givati, T. (2006). Holocaust exposure and disordered eating: A study of multi-generational transmission. *European Eating Disorders Review, 15*(1), 50–57. https://doi.org/10.1002/erv.730.

9 Treating Polycystic Ovarian Syndrome in Black Women With Eating Disorders

Sasha Ottey

Introduction

Polycystic ovary syndrome (PCOS) is the most common endocrine disorder in women. It is a complex hormone, metabolic, and reproductive disorder (http://www.pcoschallenge.org/what-is-pcos/). There is a strong genetic component, with 70% heritability in the development of PCOS (Mykhalchenko et al., 2017). Estimates for the prevalence of PCOS vary anywhere from 4% to 21% of the female population, depending on the diagnostic criteria used and geographic location (Brakta et al., 2017). A PCOS diagnosis is most often made if a woman or girl has two out of three of the following: (1) irregular or absent menstrual cycles/ovulation; (2) hyperandrogenemia or hyperandrogenism, with symptoms such as hirsutism (excess facial and body hair growth), androgenic alopecia (male or female pattern hair loss), or acne; or (3) polycystic ovaries (multiple immature follicles) as seen on transvaginal ultrasound in adult women. PCOS is also a diagnosis of exclusion in which other disorders with similar symptoms such as nonclassic adrenal hyperplasia or a pituitary tumor should be ruled out. Other characteristics of PCOS include subfertility or infertility, increased risk for anxiety, depression, eating disorders, other mental health disorders, insulin resistance, weight gain, and other features of metabolic syndrome. Despite what the name polycystic ovary syndrome may suggest, PCOS is not just a disorder of the reproductive system and does not go away after reproductive years or a hysterectomy. PCOS can affect other organs systems such as the brain, skin, fat, blood vasculature, pancreas, liver, and others (National Institutes of Health, 2012). According to the Centers for Disease Control and Prevention, more than half the women with PCOS will develop type 2 diabetes or prediabetes by age 40. Women with PCOS also have a four to seven times higher risk for heart attack compared to women the same age who don't have PCOS (https://www.cdc.gov/diabetes/library/spotlights/pcos.html). African Americans with PCOS have a greater propensity for obesity and hypertension and have a significantly elevated burden of cardiovascular disease risk factors (Lo et al., 2006; Mensah, Mokdad, Ford, Greenlund, & Croft, 2005). Despite its prevalence and risk profile, PCOS is still not well understood, and 50% of women are going undiagnosed, putting them at increased risk for comorbid disorders such as type 2 diabetes, hypertension and endometrial cancer (Gupta, Gupta, & Mueen Ahmed, 2018). Furthermore, research data on Black women with PCOS globally, including genome-wide association studies, is notably lacking. Thanks to a collaboration between Professor Richard Adanu at the University of Ghana, Dr. Christian Makwe at the University of Lagos, and Dr. Ricardo Azziz, formerly of the State University of New York, the first PCOS studies in Sub-Saharan Africa commenced in Ghana and Nigeria in 2018, 83 years after the disorder was first described by Drs. Stein and Leventhal. This study aims to better assess the public health and economic implications of PCOS; determine the phenotype of PCOS in the region, allowing for improved screening methods; compare data between Ghanaian and African American and other women to better understand how environmental or ethnic factors influence PCOS; and to better understand the genetics of PCOS.

PCOS in Black Women

So what do we know about Black women's experiences living with polycystic ovary syndrome and the physical and psychosocial challenges that accompany the disorder? Even though the majority of PCOS research so far has included Caucasian and Asian women, we know that Black women experience all the same symptoms, with disproportionately elevated risk for developing hypertension, weight gain, and other cardiovascular risk factors (Lo et al., 2006; Mensah et al., 2005). Women with PCOS have a three-fold greater risk for developing endometrial cancer, which has twice the mortality rate in Black women (Barry, Azizia, & Hardiman, 2014; Long, Liu, & Bristow, 2013). Black women also experience the mental health disorders associated with PCOS such as binge eating disorder, anxiety, and depression.

Black women with PCOS have some unique ethnic and cultural challenges. PCOS Challenge: The National Polycystic Ovary Syndrome Association, conducted a nonscientific member survey of 20 Black women in the United States. The survey respondents shared their opinions and feedback on how they think their races and ethnicities influenced their experiences with PCOS. The most common challenges that they identified were access to proficient health care, access to healthy food options, mistrust of health care providers, resistance to lifestyle changes from family members, and unwillingness to seek care for mental health.

Bad Experiences and Lack of Trust in the Medical Community

Some women described the long, turbulent history between Black people and the medical system (e.g., segregated hospitals, Tuskegee Experiment, the statistic that Black women in the US are 243 percent more likely to die from pregnancy- and childbirth-related causes than White women in the US) as well as the prevalent weight bias and discriminatory practices that are both overt and perceived in interactions with providers. Along this line, an insightful TEDMED talk by Dr. Peter Attia highlights his [mis]treatment of a patient based on assumptions that he made because of weight bias (Martin, 2017; Attia, 2013). Black women often experience not only weight bias but also racial bias, which compounds the fears and frustrations associated with seeking care. One of the survey's respondents mentioned that it took longer for her to get diagnosed with PCOS and that her symptoms were overlooked because her doctor assumed that being bigger was normal for her based on her race and family history. One common complaint for women with PCOS that is not unique to Black women is the general treatment by doctors, especially in language about weight and weight loss.

> I am fed up with the medical community. Unlike a lot of black women, I do have health insurance, but to visit specialist after specialist with horrible bedside manners who tell me I will die in the next few years if I don't lose weight is not my idea of helping me to control my condition. I can now understand why my grandmother didn't like doctors and chose herbs over medical fluff.
>
> —RG

Related to RG's grandmother's inclination for herbs over modern medicine, the preference for home or "natural" remedies still seems to prevail among Black families.

A Weighty Issue

Due to the complexity of the endocrine and metabolic disturbances in PCOS, some women and teens with PCOS can experience rapid weight gain and difficulty losing weight. When women with PCOS gain weight, the major focus from the health care community regarding weight is, "You need to lose weight. Eat less and exercise more. Even 5 to 10% weight loss can help you get pregnant or feel better." This is, after all, what the research shows. Looking closely at the weight-loss methods in some of these research studies reveals extreme calorie restriction, medical weight-loss programs, bariatric surgery, and short-term methods to produce weight loss and determine a specific outcome. There are few good-quality studies on the lifestyle modifications in PCOS. Ultimately, the studies also show that there is no one "diet" or exercise program that works the same for everyone with PCOS. However, most women with PCOS try multiple "diets" or change their lifestyles, attempting to accomplish the weight loss that will help them get pregnant or feel better.

Put Some Meat on Those Bones

Most larger body types are often seen as acceptable or desirable within the Black community. Sometimes family and others around may even discourage some of the healthy lifestyle changes for fear that one may "lose too much weight" and "look sick."

> Black women who gain weight in their thighs, butt and even a bit around the midsection may be viewed as "thick." These curves are welcomed and admired by many black men.
>
> —ND

Some even get praised for gaining weight.

> I've always been super small (size 0 for years) and danced for years. So when I stopped dancing and the weight started, my family was overjoyed that now I "look healthy."
>
> —ST

One of the most common conflicts with their families was when they chose to make lifestyle changes including food and exercise. There is sometimes little support for eating "that bland" food, especially from the older generation.

> Common meals in the black community often consists of foods that are fried, loaded with carbs and followed by sweet, rich desserts. This includes fried fish, fried chicken, cornbread, macaroni and cheese, pound cake, red velvet cake, pie, and finished with a sweet beverage like iced tea, Kool-Aid, or punch. Even outside of a PCOS diagnosis, these meals wreak havoc on the body. Trying to change my eating habits to avoid some of these foods can cause some conflict.
>
> —ND

It's a Family Affair

With PCOS being a genetic condition, many of the respondents observed that their mothers or aunts had similar symptoms of weight gain, infertility, excess facial and body hair, or male pattern hair loss but were never diagnosed. Most had developed diabetes, hypertension, and other comorbid conditions of PCOS. Another perspective was that having diabetes, heart disease, and other chronic diseases has almost become accepted as a part of the Black experience. Many people don't talk about their health with their family or friends.

> One may not readily find the opportunities to openly discuss health concerns with friends and/or family. In the Black community, it seems as if it is common and acceptable to have high blood pressure, high cholesterol and diabetes, so there is no reason to talk about it.
>
> —ND

PCOS, Mental Health, and the Plight of the "Strong Black Woman"

One of the most frequently reported burdens was the pressure to "stay strong," keep your problems to yourself, hold your head up high, pray about it, and leave your troubles to God. PCOS can wreak havoc on mental health. Common mental health challenges include mood disorder, body image issues, anxiety, depression, binge eating disorder, and bipolar disorder (Sirmans & Pate, 2014). Mental and emotional wellness should be included in the health care and management of women and girls with PCOS.

As a black woman, anxiety can be often translated as the stereotypical "angry black woman," when sometimes it is just mere overload of life. Especially when you have PCOS. Once again, our culture as black people is to hide the problems, hide the secrets, hide the fears—keep them quiet and deal. In the black community, depression, anxiety and eating disorders are deemed taboo, hush-hush—a "white person's problem." Throughout history, we have had to demonstrate large amounts of strength on so many levels that depression was ignored and pushed under the rug so to speak. Thus, when it comes to depression, it is not common for black people to talk about their problems or take medication.

—RG

As a black woman, the last thing you may want to admit to is your struggle with anxiety, depression or low self-esteem. Some may even avoid seeking medical attention and counseling to better themselves. If they do, they may seek assistance in secrecy and not openly discuss it.

—ND

The Advocate—The New Black Woman With PCOS

Many Black women with PCOS often feel conflicted, unsupported, and as if "the cards are stacked against us." This is true for many women with PCOS regardless of race and ethnicity. However, there are signals that the modern woman is using the tools at her disposal to educate herself, her family, and her health care team. Many women are learning from relatives' mistakes and are refusing to passively accept that it is just "a matter of time" before high blood pressure and diabetes become a part of their medical records and way of life. Despite the history, pushback, and hurdles, Black women are now more open-minded about modern medicine and seek out access to proper care and healthy foods. Black women contribute to science and participate in research as both scientists and subjects and are more empowered to advocate for and take control of their own bodies and health.

References

Attia, P. (2013). Is the obesity epidemic hiding a bigger problem? *TEDMED 2013*. Retrieved from www.ted.com/talks/peter_attia_what_if_we_re_wrong_about_diabetes.

Barry, J. A., Azizia, M. M., & Hardiman, P. J. (2014, September 1). Risk of endometrial, ovarian and breast cancer in women with polycystic ovary syndrome: A systematic review and meta-analysis. *Human Reproduction Update, 20*(5), 748–758. https://doi.org/10.1093/humupd/dmu012.

Brakta, S., Liczneva, D., Mykhalchenko, K., Imam, A., Walker, W., Diamond, M. P., & Azziz, R. (2017, December 1). Perspectives on polycystic ovary syndrome: Is polycystic ovary syndrome research underfunded? *The Journal of Clinical Endocrinology and Metabolism, 102*(12), 4421–4427. https://doi.org/10.1210/jc.2017-01415.

Centers for Disease Control and Prevention. *PCOS and diabetes, heart disease, stroke*. Retrieved from www.cdc.gov/diabetes/library/spotlights/pcos.html.

Gupta, R., Gupta, B. M., & Mueen Ahmed, K. K. (2018). Polycystic ovary syndrome research: A scientometric assessment of global publications output during 2007–16. *OGH Reports, 7*(1). https://doi.org/10.5530/ogh.2018.7.1.3.

Lo, J. C., Feigenbaum, S. L., Yang, J., Pressman, A. R., Selby, J. V., & Go, A. S. (2006). Epidemiology and adverse cardiovascular risk profile of diagnosed polycystic ovary syndrome. *The Journal of Clinical Endocrinology and Metabolism, 91*(4), 1357–1363.

Long, B., Liu, F. W., & Bristow, R. E. (2013, September). Disparities in uterine cancer epidemiology, treatment, and survival among African Americans in the United States. *Gynecologic Oncology, 130*(3), 652–659. https://doi.org/10.1016/j.ygyno.2013.05.020.

Martin, N. (2017). LOST MOTHERS: Nothing protects black women from dying in pregnancy and childbirth. *ProPublica*. Retrieved from www.propublica.org/article/nothing-protects-black-women-from-dying-in-pregnancy-and-childbirth.

Mensah, G. A., Mokdad, A. H., Ford, E. S., Greenlund, K. J., & Croft, J. B. (2005). State of disparities in cardiovascular health in the United States. *Circulation, 111*(10), 1233–1241.

Mykhalchenko, K., Lizneva, D., Trofimova, T., Walker, W., Suturina, L., Diamond, M. P., & Azziz, R. (2017). Genetics of polycystic ovary syndrome. *Expert Review of Molecular Diagnostics, 17*(7), 723–733. https://doi.org/10.1080/14737159.2017.1340833.

National Institutes of Health. (2012, December 3–5). Evidence-based methodology workshop on Polycystic Ovary Syndrome. *Executive Summary*. Retrieved from https://prevention.nih.gov/docs/programs/pcos/FinalReport.pdf.

PCOS Challenge: The National Polycystic Ovary Syndrome Association. *What is PCOS*. Retrieved from www.pcoschallenge.org/what-is-pcos/.

Sirmans, S. M., & Pate, K. A. (2014). Epidemiology, diagnosis, and management of polycystic ovary syndrome. *Clinical Epidemiology, 6*, 1–13. https://doi.org/10.2147/CLEP.S37559.

10 Psychiatric Medications and the Treatment of Eating Disorders in African American Women

Rashida Gray

Introduction

Psychiatric treatment and care is an integral part of an interdisciplinary approach for the treatment of patients with eating disorders (EDs). Patients may present with anxiety, suspicion, or apprehension about the evaluation. The role of psychiatrists in the care of patients with EDs may vary, but typically they conduct a psychiatric evaluation, determine psychiatric diagnosis(es), and develop a treatment plan. Thus, African American women with EDs may be referred to or interact with a psychiatrist during the treatment course. African American women have often received negative messaging about psychiatry, mental health, mental illnesses, psychiatrists, and psychiatric medications. This messaging comes from the community, family, Black church, the larger media, friends, and their knowledge of the history of African Americans and the US health care system. Moreover, a small number of African American female psychiatrists are currently practicing in the United States. This fact means that when an African American woman is referred to a psychiatrist, she will interact with a psychiatrist that does not share her gender, race, history, culture, and/or life experience. These differences are highly notable and may be emotionally distressing to the patient. Nevertheless, the psychiatrist may be unaware of this transference and interpersonal dynamic. This dynamic and the psychiatrist's lack of awareness and/or ability to address such circumstances contribute to the patient's feelings of mistrust, skepticism, fear, and feeling misunderstood and limit the building of connection with the psychiatrist. Psychiatrists of color may not have the same obstacles to build connection and trust but are still representatives of a field that is greatly mistrusted by most African Americans. The clinical benefits of psychiatric treatment depend on the strong foundation of a trusting therapeutic relationship between the patient and the psychiatrist. This trust helps patients to engage and believe in the treatment recommendations, especially medications. African American female patients, like most patients, want to improve their health and life. They also want to collaborate with a health care practitioner who is willing to provide competent psychiatric care.

Many people are unaware of what happens in a psychiatric evaluation. Beyond curiosity and concern over the psychiatrist, an African American female patient may also be curious and concerned about the office, the process of a psychiatric evaluation, her safety, or fear of loss of autonomy.

She may arrive at the session with many questions:

- Will I have to lie on a couch?
- Will the medications make me feel like a zombie? Or will I become addicted to the medication?
- Will I be declared "crazy"?
- Could I be put in a straitjacket?
- How can they understand my life if they are White? Or never experienced racism?
- What do I do if they say something that is racially or gender insensitive?

A comprehensive psychiatric evaluation includes a medical history, family history, psychiatric history, evaluation of current psychiatric symptoms, mental status exam, social and developmental history, possible physical exam, medical records, available imaging, and lab studies. Physicians gather this information to determine whether any nonpsychiatric medical diagnosis requires consideration. They also assess which psychiatric diagnosis correlates with the symptoms reported and whether medication and/or therapy is needed to improve or resolve a patient's symptoms. All of the above should be discussed and explained with the patient, particularly a skeptical African American female patient who may be feeling very vulnerable and may not automatically trust the process or the physician. A psychiatrist's treatment plan may include psychotherapy recommendations if those are not already in place, lifestyle changes, medical recommendations such as lab work, referrals to specialists, and recommendations for psychiatric medications if indicated.

When African Americans are referred to a psychiatrist, they may bring varying degrees of past experiences, preconceived notions, family histories, and ethnic and culturally informed ideas and overall knowledge about the US mental health care system, psychiatrists, and psychiatric medications. African Americans have a long and traumatic history with the US health care system, including psychiatry (Cuevas & O'Brien, 2019; Kennedy, Mathis, & Woods, 2017; Kato, Borsky, Zuvekas, Soni, & Ngo-Metzger, 2018; Zimmerman & Anderson, 2019). Even if African American women with EDs are able to move past the stigma, fear, and other barriers to access psychiatric treatment, they may bring generational history, fear, and mistrust into the session and the treatment relationship with the psychiatrist.

African American Fear and Mistrust of Mental Health Care

Former US Surgeon General David Satcher stated in his report on mental health in the US, "Research documents that many members of minority groups fear, or feel ill at ease with, the mental health system" (Satcher, 2000, p. 80). African Americans' avoidance and mistrust of the health care system are contributing barriers to medical and mental health treatment (U.S. Department of Health and Human Services, 2001). This mistrust is connected to the history of physicians, nurses, hospitals, and researchers mistreating African Americans by using pseudoscience to characterize them as inferior in intellect, morals, and abilities and subjecting them to inhumane medical care and withholding treatment even when available. Since the arrival of enslaved Africans, African American women have been victimized by physicians. Such inhumane practices included performing heinous gynecological surgical experimentation on enslaved women by Dr. J. Marion Sims (Suite, La Bril, Primm, & Harrison-Ross, 2007), involuntary sterilizations of Black women, and allowing African American men for 40 years in Tuskegee, Alabama, to develop advanced stages of syphilis and transmit it to their wives and children while researchers withheld treatment and waited for death in order to perform autopsies. Although today's African American female patient is not the direct victim of these abuses, the stories, the emotions, and associated meanings have been shared within families, on front porches, across neighborhoods and communities, and in churches and schools, thus leading to generations of mistrust, fear, and foregoing of much-needed medical care.

For African American women, engaging with the health care system has always felt like a gamble. A gamble is taken often after other options have failed, such as prayer and relying on one's faith, over-the-counter remedies, naturopathic/herbal remedies, seeking advice from family and friends, and the use of denial and avoidance. This avoidance or delay in seeking medical care is easily mischaracterized as irresponsible, uninformed, or lacking concern for one's health if the fear and skepticism are not considered.

Many researchers have shown a "positive correlation between racism and overdiagnosis of serious and underdiagnosis of less serious mental disorders" in minority, marginalized populations. Studies in the 1970s, as well as recent studies, reflect an overdiagnosis of schizophrenia and underdiagnosis of mood disorders in African Americans, Afro-Caribbeans, and Latinx (Coleman & Baker, 1994; Friedman & Paradis, 2002; Gara, Minsky, Silverstein, Miskimen, & Strakowski, 2019). The idea that race may lead to a medical mishap, mistreatment, or misdiagnosis remains relevant in the lives of African American women.

Today, in the US health care system, there is evidence of health care disparities and inequities based on gender and race (Zimmerman & Anderson, 2019). Such disparities and inequities place the responsibility on the representatives of health care to address their own internal racial biases, be intentional in building trust, acknowledge the painful history and past mistakes of the US health care system to which African Americans have fallen victim, and provide space for the discussion of racially latent experiences and perceptions of health care (Suite et al., 2007).

Engaging African American women in mental health treatment requires the understanding of these traumas and resulting mistrust, particularly regarding psychiatric medications. Some evidence exists that when physicians or other health care providers acknowledge the person's African American ethnicity as a part of one's identity and life experience, this may improve the therapeutic relationship, adherence with treatment, and overall outcomes (Cuevas & O'Brien, 2019).

Eating Disorders and African American Women

Few studies have explored EDs in African Americans (Taylor, Caldwell, Baser, Faison, & Jackson, 2007). Eating disorders, as delineated and defined in the *Diagnostic and Statistical Manual-V*, include bulimia nervosa, anorexia nervosa, binge eating disorder, other specified feeding or eating disorder (OSFED), unspecified feeding or eating disorder (UFED), and avoidant/restrictive food intake disorder (ARFID). Diagnostically, all these disorders require health care providers to have a high index of suspicion, ability to assess and make an EDs diagnosis, knowledge of the various cognitive distortions behind the abnormal eating patterns, and awareness of EDs patients' varying body types and sizes. A common assumption within and outside of health care is that patients suffering from EDs are Caucasian females, middle- and upper-class SES, underweight, thin, and suffering medical conditions related to lack of nutrition, purging, and low weight. Although African American women can suffer any eating disorder, and by definition may be underweight, normal weight, or overweight, depending on the type of the disorder. Several studies have consistently shown significantly lower rates of anorexia nervosa in the African American community. When clinicians are presented with matching clinical examples of disordered eating, they are more likely to correctly diagnose an eating disorder if the patient is a Caucasian female. Nevertheless, they usually do not characterize the eating patterns as abnormal or an eating disorder if the patient is African American or Hispanic (Gordon, Brattole, Wingate, & Joiner, 2006). Studies have also demonstrated higher rates of binge eating disorder (BED) in African American women compared to Caucasians. Other studies that focused on understanding EDs in African Americans have identified differing demographics, age of onset, duration of illness, and other clinical characteristics (Taylor et al., 2007).

Consequently, the misdiagnosis or lack of diagnosis correlates with the lack of evidence-based treatment recommendations and referrals for many minority groups, including African American women. Consistent with other mental health conditions such as depression, people of color are less likely to receive evidence-based treatment for EDs (Becker, Franko, Speck, & Herzog, 2003; Marques et al., 2011; Wade, Keski-Rahkonen, & Hudson, 2011).

The gold standard of treatment for all EDs is psychotherapy. Nonetheless, some EDs, specifically BED and bulimia nervosa, have stronger data to support the use of pharmacotherapy combined with psychotherapy, compared to either treatment alone (American Psychiatric Association, 2006; Gianini, Broft, & Devlin, 2016; Agras, 2017). Pharmacotherapy alone is also recommended for eating-disordered patients when there is no option for psychotherapy due to factors limiting access. Limited access is a likely occurrence for many African American women because of costs, transportation, limited therapists trained to treat EDs, and difficulty arranging the necessary time commitment due to the significant caretaking roles for African American women, in addition to other social determinants.

Psychiatric Medications

Approach to Prescribing Psychiatric Medications for the African American Woman

Once a therapeutic relationship between a psychiatrist and the patient has been established, the prescribing physician or nurse practitioner should ensure adequate time for explaining the rationale for choosing medications, the basics of how medications work, the potential benefits, and potential side effects. They should be prepared for questions that may seem paranoid to the uninformed but are based in history, genuine misunderstanding, and normal fear. Even with a good understanding of her diagnosis and a trusting relationship with her health care practitioner, a client may be concerned about being labeled "crazy" because a psychiatric medication has been recommended, or she may believe that the medication can cause her to "go crazy" or change "who I am, my personality." She may worry about "being a zombie" based on a relative or neighbor's reaction to medications. African American women may fear that they will "become addicted" to prescribed medications that are not associated with abuse or misuse as they may watch family members or neighbors descend into an addiction to illicit drugs. Trust, compassion, information, and a safe space are needed to discuss fears and allow collaboration. Such criteria are instrumental in helping the patient agree to take medications, consistently take them as prescribed, and feel comfortable to address concerns with the health care practitioner before stopping or self-adjusting the dose. A health care practitioner may feel that a 60% reduction in symptoms is a success, but a patient who expected a cure may be disappointed. Similarly, without a discussion of side effects, the patient may feel mistreated or deceived if they develop significant weight gain, fatigue, or other physical changes due to medication side effects. Psychiatrists and other health care professionals prescribing medications are constantly navigating the balance of risks versus benefits with medications, but this must include the patient's concerns and her vision of treatment goals.

Psychiatric medications carry an inordinate level of stigma burden in our society because of misconceptions, historical misuse, side effects, and the stigma associated with mental illness. This burden is very distinct from other categories of medications and can be an enormous hurdle for African Americans, who may need psychiatric medications.

Psychiatric medications are categorized based on their pharmacology and the types of disorders that they treat, although some medications are used for several different psychiatric conditions or even medical conditions. Currently, there are no FDA-approved medications for most of the EDs listed in the *Diagnostic and Statistical Manual-V*. A variety of medications are prescribed off label to reduce the behaviors associated with EDs. These medications include selective serotonin reuptake inhibitors (SSRIs) as the most commonly prescribed stimulants and typically prescribed for treatment of attention deficit disorder, anticonvulsants, and others. There is one FDA-approved medication, lisdexamfetamine, for BED that is more common in African American women (Taylor et al., 2007). Medications prescribed for weight reduction have also been studied in EDs associated with obesity and are believed to have a role in treatment, although being controversial and likely appropriate for a small number of patients with obesity and eating disorders. The limited research and evidence of only partial improvements seen with psychiatric medications warrant a full discussion with African American female patients about the realistic potential benefits and risks.

Binge Eating Disorder

Owing to the high rates of obesity in patients with BED (roughly 50% according to Ogden, Carroll, Fryar, & Flegal, 2015) and the higher prevalence for obesity among African American women (Didie & Fitzgibbon, 2005), physicians should be screening their obese, morbidly obese, and overweight African American patients for symptoms of BED and referring them to appropriate health care providers, therapists, or eating disorder treatment centers. It is also important to note that 50% of BED patients are normal weight and infrequently seek help.

Binge eating disorder is more prevalent in minority communities compared to Caucasian communities and is the most common eating disorder diagnosed in minority communities (Eisenberg, Nicklett, Roeder, & Kirz, 2011; Taylor et al., 2007). Psychotherapy alone is more efficacious than pharmacotherapy alone, but there is limited research available regarding combined treatment. Psychotherapy, along with nutrition-focused behavioral modification, is considered the first-line treatment, while SSRIs are the most commonly prescribed medication. As previously mentioned, lisdexamfetamine is the only FDA-approved medication for BED. Some medications also show promise due to assisting with weight loss but are not specifically indicated for BED. These medications may include antidiabetic medicine, anorexiants, anticonvulsant, and lipase inhibitors. The antidiabetic medicines glucagon-like peptide-1 agonists, liraglutide and exenatide, increase insulin release, decrease glucagon release, and suppress appetite. Liraglutide and exenatide are indicated for weight loss and diabetes. Anorexiants, such as lorcaserin and phentermine, which reduce appetite, have also shown benefit for controlling weight. Physicians may also want to consider topiramate, an anticonvulsant that has some weight loss benefits, in addition to orlistat, a lipase inhibitor (Bodell & Devlin, 2010).

Due to the high comorbidity of other psychopathologies, it is highly likely that patients with BED may benefit from a psychiatric medication to address coexisting psychiatric disorders. In the US, about 49% of patients with BED had a lifetime history of three or more comorbid psychiatric disorders (i.e., social anxiety, substance abuse, and mood disorders; Hudson, Hiripi, Pope, & Kessler, 2007).

Physicians may also want to consider prescribing one of the medications associated with some positive benefits for a reduction in frequency, severity, or duration of binge episodes or associated with weight reduction. Although there is limited data, the research reflects the greatest benefit when there is a combination of medications and psychotherapy, which can target the cognitive distortions, compulsive behaviors, and necessary coping strategies. Conversations with African American women should provide information about realistic outcomes, the potential limited outcomes of taking medications without therapy, and the long-term risks without treatment. True informed consent, respectful of an African American woman's autonomy and desire to make informed decisions about her health care help reduce the negative misconceptions they may possess about mental health care, improve adherence, and reduce stigma.

Anorexia Nervosa

Anorexia nervosa (AN) infrequently affects African American women. It is more likely to occur in younger demographics than older African American women. Treatment guidelines primarily recommend psychotherapy and nutritional rehabilitation because studies have shown limited benefits from medications. Medications have been shown to have minimal benefit in reducing the distorted cognitions associated with the illness or improving food intake or enhancing weight gain. Multiple randomized trials suggest that the antipsychotic olanzapine modestly improves weight. Additionally, no medication has shown benefit in the area of prevention or delaying onset of subsequent episodes of AN (Attia, 2012; National Institute for Health and Care Excellence, 2017). In line with the other EDs, psychiatric medications are commonly prescribed to AN patients to treat comorbid conditions, like major depression.

Bulimia Nervosa

Bulimia nervosa (BN) has been shown to respond well to combined treatment with pharmacotherapy and psychotherapy, thus reducing the frequency of binging and purging behaviors (Agras, 2017; Bacaltchuk, Hay, & Trefiglio, 2001; Gianini et al., 2016). Medication efficacy in BN has been typically defined as a reduction of symptoms by 50% to 75% (Bacaltchuk et al., 2001). Selective serotonin reuptake inhibitors are the recommended first-line medications, with fluoxetine being the most commonly studied medication, although other

SSRIs are thought to be just as effective (Gianini et al., 2016; National Institute for Health and Care Excellence, 2004; Shapiro et al., 2007). Most treatment guidelines recommend fluoxetine as the first-line medication for BN, and it is typically dosed up to 60 mg. This is higher than the typical dosing when fluoxetine is used to treat depression. No studies compared SSRIs head to head for the treatment of BN. However, other SSRIs, including escitalopram, sertraline, and fluvoxamine, have shown promise and are considered second-line treatment (National Institute for Health and Care Excellence, 2004). The third-line treatment includes tricyclic antidepressants, monoamine oxidase inhibitors, trazodone, and topiramate (National Institute for Health and Care Excellence, 2004).

Psychiatric Medications and Eating Disorder Comorbidities

Psychiatric medications are also prescribed to patients with EDs to treat comorbid psychiatric conditions that commonly co-occur, such as posttraumatic stress disorder, major depressive disorder, and generalized anxiety disorder (American Psychiatric Association, 2006). Such conditions are more common in female patients. Comorbidity is the rule rather than the exception for patients with EDs (Jacobi et al., 2004; Taylor et al., 2007). There are no studies showing a difference in the rates of comorbidity in African American women compared to Caucasian women. The types of medications commonly prescribed for comorbidities include antidepressant medications, antianxiety medications, sleep aids, mood stabilizers/anticonvulsants, and antipsychotic medications. However, bupropion, an antidepressant, is the only medication contraindicated in all patients with EDs due to an increased risk of seizures. Due to the high risk of medical comorbidities and medical complications secondary to EDs, a physician must complete a full medical evaluation, including lab studies, before starting medications. Women of color showed similar efficacy with psychiatric medications in disorders such as major depression and generalized anxiety disorder, although limited research compared their effects on eating disorder symptoms response to medications across ethnicities.

The psychotherapist, nutritionist, or primary care physician often is the health care practitioner with the responsibility of referring a patient to see a psychiatrist. This fact highlights their important role in providing the initial information about mental health care, psychiatric medications, and the role of a psychiatrist in their treatment. They must be aware that African American patients may harbor mistrust and misunderstanding about psychiatrists and psychiatric medications. Patients are much more likely to agree to medications if the initial recommendation comes from a health care provider with whom there is a strong and trusted relationship. Health care providers must also be mindful of their own racial, gender, and mental health biases and stigma that they may possess. African American women may also have internalized the notions that EDs do not affect them and may need greater levels of education, support, and informed guidance to begin accepting the diagnosis and treatment.

Considerations when prescribing or discussing psychiatric medications with African American women with EDs are as follows:

- Building trust through therapeutic relationship building and respecting and acknowledging an African American women's ethnicity and possible mistrust of mental health care.
- Inquiring about her and her family's perception of mental health care.
- Explaining that psychiatric medications are more likely to be helpful than harmful to patients and are rigorously studied for many years before being approved for use, just like other medications.
- Discussing realistic expected outcomes, treatment goals, and potential side effects at multiple stages of treatment, particularly in the beginning. Being dismissive of a patient's report of side effects or a patient expecting unrealistic outcomes can cause irreparable harm to the relationship and may reinforce mistrust.
- Addressing the risk of psychiatric medications causing weight gain prior to starting medications and the medications with the highest risk of weight gain should be carefully considered.
- Finding the right medication and dose. This approach requires a trusting and working relationship with the psychiatrist and may require several follow up visits to review the overall goal and expectations of the medication frequently.
- Considering a combination of therapy and medications, since it has been shown to have a synergistic effect.
- Discussing concerns about the medications, either from the patient or therapist. The discussion should be focused on empowering the patient to seek answers from the psychiatrist and should not feed into negative, pejorative, and overly generalized criticism of the mental health care system.
- Considering that EDs have historically not been associated with African American women, and she may be surprised to receive the diagnosis.
- Having the ability to shift negative perceptions of mental health, engage more African American women in much-needed psychiatric treatment, and improve the overall health of African American women.

References

Agras, W. (2017). Treatment of eating disorders. In A. F. Schatzberg & C. B. Nemeroff (Eds.), *The American Psychiatric Association publishing textbook of psychopharmacology*. New York: American Psychiatric Association.

American Psychiatric Association. (2006). *Treatment of patients with eating disorders* (3rd ed.). Washington, DC: American Psychiatric Association.

Attia, E. (2012). In the clinic. Eating disorders. *Annals of Internal Medicine, 156*(7), ITC4. https://doi.org/10.7326/0003-4819-156-7-201204030-01004.

Bacaltchuk, J., Hay, P., & Trefiglio, R. (2001). Antidepressants versus psychological treatments and their combination of bulimia nervosa. *Cochrane Database of Systematic Reviews, 4*, CD003385.

Becker, A. E., Franko, D. L., Speck, A., & Herzog, D. B. (2003). Ethnicity and differential access to care for eating disorder symptoms. *The International Journal of Eating Disorders, 33*(2), 205–212. https://doi.org/10.1002/eat.10129.

Bodell, L. P., & Devlin, M. J. (2010). Pharmacotherapy for binge eating disorder. In C. M. Grilo & J. E. Mitchell (Eds.), *The treatment of eating disorders* (p. 402). New York: Guilford Press.

Coleman, D., & Baker, F. M. (1994). Misdiagnosis of schizophrenia in older, black veterans. *The Journal of Nervous and Mental Disease, 182*(9), 527–528. https://doi.org/10.1097/00005053-199409000-00008.

Cuevas, A. G., & O'Brien, K. (2019). Racial centrality may be linked to mistrust in healthcare institutions for African Americans. *Journal of Health Psychology, 24*(14), 2022–2030. https://doi.org/10.1177/1359105317715092.

Didie, E. R., & Fitzgibbon, M. (2005). Binge eating and psychological distress: Is the degree of obesity a factor? *Eating Behaviors, 6*(1), 35–41. https://doi.org/10.1016/j.eatbeh.2004.08.007.

Eisenberg, D., Nicklett, E. J., Roeder, K., & Kirz, N. E. (2011). Eating disorder symptoms among college students: Prevalence, persistence, correlates, and treatment-seeking. *Journal of American College Health, 59*(8), 700–707. https://doi.org/10.1080/07448481.2010.546461.

Friedman, S., & Paradis, C. (2002). Panic disorder in African-Americans: Symptomatology and isolated sleep paralysis. *Culture, Medicine and Psychiatry, 26*(2), 179–198. https://doi.org/10.1023/a:1016307515418.

Gara, M. A., Minsky, S., Silverstein, S. M., Miskimen, T., & Strakowski, S. M. (2019). A naturalistic study of racial disparities in diagnoses at an outpatient behavioral health clinic. *Psychiatric Services, 70*(2), 130–134. https://doi.org/10.1176/appi.ps.201800223.

Gianini, L., Broft, A., & Devlin, M. (2016). Treatment of binge eating, including bulimia nervosa and a binge-eating disorder. In B. T. Walsh, E. Attia, D. R. Lasofer, & R. Sysko (Eds.), *Handbook of assessment and treatment of eating disorders* (p. 279). Arlington, VA: American Psychiatric Association.

Gordon, K. H., Brattole, M. M., Wingate, L. R., & Joiner, T. E. (2006). The impact of client race on clinician detection of eating disorders. *Behavior Therapy, 37*(4), 319–325. https://doi.org/10.1016/j.beth.2005.12.002.

Hudson, J. I., Hiripi, E., Pope, H. G., & Kessler, R. C. (2007). The prevalence and correlates of eating disorders in the National Comorbidity Survey Replication. *Biological Psychiatry, 61*(3), 348–358. https://doi.org/10.1016/j.biopsych.2006.03.040.

Jacobi, F., Wittchen, H.-U., Holting, C., Höfler, M., Pfister, H., Müller, N., & Lieb, R. (2004). Prevalence, co-morbidity and correlates of mental disorders in the general population: Results from the German Health Interview and Examination Survey (GHS). *Psychological Medicine, 34*(4), 597–611. https://doi.org/10.1017/s0033291703001399.

Kato, E., Borsky, A. E., Zuvekas, S. H., Soni, A., & Ngo-Metzger, Q. (2018). Missed opportunities for depression screening and treatment in the United States. *Journal of the American Board of Family Medicine, 31*(3), 389–397. https://doi.org/10.3122/jabfm.2018.03.170406.

Kennedy, B. R., Mathis, C. C., & Woods, A. K. (2007). African Americans and their distrust of the health care system: Healthcare for diverse populations. *Journal of Cultural Diversity, 14*(2), 56–60.

Marques, L., Alegria, M., Becker, A. E., Chen, C.-N., Fang, A., Chosak, A., & Diniz, J. B. (2011). Comparative prevalence, correlates of impairment, and service utilization for eating disorders across US ethnic groups: Implications for reducing ethnic disparities in health care access for eating disorders. *The International Journal of Eating Disorders, 44*(5), 412–420. https://doi.org/10.1002/eat.20787.

National Institute for Health and Care Excellence. (2004). *Eating disorders: Core interventions in the treatment and management of anorexia nervosa. Bulimia nervosa and related eating disorders.* Clinical Guideline 9. Leicester, UK: National Institute for Health and Care Excellence.

National Institute for Health and Care Excellence. (2017). *Eating disorders: Recognition and treatment.* Retrieved from www.nice.org.uk/guidance/ng6.

Ogden, C. L., Carroll, M. D., Fryar, C. D., & Flegal, K. M. (2015). *Prevalence of obesity among adults and youth: United States, 2011–2014* (NCHS data brief No. 219). New York: U.S. Department of Health and Human Services.

Satcher, D. (2000). Mental health: A report of the Surgeon General. *Professional Psychology, 31*(1), 5–13.

Shapiro, J. R., Berkman, N. D., Brownley, K. A., Sedway, J. A., Lohr, K. N., & Bulik, C. M. (2007). Bulimia nervosa treatment: A systematic review of randomized controlled trials. *The International Journal of Eating Disorders, 40*(4), 321–336. https://doi.org/10.1002/eat.20372.

Suite, D. H., La Bril, R., Primm, A., & Harrison-Ross, P. (2007). Beyond misdiagnosis, misunderstanding and mistrust: Relevance of the historical perspective in the medical and mental health treatment of people of color. *Journal of the National Medical Association, 99*(8), 879–885.

Taylor, J. Y., Caldwell, C. H., Baser, R. E., Faison, N., & Jackson, J. S. (2007). Prevalence of eating disorders among Blacks in the National Survey of American Life. *The International Journal of Eating Disorders, 40*(Suppl.), S10–4. https://doi.org/10.1002/eat.20451.

U.S. Department of Health and Human Services. (2001). *Mental health: Culture, race, and ethnicity: A supplement to Mental health, a report of the Surgeon General: Executive summary.* Retrieved from www.ahci.org/Documents/Report.

Wade, T. D., Keski-Rahkonen, A., & Hudson, J. I. (2011). Epidemiology of eating disorders. In M. T. Tsuang, M. Tohen, & P. B. Jones (Eds.), *Textbook of psychiatric epidemiology* (Vol. 15, pp. 343–360). Chichester, UK: John Wiley & Sons.

Zimmerman, F. J., & Anderson, N. W. (2019). Trends in health equity in the United States by race/ethnicity, sex, and income, 1993–2017. *JAMA Network Open, 2*(6), e196386. https://doi.org/10.1001/jamanetworkopen.2019.6386.

Part III

Nutrition and Weight Concerns

11 Cultural Competence

Considerations in the Treatment of African American Women With Eating Disorders

Goulda Downer

The American Psychiatric Association (2013; Parekh, 2017) reports that eating disorders are illnesses in which people experience severe disturbances in their eating behaviors and related thoughts and emotions. Hallmarks of the illness which are associated with maladaptive eating regulation responses are a preoccupation with food and weight. Eating disorders are most commonly seen in women between the ages of 12 and 35. These disorders have the highest mortality rate of any mental illness (Smink, Van Hoeken, & Hoek, 2012).

Despite erroneous assumptions about the absence of the disorders in Black women, it is readily acknowledged that genetics (Berrettini, 2004; Trace et al., 2013) environmental factors, and personality traits all combine to create risk for development of eating disorders (Culbert et al., 2015), proving that no one is exempt from the disorders. Yet the lack of both diverse behavioral therapists with the requisite cultural competency knowledge and skills to treat Black women are among the main barriers to effective treatment.

The basic premise of culturally competent (CC) care for AA women with EDs is that individuals have a right to cultural beliefs, values, and practices, and these factors should be respected, understood, and considered when rendering quality care. By utilizing tools that expand on ways to achieve CC clinical care, MHPs can gain a better understanding of general cultural starting points for approaching, learning about, and interacting within the AA culture. And understanding and negotiating with individuals about the various social and cultural factors that influence their ability to identify and prevent EDs can serve to improve clinical outcomes and foster greater patient satisfaction.

For MHPs to provide care that is culturally responsive, meaningful, acceptable, accessible, and useful, an understanding of how one's own cultural values, beliefs, and assumptions not only influence but affect the care provided to patients is key. Acknowledging the presence of common attributes and the ability to enlarge the view of culture beyond ethnic differences to include religion, gender, age, race, sexual orientation, social class, socioeconomic, and disability are also critical. Furthermore, understanding that culture encompasses a systems-wide variable in family-, community-, and region-oriented support while avoiding stereotyping groups of people and instead addressing the moral and ethical obligation to provide support to all patients is the professional duty of the MHP. In so doing, the impact of the services offered is strengthened.

At the point of delivery, CC MHPs should be (1) knowledgeable about cultural differences among and within the AA community and their impact on attitudes and behaviors; (2) sensitive, understanding, nonjudgmental, and respectful in dealing with people whose culture is different from their own; (3) flexible and skillful in responding and adapting to different cultural contexts and circumstances; and (4) able to incorporate an understanding of the needs of the target AA women population and to design and deliver services accordingly. The impact of these interventions is anticipated to achieve greater adherence, thereby improving anticipated clinical outcomes without unnecessary risk.

Attitudes of health care providers can directly impact the ability of ethnic and racial minorities who seek or use health care services. Health care providers themselves may hold biases that can become barriers to care. However, the care provider who understands that beliefs about disease, health, and perceived causes of sickness stem, in part, from an individual's culture and to be effective, health care services should be responsive to and respectful of cultural and linguistic needs is on the path of cultural awareness. Thus, CC is aimed at helping care providers gain a greater understanding and awareness of how culture may influence their attitudes, behavior, and health care policies.

BE SAFE Core Elements

To help clinicians better understand how CC can improve quality of care and health outcomes while simultaneously eliminating health disparity, the BE SAFE (McNeil, 2005) Model of Cultural Competence is recommended. The mnemonic BE SAFE is a framework that uses culturally pluralistic content and perspectives based on the following six core elements, namely, (1) barriers to care, (2) ethics, (3) sensitivity of the provider, (4) assessment, (5) facts, and (6) encounters. The model addresses specific barriers related to cultural practices and the health care system. BE SAFE provides a deeper understanding of cultural competency as it relates to providing quality care and to assist individuals develop their understanding of intraethnic variations and the role that culture and values, beliefs, and customs of individuals play in health equity.

This concept discusses each of these six core elements in order to provide health care professionals with a culturally relevant framework that will assist them in providing quality health care services to ethnic and racial minorities such as African Americans. While initially developed to address HIV disparity among ethnic and racial minorities, the tenets of the BE SAFE module can be seamlessly adopted for use in addressing health disparity in a culturally competent manner. The model is intended to familiarize providers with a basic understanding of the African American patient and his or her cultural background and beliefs.

Barriers

Barriers to care is defined as real or perceived gaps to providing quality care that are compounded by the relationship that ED has to ethnicity. These barriers include access to care issues, stigmas surrounding health care services, support systems, bias in medical decision making, and African American mistrust of the medical community. For example, the mistrust that African Americans have for the medical community is reflected in the disparities because of generational trauma by the Tuskegee experiment (McCallum, Arekere, Lee Green, Katz, & Rivers, 2006). And although specific examples are often given for African American mistrust, there is evidence that it stems from centuries of medical mistreatment and abuse (Byrd & Clayton, 2003).

Regardless of the origin, barriers may impair outcomes by increasing patients' emotional anxiety and physical stress and may also serve to reduce the likelihood of seeking follow-up care. For the care provider, a lack of awareness of ED and of health-seeking behaviors, along with gaps to providing culturally appropriate quality care, when compounded by a lack of diversity in field of mental health, may all contribute to unnecessary health challenges for AA women.

Barriers:

- Prejudice/provider bias
- Socioeconomic status
- Ethnicity (racism in health care)
- Support systems deficit characterized by ignorance, poverty, crime, violence
- Gender bias
- Mistrust of the medical community (e.g., Tuskegee Experiment metaphor)
- Access-to-care issues
- Stigmas, lack of awareness about ED
- Clinician bias, lack of objectivity
- Stereotyping, racism, fat shaming
- Bias in medical decision making
- Education literacy and its association to recommended treatment adherence
- Lack of diversity in health care leadership and workforce
- Systems of care poorly designed for diverse patient populations
- Poor cross-cultural communication between providers and patients
- Mental illness—using food as a coping mechanism

Ethics

Ethics addresses the human condition as it applies to morality of beliefs, values, and behavior. Providers must give priority to professional duty, valuing of different cultures, and issues relevant to honesty, confidentiality, research, etc. The sources of ethics include reason, individual experiences, and societal experiences. Most of these experiences may include lived experiences that, when combined, constitute a person's culture. Thus, having ethics is a germane component of a cultural competency model.

It is the duty of health care professionals to not only do their best for their patients but also to do no harm. These are the principles on which beneficence and benevolence are built. This conduct can also be considered components of natural law—the ethical principle emphasizing the desire of all humans to do what is morally good. These principles support the valuing of different cultures.

Other important issues in the care of AA with ED include truth telling, confidentiality, research, dealing with health complications, and the responsibility of health care professionals. These issues often create dilemmas between the different ethical layers, including the ethics of the individual, institution, and society.

In summary, the importance of ethics in determining the morally good practice of a health care professional in acknowledging and learning about the patient's culture is a construct of the cultural competency model.

Ethics:

* Morality, values
* Belief systems—behaviors driven by individual experiences and social influences
* Professional ethics—do no harm and to do the best for the patient (principles of beneficence and benevolence)
* Truth telling; honoring patient's perspective and autonomy
* Principles support the valuing of different cultures
* Honesty
* Accountability for judgments and actions
* Encompasses more than physically caring for patients
* Includes public interest in the health care system as a whole and in its ability to provide appropriate services for all people
* Embraces promotion of health in basic life patterns
* Desire (moral obligation)
* Humanizing (value of providing care)

Sensitivity

Sensitivity of the provider addresses the need for providers to examine their own prejudices and biases toward other cultures and determine where they are along a continuum that ranges from unconscious to conscious competence. In cultural awareness, the provider becomes aware and is sensitive, responsive, and appreciative of the values, beliefs, customs, heritage, and problem-solving strategies of a patient's culture. The approach requires constant review of one's own prejudices and biases toward other cultures. It also demands an in-depth exploration of one's own cultural background. The importance of this construct is aimed at preventing the health care professional from engaging in the phenomenon of cultural imposition—the tendency to impose one's values on another culture (Campinha-Bacote, 1988).

Before one can begin to understand another's culture, it is important to identify one's biases and to determine where they lie. The provider should assess her/his biases along a continuum that ranges from unconscious to conscious competence. Unconscious incompetence (Leininger, 1988) is evidenced when a health care professional is not aware that cultural differences exist, whereas conscious incompetence is reflected where the health care professional does not understand another's culture but is aware of this lack of understanding and that differences do exist. Further along the continuum is the consciously competent health care professional who becomes knowledgeable about cultural differences but is still in the process of learning about another culture. Finally, the health care professional may become unconsciously or consciously competent when the knowledge of cultural differences is regularly and appropriately incorporated in one's behavior and interaction with a patient of a different culture.

Sensitivity:

• Examination of one's own biases and prejudices: race, ethnicity, obesity, sexual orientation, language, health issue, gender, etc.
• Exploration of one's cultures
• Creation of shared understandings and shared context
• Examining one's prejudices and biases toward other cultures
• Working to avoid engaging in the phenomena of cultural imposition
• Caring for difficult patients
• Sensitivity not just to others' personal cultural beliefs, practices, and values but also to their own belief systems.
• Cultural humility

Assessment

Assessment addresses the ability to collect relevant data regarding a patient's health history and presenting health challenges in the context of the patient's cultural background. Included is the understanding that patients have a right to have their specific cultural beliefs, values, and practices.

Assessment:

• Collection of relevant patient information
• Use of systemic appraisal approach
• Presentation of the patient in the context of the patient's own cultural background
• Use of culturally appropriate measurements and tools

Culturally Based Assessments and Treatment Plans

• Cultural assessment: Systematic evaluation or assessment of individuals, groups, and communities as to their cultural values, beliefs, and practices to determine explicit needs and intervention practices within the cultural context of the people being evaluated.
• Personal values and attitudes: Are you currently including those practices that promote mutual respect between you the MHP and patients (e.g., screening materials for offensive cultural, ethnic or racial stereotypes,

being aware and intervening, when appropriate, on behalf of patients when organizations conduct themselves in culturally insensitive manner)?
- Communication style: In order to communicate effectively, are you sensitive to using alternatives to written communications (particularly for patients with low literacy skills or for those with English as a second language)? How are your nonverbal cues?
- Learning environment: Are you currently establishing culturally and linguistically responsive interior design, posters, pictures and artwork, as well as magazines, pamphlets, videos, films, etc. that deliver culturally targeted messages and are literacy sensitive?
- Community participation: Are you currently aware of issues or concerns in the community of patients you serve, and are you working with appropriate community organizations to develop and implement programs?
- Policies and procedures: Are you including written policies, mission statement, goals, and objectives for cultural and language philosophies and practices?
- Patient-sensitive clinical practice: Are you developing a practice that acknowledges the importance of culture while avoiding the misuse of scientific information and stereotyping groups?
- Appraisal: spiritual, social, mental/emotional, physical, occupational, etc.

Data-Gathering Strategies

- Recognize that differences and similarities are present inside and outside cultures
- Sharpen listening skills
- Ask questions to clarify perceptions
- Utilize various culturally appropriate resources in care provision

Facts

To design an accurate ED treatment plan, the health care professional must individualize key characteristics to their patients. These include and are not limited to an understanding of physiology, behavior, and the patient's perception of his or her illness. An understanding from the perspective of the individual's culture, including acceptance of weight variations, world views, and culturally specific behavioral patterns, is all important.

Facts:

- Culturally specific behavioral patterns; biologic variations based on ethnicity, worldviews
- Variations in drug interactions and efficacy
- Influence of spirituality, discrimination and stigmas, support systems
- MHP must individualize these characteristics to their patients
- Values
- Beliefs

- Lifeways
- Practice/customs
- Physiological, anatomical, and pharmacological (biocultural ecology)
- All information/facts about the individual/culture (Purnell's 12 Domain-1998; Purnell, 2002)

Encounters

Achieving effective encounters with patients from ethnically and culturally diverse backgrounds is a core component of cultural competence in the clinical setting. Encounters are necessary face-to-face interactions that allow health care professionals to effectively engage in cross-cultural interactions with culturally diverse populations (Campinha-Bacote, 1998).

   Many encounters with specific ethnic groups are needed to effectively interact with those groups. Factors such as language, cultural norms, and concepts of personal space are important variables to consider when encountering African American patients. Encounters address the fact that MHPs have a duty to achieve effective sessions with all of their patients. When MHPs are unsure how to proceed, factors such as language, cultural norms, the role of spirituality, and concepts of personal space should be discussed during a patient's first visit. Encounters include the ability to obtain valuable information with the individual in her settings to yield culturally appropriate interventions and promote results-based programs.

Encounters:

- Cultural norms
- Concepts of personal space
- Eye contact
- Touch
- Effective interpersonal strategies
- Learning styles
- Language considerations and the appropriate use of interpreter and translation services

Characteristics of Culturally Competent Service Delivery

- Knowledgeable about cultural differences and their impact on attitudes and behaviors
- Sensitive, understanding, nonjudgmental, and respectful in dealing with people whose culture is different from our own
- Flexible and skillful in responding and adapting to different cultural contexts and circumstances
- Culturally appropriate service delivery incorporates an understanding of the needs of the target patient populations and designs services accordingly
- Culturally accessible service delivery, in essence, "opens the doors" to services for all patients

Culturally Competent Health Care System

- Respond to current and projected demographic changes
- Help eliminate long-standing health disparities
- Provide culturally competent patient health-related information/education
- Expand choices and access to high-quality clinicians by the public in general
- Achieve greater patient adherence to medical advice, thereby increasing patient compliance

Outcomes

- Improved quality of care
- Improved patient satisfaction
- Trust established
- Increased participation in programs
- Increased collaboration
- Increased cultural awareness and sensitivity
- Cultural appreciation developed

Conclusion

Culture is a way of life developed and shared by a group of people and passed down through generations. The US is diversifying, and the mental health field needs to do the same in an effort to meet the nation's needs. Until then, the process of closing the racial/ethnic gap in this field begins with understanding the experiences of those who are in it. CC, then, is key among the myriad strategies for improving quality of care to AA women with ED. We must demand that AA women be included in eating-disorder prevention and treatment programs. It is also imperative that we educate MHPs about the unique cultural factors associated with eating disorders among AA women so that they may be addressed head-on! This can be achieved by improving teaching and training of MPHs about the CC needs of AA women. In so doing, MPHs will be able to be better equipped to detect and manage eating disorders in their practices and ensure high standards of care for their patients. A diverse, culturally competent mental health workforce, as well as provider and patient education, are key factors to eliminating mental health care disparities for AA women with ED.

Cultural competence is the ability to work effectively across cultures in a way that acknowledges and respects the culture of the person or organization being served. The BE SAFE Model of Cultural Competence offers health care professionals caring for this population a practice model that enhances their level of cultural competency. This model asserts that health care professionals begin their journey toward becoming culturally competent by:

- Addressing overt and covert barriers to care
- Assessing their level of awareness and sensitivity toward AA women with ED

- Conducting a cultural assessment
- Obtaining knowledge about this cultural group
- Maintaining effective clinical encounters

Culturally appropriate service delivery incorporates an understanding of the needs of the target patient populations and designs services accordingly. Likewise, culturally accessible service delivery, in essence, "opens the doors" to services for all patients. We must remember that cultural competence is a journey—not a destination; a process—not an event; and a process of becoming competent, not being culturally competent.

- To care for someone, I must know who I am.
- To care for someone, I must know who the other is.
- To care for someone, I must be able to bridge the gap between myself and the other.

What is culturally competent care? Culturally competent care is about the creation of an environment in which the best health care practices can be safely and conscientiously implemented; it affirms all persons and shows contempt to no one for any reason; it supports and assists each person by incorporating behaviors and interactions from the medical personnel that serves to help restore the individual's well-being.

—Goulda A. Downer, 2012

References

American Psychiatric Association. (2013). *Diagnostic and statistical manual of mental disorders* (5th ed.). Washington DC: American Psychiatric Association.

Berrettini, W. (2004). The genetics of eating disorders. *Psychiatry* (Edgmont), *1*(3), 18–25. Retrieved from www.ncbi.nlm.nih.gov/pmc/articles/PMC3010958/.

Bulik, C. M., Sullivan, P. F., & Kendler, K. S. (1998). Heritability of binge-eating and broadly defined bulimia nervosa. *Biological Psychiatry, 44*, 1210–1218.

Byrd, W. M., & Clayton, L. A. (2003). Racial and ethnic disparities in healthcare: A background and history. In *Unequal treatment: Confronting racial and ethnic disparities in health care*. Retrieved from www.nap.edu/read/10260/chapter/20.

Campinha-Bacote, J. (1998). Cultural diversity in nursing education: Issues and concerns. *Journal of Nursing Education, 37*(1), 3–4. Retrieved from www.healio.com/nursing/journals/jne/1998-1-37-1/%7B0d099df78f2e-437e-8496 814795433b68%7D/cultural-diversity-in-nursing-education-issues-and-concerns.

Campinha-Bacote, J. et al. (2005). *Transforming the face of health professions through cultural and linguistic competence education: The role of the HRSA centers of excellence*. Washington, DC: U.S. Department of Health and Human Services, Health Resources and Services Administration. http://www.hrsa.gov/culturalcompetence/cultcompedu.pdf.

Culbert, K. M., Racine, S. E., & Klump, K. L. (2015). Research review: What we have learned about the causes of eating disorders—a synthesis of sociocultural, psychological, and biological research. *Journal of Child Psychology and Psychiatry, 56*(11), 1141–1164.

Hudson, J. I., Hiripi, E., Pope, H. G., & Kessler, R. C. (2007). The prevalence and correlates of eating disorders in the national comorbidity survey replication. *Biological Psychiatry, 61*(3), 348–358.

Leininger, M. M. (1988). Leininger's theory of nursing: Cultural care diversity and universality. *Nursing Science Quaterly, 1*(4), 152–160. Retrieved from https://journals.sagepub.com/doi/10.1177/089431848800100408.

McCallum, J. M., Arekere, D. M., Lee Green, B., Katz, R. V., & Rivers, B. M. (2006). Awareness and knowledge of the U.S. public health service syphilis study at Tuskegee: Implications for biomedical research. *Journal of Health Care for the Poor and Underserved, 17*(4), 716–733. Retrieved from www.ncbi.nlm.nih.gov/pmc/articles/PMC1828138/.

McNeil, J., ed. (2005). BE SAFE: *A cultural competency model for African Americans.* National Minority AIDS Education and Training Center. Washington, D.C.: Howard University Washington. Retrieved from https://targethiv.org/sites/default/files/file-upload/resources/BESAFE_AfrAmr.pdf.

Parekh, R. (2017). *What are eating disorders?* Retrieved from www.psychiatry.org/patients-families/eating-disorders/what-are-eating-disorders.

Purnell, L. (2002). *The Purnell Model for cultural competence.* Retrieved from www.researchgate.net/publication/11265758_The_Purnell_Model_for_Cultural.

Smink, F. R., Van Hoeken, D., & Hoek, H. W. (2012). Epidemiology of eating disorders: Incidence, prevalence and mortality rates. *Current Psychiatry Reports, 14*(4), 406–414.

Trace, S. E., Baker, J. H., Peñas-Lledó, E., & Bulik, C. M. (2013). The genetics of eating disorders. *Annual Review of Clinical Psychology, 9*, 589–620. Retrieved from www.annualreviews.org/doi/10.1146/annurev-clinpsy-050212-185546.

12 Only a Dog Wants a Bone! The Other End of the Eating Spectrum

Overweight and Obesity

Dawn McMillian

Introduction

A lot of attention has been paid to anorexia nervosa and bulimia, the most commonly known eating disorders, and how they affect African American women's physical and mental health. Anorexia nervosa is an eating disorder characterized by weight loss; difficulties maintaining an appropriate body weight for height, age, and stature; and, in many individuals, distorted body image. People with anorexia nervosa generally restrict the number of calories and the types of food that they eat (NEPA, 2019). Conversely, bulimia is an emotional disorder in which bouts of extreme overeating are followed by depression and self-induced vomiting, purging, or fasting (NEPA, 2019). While African American women can suffer from either of these conditions, they have traditionally been thought to have a much greater satisfaction with their bodies and therefore less tendency to engage in disordered eating or related practices and to be less likely to diet and to have an overall more positive body image (Sanderson, Lupinski, & Moch, 2013). Since most research focuses on anorexia nervosa and bulimia, not much attention is paid to overconsumption (in the form of compulsive overeating or emotional eating) in the African American female population. Compulsive overeating is described as frequent episodes of uncontrollable eating in which a person continues to eat food long after feeling full and even to the point of feeling sick. Compulsive overeaters may meet criteria for binge eating disorder (BED), which is a formal diagnosis. "Emotional eating" is another term that is frequently used to describe this phenomenon. It refers to instances when a person turns to food for comfort rather than hunger. In most instances of emotional eating, the person is under some form of stress. Emotional eating can also refer to instances when a person uses food as a reward, after a hard day at work, or when they feel lonely or depressed. Whatever the reason for emotional eating, it is important that the person realizes that eating and food are being used as an emotional coping strategy (Mirror Mirror, 2019). In actuality, African American women have been found to be equally or more likely than their White counterparts to binge eat (Striegel-Moore et al., 2002), and this affects African American women negatively in myriad ways.

Overconsumption of unhealthy food and its resulting effects of overweight and obesity increases the risk of various diseases such as diabetes, hyperlipidemia, and hypertension. A healthy diet is key to good nutrition and is necessary for a long and healthy life, on average. Eating nutrient-dense foods and balancing energy intake with the necessary physical activity to maintain a healthy weight is essential at all stages of life. Unbalanced consumption of foods high in calories (sugar, starch, or fat) and low in essential nutrients contributes to energy excess, overweight, and obesity. The amount of the energy consumed in relation to physical activity and the quality of food are key determinants of nutrition-related chronic disease (Armstrong, 2002). African American women are particularly affected by diseases related to insulin resistance and suffer from high rates of cardiovascular disease (CVD), high blood pressure, type 2 diabetes, stroke, and death from hypertension-related complications. African American women are three times more likely to die from complications related to hypertension than White women (40.0% versus 14.9%), three times more likely to die from type 2 diabetes, and 1.4 times more likely to die from CVD than White women (Ferdinand, 2008). In the majority population, the occurrence of these diseases is met with universal concern and dedication to eradication. However, too frequently, these same diseases in the African American community are met with apathy by the affected communities' membership: "*Girl, you know Black women just thick*"; resignation: "*I'm just built like Big Momma . . . I'm big boned*"; and, at worst, a "membership requirement" for being an African American person in America: "*Everyone in my family gets diabetes at some point.*" African Americans do themselves a disservice by just accepting large numbers of diagnoses of these conditions in their communities as inevitable when they can significantly decrease the occurrence rates and reverse the adverse health effects by changing their diets and eating behaviors. Coke-bottle curves can come with a health cost.

It is well established in the field of nutrition and dietetics that overconsumption of food, specifically high-calorie, low-nutrient foods, results in excessive weight gain. In the majority population, overweight and obesity carry a negative connotation, can often result in ridicule, and are not a body type sought after by most females. Many White women are pressured from an early age to maintain a thin, almost underweight appearance. Many White women have been on their first "diet" by elementary or middle school, usually at the urging of a family member or friend. Studies examining ethnic differences in attitudinal body image have found that White women are more negative in their attitudes toward their weight and overall appearance than are African American women. For instance, they tend to be more dissatisfied with their weight even when their weight is within normal range (Desmond, Price, Hallinan, & Smith, 1989; Lovejoy, 2001; Perez & Joiner, 2003). This resulting social pressure to be "thin" is commonly manifested in some individuals as anorexia, bulimia, and/or excessive exercising.

On the other hand, historically in the African American community, being overweight has not been looked upon as such a negative phenotype. If an African American child starts to lose weight, it is very likely to be noticed by the mother relatively quickly and met not with praise but with great concern, extra portions at mealtimes, and questions of "Are you feeling all right, baby?" Studies that have been conducted on African American females in middle school, high school, and college have suggested they might have a more positive body image than White women due to a broader and more flexible definition of beauty within their culture, which in turn is connected to a positive body image (Wood-Barcalow, Tylka, & Augustus-Horvath, 2010). A similar study done at a historically Black college/university (HBCU) found that African Americans had a more tolerant attitude about weight gain and body image, felt less social pressure about weight, and their desired body image was not related to health, it was related to "a look." Orenstein (2000) found that African American girls at a predominately African American school did not experience the pressures of being thin and did not feel that body image is a problem for them (Sanderson et al., 2013). African American women are constantly praised for their ample hips, thick thighs, and overfat figures. We've all heard the saying, "Only a dog wants a bone!" coming from both African American males and females alike as an expression of appreciation for a African American woman's sometimes overweight or overfat physique. This is a flattering confidence and self-esteem builder to many women, but it may be setting them up for health issues in the long run.

The more flexible conceptions of beauty and the atmosphere of mutual appreciation expressed within the African American community in regards to weight, the more pride African American women have in their self-image (Lovejoy, 2001; Shuttlesworth & Zotter, 2011). According to Kumanyika et al., approximately 40 percent of African American women who were moderately to severely overweight by medical standards considered their figures to be attractive or very attractive (Kumanyika, Wilson, & Guilford-Davenport, 1993), whereas their White counterparts would feel the opposite. Furthermore, other studies have found that African American women tend to have higher levels of satisfaction with their overall weight and body size compared with White, Latino, Asian, and Native American women. This holds true even though African American women tend to be heavier, on average, than women in any of these other ethnic groups (Akan & Grilo, 1995; Story, French, Resnick, & Blum, 1995; Lovejoy, 2001).

On the flip side, African American women having a positive attitude toward regular aerobic exercise and healthy eating can sometimes be seen as an attempt to emulate "White" people and a rejection of the traditional African American female shape, putting African American women in the crosshairs for ridicule and harassment by their own community members. How many times have you heard African American folks scoff when the suggestion of "working out" is brought up? Many African American women ascribe that activity to White women and exclaim, "I don't want to lose any weight in the *wrong places*!" There is also a sector of African American females to whom haircare contributes to this aversion to exercise. Many African American women spend a significant amount of money on their haircare, whether it be relaxers, weaves, or wigs. These styles are not as easily maintained when coupled with frequent perspiration. Therefore, many African American women choose to keep their carefully coiffed hairstyles intact rather than exercising their bodies, which can lead to them being beautiful to look at on the outside but wreaking havoc on their internal health.

Similar to other cultures, African American women take into consideration what the males in their community deem "attractive" when judging their own external look, and the influence of male partners is strong. For example, while African American adolescent girls identify style and attitude as key markers of beauty, they are simultaneously "aware that African American boys had more specific physical criteria for an 'ideal girl' than they had themselves" (Parker et al., 1995, p. 108). Thus, it seems that the physical traits that African American women embody and claim to prefer are often a reflection of African American men's desires. This can be seen most clearly in the over exaggerated curves worn by "celebrities" (Cardi B, Kim Kardashian, and Nicki Minaj, just to name a few) that are emulated in droves by African American women after they are openly admired en masse by African American men.

Food preparation is almost a religious experience in the African American community, and this task is almost exclusively handled by African American females. Common hallmarks of the African American diet are processed foods, saturated fat, added sugars, and added sodium, all of which are also positively correlated with overweight and obesity. A common barrier to health that African American women struggle with is the adjustment of food selection, preparation, and portion control to improve health. There are recipes that cross generations, like Granny's fried fish or Madea's pound cake, that people are loath to adapt into a healthier version, because the taste (and nostalgia) will forever be lost. Remember, food is also a way to feel pleasure in the African American community. When families gather around the table in the evenings after school and work, they can "escape" from a difficult day into a bountiful dinner comprised of large portions of meats and processed grains, which are frequently prepared in an unhealthy way. If vegetables are served, they have usually been cooked to the point of losing most of their nutritional value and have been seasoned with high-sodium spices and/or large amounts of butter, which is the hallmark of a high-fat diet. Many African American females, as stated earlier, suffer from emotional eating, so if they've had a bad day, what better way to cap it off than a hearty meal when they get home? Food is the elixir that cures all . . . sadness, depression, anger, and frustration.

Cultural traditions also play a role in how African American women view food and weight. In the African American community, food always takes center stage at weddings, funerals, birthdays, holidays, reunions, etc. It is seen as a way to express—and, importantly, to *receive*—love. A mother shows her love for her children by feeding them filling food and demonstrates that she's maintaining a happy, *secure* household by having rotund, well-fed children. Some believe this behavior comes from slavery, when being able to feed your family well was not guaranteed and food was a rare pleasure for folks who led a frequently joyless existence. In many African American households, if an individual is losing weight (or has a low body weight), it is synonymous with illness, drug addiction, and a host of other undesirable conditions like HIV or AIDS. These things are stigmas in the African American community, while the well-fed, overweight individual is associated with prosperity and health.

Conversely, another prevalent issue in the younger African American female generation is the complete lack of cooking knowledge itself, which results in increased consumption of processed, ready-to-eat foods, another contributor to poor health in the African American community. Some studies show that the lack of access to full-service supermarkets in their communities that offer a variety of healthy food options at affordable prices (Morland, Diez Roux, & Wing, 2006; Sutherland, 2013), combined with the numerous convenience and corner stores as well as fast-food restaurants that offer foods high in calories, sugar, starches, sodium, and fat at relatively low cost, are the main culprits in this equation. Similar to the rest of the US population, African American females shop where they live. If a person doesn't have ready access to healthy foods, they usually end up purchasing unhealthy foods, which results in an unhealthy diet. An unhealthy diet leads to an unhealthy individual.

An additional barrier is that many young and middle-aged African American females think, incorrectly, that it is "too expensive to eat healthy" and strategically placed marketing bolsters that impression. How many commercials and memes have you seen that compare a $5 fresh fruit cup with a dollar-menu serving of French fries? When you are balancing a tight budget for a family of four, how easy is it to persuade you that the dollar menu is your best bet? While there are definitely price inequities when shopping for prepared foods that definitely contribute to an unhealthy food environment, African American women must also educate themselves on food preparation and make healthier choices when shopping when healthy resources are available to them. Planning ahead is key. Making grocery lists, researching healthy recipes on the internet or in cookbooks, and keeping your pantry stocked with the staples of a healthy diet along with a variety of healthy snacks can help African American women improve their nutrition environment. If you are surrounded by healthy food, you will eat healthy food.

Another unhealthy relationship that African American women can have with food is illustrated by emotional or stress-related eating. African American women seeking mental health assistance is heavily stigmatized in our community. Due to this, instead of reaching out for behavior and mental health counseling, many African American women self-medicate in a variety of ways . . . one of which is compulsive overeating or emotional eating. African American women's eating problems have also been conceptualized as a means of coping with the emotional pain of a variety of oppressions, including sexism, racism, poverty, and sexual abuse (Avery, 1990; Bray, 1992; Lovejoy, 2001). Many African American women find it hard to admit they are overworked, overwhelmed, underloved, and depressed. So instead of complaining or asking for help, many African American women try to *keep on keepin' on* while they medicate their pain in self-destructive ways: overeating, smoking, drinking, or using drugs (Mitchell & Herring, 1998, p. 67). Because overweight African American women are not as stigmatized by the larger society or by their own culture as are White women (Hebl & Heatherton, 1998), an African American woman's "survival strategy" of overeating would remain invisible to many around her (Beauboeuf-Lafontant, 2003). Food has long been used as a tonic for pain in our community, so in times of stress or trouble, many African American women turn to the one thing that has let them experience physical pleasure for most of their lives: food. Ironically enough, the pendulum has swung too far in one direction, resulting in the cultural normalization of obesity and the erroneous belief that the development of the associated illnesses is as inevitable as the Black, beautiful skin we are in and not able to be prevented or reversed by changing our eating and exercise behaviors.

Most African American women closely identify with the image of the *strong Black woman*— the African American woman who struggles to "make a way outta no way," who single-handedly raises her children, works multiple jobs, and supports an extended family. As Angela Mitchell and Kennise Herring (1998) wrote, "If there's one prevailing image we have of ourselves, it's that we can survive anything. We get that image from our mothers, who frequently shield us from the truth of their feelings." Weight management is not deemed very important to many African American women because they have too many other things to worry about. Many of them are managing homes as single parents, trying to raise children as single parents, and trying to make financial ends meet. Survival is what their concern is, not being a healthy size or weight (Beauboeuf-Lafontant, 2003). When African American females are able to embrace their unique, God-given body shapes in combination with a healthy diet and regular exercise, they will be well on their way to eradicating many of the nutrition-related diseases plaguing their community, spurred by their own disordered eating behaviors.

References

Akan, G. E., & Grilo, C. M. (1995). Sociocultural influences on eating attitudes and behaviors, body image, and psychological functioning: A comparison of African-American, Asian-American, and Caucasian college women. *International Journal of Eating Disorders, 18*, 181–187.

Armstrong, T. (2002, February). *Diet, nutrition and the prevention of chronic diseases.* Retrieved from www.who.int/dietphysicalactivity/publications/trs916/summary/en/.

Avery, B. Y. (1990). Breathing life into ourselves: The evolution of the national Black women's health project. In E. White (Ed.), *The Black woman's health book.* Seattle, WA: Seal.

Beauboeuf-Lafontant, T. (2003). Strong and large Black women? exploring relationships between deviant womanhood and weight. *Gender and Society, 17*(1), 111–121.

"Binge Eating Disorder." National Eating Disorders Association (NEPA). Retrieved October 19, 2019 from www.nationaleatingdisorders.org/learn/by-eating-disorder/bed.

Bray, R. (1992, January). Heavy burden. *Essence*, 52–56.

Desmond, S. M., Price, J. H., Hallinan, C., & Smith, D. (1989). Black and White adolescents' perceptions of their weight. *Journal of School Health, 59*, 353–358.

Ferdinand, K. C. (2008). Obesity and the metabolic syndrome in African American women. *Journal of the CardioMetabolic Syndrome, 3*, 126–128.

Hebl, M., & Heatherton, T. (1998). The stigma of obesity in women: The difference is black and white. *Personality and Social Psychology Bulletin, 24*, 417–426.

Kumanyika, S., Wilson, J. F., & Guilford-Davenport, M. (1993). Weight-related attitudes and behaviors of Black women. *Journal of the American Dietetic Association, 93*, 416–422.

Lovejoy, M. (2001). Disturbances in the social body: Differences in body image and eating problems among African American and White women. *Gender & Society, 15*, 231–261.

Mirror Mirror Eating Disorder Help. (2019). *Compulsive eating*. Retrieved October 19, 2019 from www.mirror-mirror.org/compulsive.htm.

Mitchell, A., & Herring, K. (1998). *What the blues is all about: Black women overcoming stress and depression*. New York: Perige.

Morland, K., Diez Roux, A. V., & Wing, S. (2006). Supermarkets, other food stores, and obesity: The atherosclerosis risk in communities study. *American Journal of Preventive Medicine, 30*, 333–339.

National Eating Disorders Association. (2019). *Anorexia nervosa*. Retrieved October 19, 2019 from www.nationaleatingdisorders.org/learn/by-eating-disorder/anorexia.

Orenstein, P. (2000). *Schoolgirls: Young women, self-esteem, and the confidence gap*. New York: Anchor Books.

Parker, S., Nichter, M., Nichter, M., Vuckovic, N., Sims, C., & Ritenbaugh, C. (1995). Body image and weight concerns among African American and white adolescent females: Differences that make a difference. *Human Organization, 54*, 103–114.

Perez, M., & Joiner, T. (2003). Body image dissatisfaction and disordered eating in Black and White women. *International Journal of Eating Disorders, 33*, 342–350.

Sanderson, S., Lupinski, K., & Moch, P. (2013). Is big really beautiful? Understanding body image perceptions of African American females. *Journal of Black Studies, 44*(5), 496–507.

Shuttlesworth, M., & Zotter, D. (2011). Disordered eating in African American and Caucasian women: The role of ethnic ID. *Journal of Black Studies, 42*(6), 906–922.

Story, M., French, S. A., Resnick, M. D., & Blum, R. W. (1995). Ethnic/racial and socioeconomic differences in dieting behaviors and body image perceptions in adolescents. *International Journal of the Eating Disorders, 18*, 173–179.

Striegel-Moore, R. H., Dohm, F., Kraemer, H. C., Taylor, B., Daniels, S., Crawford, P., & Schrieber, G. H. (2002). Eating disorders in Black and White women. *American Journal of Psychiatry, 160*(7), 13.

Sutherland, M. (2013). Overweight and obesity among African American women: An examination of predictive and risk factors and weight-reduction recommendations. *Journal of Black Studies, 44*(8), 846–869.

Wood-Barcalow, N., Tylka, T. L., & Augustus-Horvath, C. L. (2010). "But I like my body": Positive body image characteristics and a holistic model for young-adult women. *Body Image, 7*, 106–116.

Part IV

Treatment Approaches and Philosophies

13 Black Women's Presence in Eating Disorder Treatment Facilities

Kena Watson

Introduction

Limited data exists on Black women's use of eating disorder treatment facilities. The most common eating disorder treated in a hospital setting is anorexia nervosa due to the need to address malnourishment and monitor vital signs. Research shows that anorexia nervosa is less likely to be diagnosed in Black women (Taylor, Caldwell, Baser, Faison, & Jackson, 2007). Research also shows that more Black women are diagnosed with binge eating disorder than with any other eating disorder; hence, more Black women enter residential treatment facilities than hospitals due to their high diagnoses of binge eating disorder. Though more Black women are treated in residential treatment facilities, several factors may hinder their access to treatment and recovery in those facilities.

Eating disorder professionals should be mindful of the internal and external barriers that may lead to underdiagnosis of eating disorders, thus limiting access to treatment for Black women. When Black women enter eating disorder treatment centers, it is imperative for eating disorder treatment professionals to provide a safe space for which Black women are able to remove the "masks" they wear daily. Eating disorder professionals should also be inclusive of tailoring interventions including but not limited to differences in body image concerns and social support appropriately. And lastly, eating disorder professionals should actively work to advocate for a non–color-blind perspective of the body positivity movement with regard to treating Black women with eating disorders.

Barriers to Accessing Eating Disorders Treatment Facilities

A factor that hinders Black women from receiving treatment in facilities is the persona they create. Research shows that between 8% to 35% of Black women struggle with binge eating yet they experience barriers related to accessing treatment facilities (Walker-Barnes, 2014). Many people including Black women engage in binge eating to self-regulate and self soothe. Self-regulating and self-soothing are typical responses to coping with stressors such as trauma. Black women who binge eat have experienced high levels of trauma, are depressed, engage in excessive caregiving, and repress their emotions. These factors are in line with upholding the "strong Black woman" (SBW) persona (Walker-Barnes, 2014). If a Black woman strongly identifies with this persona, her identification can serve as a barrier to receiving a diagnosis or any type of psychological treatment, because the treatment encroaches on her expectation that as a strong Black woman, she is supposed to be flawless. For Black women who may be struggling with SBW persona, difficulties with asking for and receiving help, limited expression of negative emotions and excessive caretaking are often under the guise of independence and strength (West, Donovan, & Daniel, 2016). The strong Black woman persona, cultural myths about who is impacted by eating disorders, and a lack of diversity result in Black women's underdiagnoses and lack of treatment (Harrington, Crowther, & Shipherd, 2010).

Even when Black women are appropriately diagnosed for an eating disorder and the necessity for treatment arises, several other barriers arise. One of these barriers is a lack of ethnic representation in Internet searches for treatment programs. Historically, a White woman is the most common image that populates images after an Internet search for treatment programs and centers, which can be alienating towards people of color. There also tends to be a lack of diversity among eating disorder professionals employed by treatment centers. Additionally, upon entering a treatment program, it is also typical for Black women to be one of few other patients if not the only patient who identifies as non-White. This absence of racial diversity among patients and staff forces many Black women to feel alienated and reluctant to enter treatment programs.

Another factor that determines whether she enters a facility includes her ability to pay for treatment. The average cost at a treatment facility typically is hundreds of dollars a day, even with insurance. When Black women consider these factors, sometimes they struggle to enter into a program in which they might feel as though the staff or their peers cannot relate to their lived experiences and how those experiences impact their recovery. Finally, most Black women's financial status might prevent them from making the type of investment that other women can afford to make to treat their eating disorders.

Eating Disorder Treatment Centers

According to research, about 43.6% of people with binge eating disorder will receive eating disorder treatment in their life (Westerberg & Waitz, 2013). People are referred to eating disorder treatment facilities in several ways. They are often referred by their outpatient therapists, dietitians, or medical physicians. They are also referred to treatment facilities by concerned family members or support persons.

After they are referred to a treatment facility, their care varies. At the inpatient level of care, or hospitalization, treatment is geared towards those who are medically unstable. For patients that present with anorexia nervosa, refeeding may be necessary to reverse the effects of malnutrition and regulate vital signs

(Garber et al., 2015). Severe levels of malnutrition are best suited for treatment at the inpatient level of care due to weight restoration needing to occur prior to beginning residential treatment.

Further, the residential level of care for eating disorder treatment is the traditional step-down process after hospitalization. In a residential facility, patients receive 24-hour care, and they receive a level of containment for eating disorder behaviors. However, intensive medical intervention is not a necessity (Bisbing, n.d). Residential treatment typically consists of meal support and supervision; individual, family, and group therapy; nutritional counseling; and culinary support with an average length of stay between six and eight weeks depending on the severity and chronicity of the eating disorder (Bisbing, n.d).

In contrast, outpatient treatment for eating disorders is more often diversity than inpatient treatment services. This level of care includes partial hospitalization and intensive outpatient programs. Because these programs do not require overnight stay, they work well for people who are able to meet their nutritional needs because they have more insight and motivation for decreasing their eating disorder behaviors and thus require little external motivation. Similarly, the duration of outpatient services is reduced. For instance, partial hospitalization programs range between five and seven days a week, about six to eight hours per day for roughly four to six weeks. Intensive outpatient programs range between three and five days a week, about three to four hours per day for roughly four to six weeks (Bisbing, n.d).

Clinical Considerations for Eating Disorder Treatment Professionals

Building rapport is key to a successful therapeutic relationship among clinicians and their patients. At the outset of fostering this relationship, it is imperative for clinicians to be mindful of incorporating culturally sensitive information into their initial assessment, such as questions pertaining to internalized cultural beauty ideals and what social support looks like in their clients' lives. For example, because Western culture is the dominant view on body image ideals, it is helpful to discuss clients' views on beauty ideals. For example, clinicians should determine whether Black women idealize the curvaceous body ideal or the thin body ideal or any possible dissatisfaction with hair type (kinky hair vs. straight hair) or skin color (light skin vs. dark skin) (Overstreet, Quinn, & Agocha, 2010). Not only do these details provide a clear picture of subtle differences in body image dissatisfaction in Black women, but they also help tailor interventions towards helping to define what self-acceptance can look like.

Asking about their experiences growing up in regard to the demographics of who they deem as social support or typical friend group can shed light into the comfort ability of reaching out to peers in treatment. One of the unspoken but valuable experiences gained in treatment centers is having access to peers who are experiencing similar issues. Depending on the makeup of a

Black woman's typical friend group, forging these types of friendships with mostly White peers in these centers may have challenges. A couple of particular challenges that many Black women face as being one of few or the only person of color include the social confines that come with being tokenized—feeling as though one must speak for the entire race—or having to constantly check in with herself about not being portrayed as the "angry Black woman" stereotype—hesitance with speaking truths for fear of being labeled angry—which is altogether draining (Robinson, 2016). Typically, home is a place where a Black woman is able to remove the masks she has to wear in the world that guard her from being attached to these sorts of labels. However, in a residential treatment center, this may not be possible, as oftentimes, patients share rooms with other patients. Not having the personal space to "take the masks off" can take a toll on one's emotional health. Checking in with the client around their feelings about this and how they feel the fit is going may help to serve as a safe space for processing this as well as relating it to how they typically function in interpersonal relationships.

Social support is an important factor in eating disorder recovery. It is important to be inclusive of the different types of support systems that may extend beyond traditional familial ties. Family therapy plays a significant role in treatment by fostering the relationships that will be beneficial to patients' continued recovery. Depending on the patient's age, family therapy may consist of partners, parents, friends, or children of the patient, extended family, and/or community members. Typically, in the Black community, there is lack of knowledge about eating disorders, and often family members play into cultural myths such as Black people not being affected by eating disorders or that only non-White people develop eating disorders. Family therapy is a useful tool in providing educational resources to dispel myths about eating disorders and ways to be supportive to their loved one in eating disorder treatment. Challenging cultural myths in family therapy may help to end the silence that many Black women with eating disorders face in their families and communities. Another widely held cultural myth in the Black community is that prayer is often viewed as the sole means for persevering through life's challenges. In the Black community, the Black church is an important social support system (Collins, 2006). With this in mind, clinicians should be open to including spiritual confidants in family therapy, particularly since they can be supportive of the patients' recovery process. Religion has been found to be a source for coping skills and providing hope and meaning through challenging times (Akrawi, Bartrop, Potter, & Touyz, 2015). Bridging the gap between spirituality and treatment can serve as a reinforcer that prayer and therapy can coexist with regard to the treatment of eating disorders.

In keeping with the fact that Black women are not monoliths and vary in levels of desire to meet with other professionals that are of the same race, it is important to ask their preference. For some, it may be comforting, and for others, it may feel further alienating if they are highly assimilated into Western culture or do not want to draw more attention to themselves as being one of few people of color. As with any client, it is imperative to assess for their needs, and in this case, being sure not to take a color-blind approach is necessary in terms of ensuring the best clinical fit for a woman of color in a treatment facility for eating disorders.

As a means of taking a non–color-blind approach to therapy, it is imperative for eating disorder professionals to actively challenge weight stigma by acknowledging that demographic differences and "White and thin privilege" may be at the root of this issue. Binge eating disorder is commonly associated with obesity: when compared with White Americans, African American women are at a 50% increased risk of obesity (Assari, 2018). Perceived discrimination, an environmental stressor, has been found to be link to binge eating disorder as a coping mechanism (Assari, 2018). Within the last decade, there has been a shift in perspective with regard to what it means to be "healthy" and how this relates to eating disorder treatment. This shift, otherwise known as the "health at every size" (HAES^{SM}) movement is one that is well regarded and grounded in body positivity. This framework normalizes the concept that all bodies—no matter the size—can and should be viewed as "healthy" and that the number on the scale is not the sole indicator for health. Prior to this shift, most of society has upheld the idea that in order to be "healthy," one must be under a BMI of 25. While the overall sentiment of the HAES approach is admirable, therein lies room for evaluation of how this perspective is clinically beneficial for people of color, specifically Black women. Little research exists that speaks to the White and thin privilege in the HAES community. One of the original tenets of the HAES approach outlines that it seeks to "provide that *all* youth and adults have opportunities to learn the importance of eating nutrient rich foods and engaging in enjoyable physical activity from a weight-neutral perspective" (Association for Size Diversity and Health, 2009, p. 2). This does not take into account the reality of food deserts and environments that facilitate foods that are "energy-dense, nutrient-poor foods that are widely available in large portion sizes and at low cost compared to healthier foods" (Penney & Kirk, 2015, p. 40).

For many eating disorder treatment providers, the HAES perspective has become more than just a movement and more of an integral part of the recovery process. Since 2013, the Association for Size Diversity and Health has revised the original principles of the HAES approach to be more inclusive of cultural implications. While the HAES perspective has fared extremely well as an alternative toward traditional means of weight management and promoting size diversity, it is imperative to continue to monitor its effectiveness for people of all races and socioeconomic statuses.

Conclusion

There is a lack of research regarding Black women's utilization of hospital services as a means for eating disorder treatment. This may be due to the lower rates of anorexia nervosa diagnosis in Black women, which is the most common diagnosis seen at the hospitalization level of care. With binge eating disorder being a more common eating disorder diagnosis for Black women, lower levels of care (partial hospitalization and intensive outpatient treatment) tend to be the treatment levels that more Black women patients are admitted to. Barriers to treatment often consist of underdiagnosis, financial constraints, and lack of diversity in treatment centers. It is imperative for eating disorder professionals to provide a space to discuss differences in beauty ideals and how they might impact a Black woman's eating disorder recovery. It is also important for eating disorder professionals to explore Black women's racial assimilation experience with living away from home as it relates to feeling the need to wear a "mask" around other patients while in treatment. Being inclusive of the dynamics of the various support systems of Black women in treatment is imperative. And last, advocating for non–color-blind approaches to the body positivity movement will be important for the continued treatment of Black women with eating disorders.

References

Akrawi, D., Bartrop, R., Potter, U., & Touyz, S. (2015). Religiosity, spirituality in relation to disordered eating and body image concerns: A systematic review. *Journal of Eating Disorders*, *3*(1). https://doi.org/10.1186/s40337-015-0064-0.

Assari, S. (2018). Perceived discrimination and binge eating disorder; Gender difference in African Americans. *Journal of Clinical Medicine*, *7*(5), 89. https://doi.org/10.3390/jcm7050089.

Association for Size Diversity and Health. (2009). *Health at every size factsheet.* Retrieved from https://www.sizediversityandhealth.org/images/uploaded/HAES%20FACT%20SHEET%20R%2010.20.pdf.

Bisbing, Z. (n.d.). *Levels of care in eating disorder treatment.* Retrieved from https://www.nationaleatingdisorders.org/sites/default/files/NEDA%20Webinar%20Levels%20of%20Treatment.pdf.

Collins, C. F. (2006). *African American women's health and social issues.* Westport, CT: Greenwood Publishing, Inc.

Garber, A. K., Sawyer, S. M., Golden, N. H., Guarda, A. S., Katzman, D. K., Kohn, M. R., . . . Redgrave, G. W. (2015). A systematic review of approaches to refeeding in patients with anorexia nervosa. *International Journal of Eating Disorders*, *49*(3), 293–310. https://doi.org/10.1002/eat.22482.

Harrington, E. F., Crowther, J. H., & Shipherd, J. C. (2010). Trauma, binge eating, and the "strong black woman." *Journal of Consulting and Clinical Psychology*, *78*(4), 469–479.

Overstreet, N. M., Quinn, D. M., & Agocha, V. B. (2010). Beyond thinness: The influence of a curvaceous body ideal on body dissatisfaction in black and white women. *Sex Roles*, *63*, 91–10.

Penney, T. L., & Kirk, S. F. L. (2015). The health at every size paradigm and obesity: Missing empirical evidence may help push the reframing obesity debate forward. *American Journal of Public Health*, *105*(5). https://doi.org/10.2105/ajph.2015.302552.

Robinson, P. (2016). *You can't touch my hair: And other things I still have to explain.* New York: Penguin Random House LLC.

Taylor, J. Y., Caldwell, C. H., Baser, R. E., Faison, N., & Jackson, J. S. (2007). Prevalence of eating disorders among Blacks in the National Survey of American Life. *International Journal of Eating Disorders, 40*(Suppl.), S10–S14.

Walker-Barnes, C. (2014). *Too heavy a yoke: black women and the burden of strength.* Eugene, OR: Cascade Books.

West, L. M., Donovan, R. A., & Daniel, A. R. (2016). The price of strength: Black college women's perspectives on the strong black woman stereotype. *Women & Therapy, 39*(3–4), 390–412. https://doi.org/10.1080/02703149.2016.1116871.

Westerberg, D. P., & Waitz, M. (2013). Binge-eating disorder. *Osteopathic Family Physician, 5*(6), 230–233.

14 The Weight of Shame

Black Women and Binge Eating Disorder

Paula Edwards-Gayfield

Growing up in a family of all Black girls, my sisters and I frequently received messages from our parents about the importance of being self-sufficient. These conversations often focused on building self-esteem and self-acceptance, but they also focused on the importance of being a strong Black woman. However, topics related to mental health—such as depression, anxiety, or eating disorders—were rarely discussed in my family and in the Black community in general. If Black girls or women struggled with a mental illness, few people would have known about their illness, or they would have suffered in silence, believing that they were creating shame in their family. The belief at that time was that eating disorders primarily took the form of anorexia nervosa (AN), and AN was a disease of White adolescent girls of high socio-economic status. The prevailing belief also informed us that these White adolescents often sought attention and desired to become the thinnest or to not gain weight. Binge eating disorder (BED) was not a focus; if you ate too much, you must be out of control, and if you gained too much weight, then you should diet. Eating disorders did not exist! That was more than 30 years ago, and unfortunately, in many Black families, that message continues to be prevalent: eating disorders do not occur in the Black community. Today, eating disorders still are taboo topics in many Black homes and in the offices of many physicians' who serve the Black community. This behavior persists even though current research suggests that Black women suffer from eating disorders at rates that are comparable to White women (National Eating Disorders Association, 2016). Black girls and Black women are not immune from eating disorders.

In my role with the Renfrew Center, I regularly go to college campuses around the country to discuss eating disorders, and I have always been warmly welcomed. Yet during a recent outreach attempt to collaborate with a historically Black college and university about eating disorders on their campus, I was told that eating disorders were not a problem. The belief that eating disorders do not affect Black women continues. While global efforts to provide education and awareness about eating disorders are improving, culturally sensitive outreach and prevention is minimal in Black communities.

Binge eating disorder (BED) is defined as engaging in recurrent binge eating episodes characterized by the consumption of large amounts of food in a discrete period, accompanied by a sense of lack of control in the absence of compensatory behaviors. Although BED is one of the most prevalent eating disorders, the power and financial resources of the advertising, diet, and fashion industries have targeted weight loss as a "cure" for obesity and have targeted obesity as a "crime." Focusing solely on obesity has resulted in missed opportunities for Black families and physicians (whether they are White or Black) to understand BED and to help individuals find resources to treat underlying emotional issues obscured by their fixation on the scale. Although many Black women have discussed their weight or health-related concerns with their primary care physicians, their conversations often result in recommendations for changes in their diets.

Medical professionals perpetuate disparities in the treatment of eating disorders between Black and White women when they ignore factors that cause weight gain in Black women. The White and Grilo Study (2005) revealed that both Black and White women were equally likely to report receiving treatment for a weight problem, but significantly fewer Black women with BED received treatment for an eating disorder. However, BED is common among Black women (Striegel-Moore, Wilfley, Pike, Dohm, & Fairburn, 2000). Because they have felt ashamed of their inability to control their cravings, many of my clients shared that they engaged in some form of binge eating for several years before seeking counseling services. What led these women to treatment for an eating disorder? Grilo, Lozano, and Masheb (2005) suggest that for Black women, it is not the frequency of the binge eating itself but, rather, it is their distress about their eating behaviors as well as their bodies that influences their decision to seek treatment.

Clinicians working with Black women with BED are encouraged to increase their own awareness and understanding of the risk factors that predict binge eating and understand the psychiatric comorbidity and emotional distress associated with BED. For instance, Black women endure multiple oppressions: racism, sexism, classism, ageism, heterosexism, and others. They also endure the demands and mixed messages of being a Black woman, and their experiences are typically in the form of microaggressions. These daily assaults—whether verbal or nonverbal, intentional or unintentional—can have a devastating impact on Black women and are experienced as a clear form of oppression. Most girls are taught that we should be seen and not heard, that we should not take up space. Roxane Gay reminds us of the message that Black women have received: "We should be slender and small. We should be pleasing to men, acceptable to society and we are to disappear" (Gay, 2017).

When working with clients, I remind them that they are the experts about themselves, thus opening the door for them to bring up difficult issues or ask some difficult questions. A client that I referred to residential treatment hesitantly inquired about asking the question, "What am I going to do about my hair? Will I be able to get it done while I'm there?" Getting your "hair done" is vital for many Black women. Although the role and meaning of one's hair is evolving, hair can provide comfort and confidence—it can be affirming and life altering; it can provide a sense of control. It is noteworthy that the importance and impact of hair on a client's identity should not be minimized or overlooked.

Clients need to be assured that their providers are sensitive to diversity. One of my former clients who was diagnosed with BED wanted to feel that it was acceptable for her to talk about herself, including her race, age, and size. She was not a "skinny, White adolescent," which she had believed represented eating disorders. This may be a familiar topic among all clients, but the intersectionality of race, gender, and oppression may further reinforce the stereotypes and shaming experiences that Black women encounter. And one more important question that Black clients have is, "Does anyone look like me?"

Stereotypes occur and are maintained when time is not taken to understand the individual and what makes her who she is. Clients' identities are so much more than their diagnoses, weight, race, or religion. Their identities are certainly much more than whether or not they have straight or curly hair. When we allow ourselves to have preconceived beliefs, we are eliminating the opportunity to learn about our clients, and hence we create a barrier to the honest communication that gets to the core of what the client needs. Black women have to navigate microaggressions, managing or adjusting themselves to address the images (Mammy, Jezebel, or Angry Black Woman) defined by others, or they must learn to create lives that are suitable for themselves.

In a book review of Melissa Harris-Perry's *Sister Citizen: Shame, Stereotypes, and Black Women in America; For Colored Girls Who've Considered Politics When Being Strong Isn't Enough*, Tejada (2013) outlined the myths that have constructed Black women's identity and how Black women may be misperceived by others. The mammy myth depicts Black women as asexual, docile, and caring for Whites while being estranged from Blacks. The myth of the Jezebel constructs Black women as hypersexual. The Sapphire myth is employed to suggest that Black women are angry and cannot advocate on their own behalf. The strong Black woman myth helps the nation to relieve itself from addressing the persistent gender and racial inequalities endured by Black women.

Consider the Black client who is experiencing internalized racism or the trauma of racism walking into your office. Her distress of being a Black girl or woman may have had damaging effects and may underlie the symptoms and behaviors she is presenting. Treatment and prevention of psychosocial distress among Black women requires practitioners to use strategies that are culturally congruent and provide services that are empowerment focused (Jones & Guy-Sheftall, 2015). Cultural congruence is a process that transpires between the provider and the client as they develop an appropriate fit in their provider–client relationship. It involves the provider accepting diversity and being culturally aware, sensitive, and competent. Patients bring their own values, perceptions, and expectations into treatment, so they influence the creation or destruction of congruence. Consequently, the congruence process is constantly developing and evolving during therapy.

Current research (Binford, Mussell, Peterson, Crow, & Mitchell, 2004; Gilbert, 1998, 2002; Masheb & Grilo, 2006) recognizes that attempts to lessen uncomfortable or perceived negative emotions are associated with binge eating episodes. One of those emotions is shame. Shame has long been a topic of discussion among many Black clients who present for treatment of BED. Black women experience internalized racism daily. How an individual is treated and the messages she receives about herself contribute to shame. Clients have shared with me some of their numerous struggles of being a Black girl or woman at school, work, home, church, or in their communities. Frequently, the question raised is her concern if she is enough for a Black man.

The National Institute for the Clinical Application of Behavioral Medicine (2017) defines shame as "an intensely painful feeling of being fundamentally flawed." Shame is a different emotion from guilt: guilt focuses on one's behavior; shame is directed against the self. Shame is a painful self-conscious emotion that results from an individual's self-evaluations that they are defective, inferior, inadequate, and unattractive because of the shaming personal characteristics or behaviors (Gilbert, 1998, 2002). These self-evaluations are repeated, reinforced, and internalized and subsequently become the automatic appraisals that Black people have about themselves. Targeting the self is one of the worst things an individual can do, as it undermines the effect of anything good that we think of ourselves.

Individuals may use many ways to avoid experiencing painful or unacceptable emotions, and, in a paradoxical effort to reduce feelings of shame, clients may turn to binge eating. This, in turn, only increases negative affect and negative self-evaluation, resulting in increased shame. Duarte, Pinto-Gouveia, and Ferreira (2017) noted that in the long term, binge eating may cause greater distress than the person was originally experiencing, and patients often find themselves in a perpetual cycle of shame and dysregulated eating.

Binge eating disorder (BED) does not include the criteria for body image disturbance, although body image issues are a critical aspect of treatment. Body image disorder has been defined by Bruch (1962) as disturbances of perception, an inability to recognize signals and sensations in the body, and delusion-like distortions of size and weight. This may be true for some Black women, but for other Black women, body image is greater than size, shape, and weight. It is more complex. Ethnic identity and acculturation issues are a struggle for Black girls. Asking clients to define their personal meaning of body image should not be overlooked. Black women may report body dissatisfaction rather than body image concerns; exploring the distinction is fundamental in assessing their concerns. For several of my clients, body dissatisfaction was closely associated with attractiveness, which is defined as having a pleasing appearance or features and qualities that people like. Aspects of attractiveness may focus on hair, skin complexion, shapeliness, the fit of clothing—essentially "looking good."

Many believe that Black women are seemingly "protected" from the thin ideal due to a historical, cultural acceptance of a shapelier figure. What might be more accurate is that there is more flexibility in determining what physical characteristics are considered to be attractive among Black women. Thinness, which oftentimes is seen as skinny, is not the only standard of beauty within the Black community. Overstreet, Quinn, and Agocha (2010) have noted that the desire to achieve a curvaceous body shape is significantly associated with body dissatisfaction. Heavy and voluptuous is not always considered synonymous with curvy. Black women are increasingly desiring a slender, curvaceous figure (full breasts and ample behinds). My adolescent clients use the colloquialism "slim thick" to describe this body type. Increasing numbers of Black women are undergoing cosmetic surgery to achieve a desired look that reflects their standard of beauty.

Clinicians are encouraged to be prepared for the challenges and responsibilities that come with treating diverse individuals. Starting recommendations include demonstrating a willingness to conduct self-reflection or signifying that you value diversity. Explore your own attitudes about people from different races, classes, and cultures. Notice what in your office promotes acceptance. Are there pictures of different body shapes and people of different races and ethnicities? Do you have seating that is comfortable for individuals who are a larger size? Treating Black women with binge eating disorder requires provider self-awareness. How do you integrate multicultural skills when working with clients? Are you culturally aware? How do you manage the dynamic of difference? Providers need to be willing to ask the difficult questions while creating an environment that is respectful, compassionate, and empowering for Black clients. A quote from Maya Angelou is a reminder: "people may forget what you said, people will forget what you did, but people will never forget how you made them feel" (n.d.).

Being Black and living in a predominately White environment may be like being a red dot on a White screen. Experience in treating eating disorders is not sufficient—providers need to be culturally competent, seek supervision, and explore treatment models that may enhance your perspective. A few suggestions to become culturally competent include developing cultural empathy— ask yourself what it is like to be different or explore ways in which you are different from your clients. Be culturally sensitive—Black women are members of several oppressed groups. Explore their experiences within and outside their cultural group or community. Consider the deviation of eating habits from those expected within one's culture. Allow your clients the opportunity, the time, and the space to assist you, the provider, in exploring what it is like to be a Black girl or woman.

"Lexi" Vignette

Lexi (not her actual name) is a 33-year-old, single, African American female who lives alone and has presented for outpatient treatment. Initially, she reports experiencing depressive symptoms, as well as instances when she felt extremely overwhelmed, questioning if she was experiencing a panic attack. Denying previous mental health treatment, Lexi claims she would have "just talked to my friends" if anything significant was happening. She shared that she is very nervous about being in counseling and worries that her family and friends will not understand. As an African American woman, Lexi strongly believes that Black people do not go to counseling—if anything, they turn to the church for support, thus reinforcing her persistent question if counseling is the right thing for her to pursue. During the initial session, Lexi discussed familial relationships, sharing that her relationship with her mother is "rocky," and she does not have a relationship with her father; sibling relationships are "okay," but she sometimes questions if she fits in. At a later session, she was able to disclose that some of her discourse reflects her siblings' beliefs that she thinks she is "better than they are" and that she "acts White." When the clinician explored this further, Lexi shared examples related to her hairstyles, the people she dated, and the area in which she lives. Essentially, the efforts she put into action to succeed seemed, to others, to be a betrayal of her race.

While exploring some of the stressors that Lexi experiences, I was told that she "just needs more self-control" and is "tired of not feeling good in her body." Additionally, she shared experiencing significant stress at work and concerns about her growth opportunities at her current company. While putting unrealistic pressure on herself and believing she cannot afford to fail, she struggles to define what failure is and has difficulty acknowledging the successes she has achieved. She explains her conundrum by stating that she has heard and believes that individuals (both outside of her race and some within her race) expect Black women to fail. If they do not fail, their attributes such as strength and assertiveness are considered to be too aggressive, and sadly, these talented women are often referred to as "bitches."

Lexi believes that for her to succeed at work, she must demonstrate her worth. As such, she routinely skips lunch because she is "too busy" to take a break. She will snack throughout the day and has noticed the increasing amount of food she consumes in the evening. She additionally shared that she snacks "heavily" at night. Lexi shared that she has gained approximately 30 pounds in the past year and has tried "almost every diet on the market." She is not happy about the weight gain and would like to do something about it. She says, "I know what to do, but I just can't figure out how to do it consistently." Attempting to implement an exercise regimen, she reports difficulty in managing her schedule, the impact on her hair, and having little energy to exercise. She additionally shares that she is frustrated with herself and doesn't understand why she is so "lazy."

The clinician discussed clinical concerns with Lexi including binge eating disorder (BED). Lexi shared that eating disorders were for White, adolescent females and women who were looking to lose weight or seek attention. She questioned the diagnosis and whether there truly were Black people, who "were not trying to be White" and had eating disorders. The clinician explored a greater examination of Lexi's beliefs about size, shape, and weight, as well as food. Messages such as being in the "clean plate club" and responses to the use of food as both reward and punishment were recalled by her. Lexi additionally struggled with comparisons amongst her family, friends and coworkers, including concerns about skin color and hair type.

This case had numerous clinical factors for consideration, including: diagnosis, clinical case formulation, "fit" between the therapist and Lexi, the appropriateness of the therapeutic approach, culturally specific clinical issues and treatment modifications, transference and countertransference, and other clinical dilemmas that may have occurred. However, one major theme was present and addressed throughout the course of treatment—shame. Shame for being in therapy, shame for not being able to get control of her life, shame for choosing unhealthy relationships, shame for her eating behaviors, and shame about her appearance and her career.

Eating disorders are emotional disorders and disorders of disconnection. Throughout the process, Lexi was increasingly aware that the binge eating behaviors functioned to regulate her emotions. She reported experiencing relief at the end of her day during binge episodes, oftentimes followed by guilt; this relief was the escape from her life stressors and her inability to "live up to" the messages that had been engrained since she was a child. The Renfrew Unified Treatment (UT) model was the therapeutic approach used with Lexi. The Unified Treatment model is an adaptation of an existing empirically supported treatment, the Unified Protocol (UP; Barlow et al., 2011) that was adapted to (1) explicitly address eating disorder symptomatology and (2) intentionally infuse relational principles into treatment (UT; Thompson-Brenner et al., in press). Utilizing the Unified Treatment Model, Lexi was able to explore her values, improve mindfulness, and begin to explore the impact of shame on her emotionally driven behaviors. The ultimate goal of treatment was to promote tolerance of difficult emotions over contexts and time in order to create sustainable change and emotional resilience for Lexi.

Experiencing shame is not uncommon among African American women. During my work with Lexi, ethnic identity, her level of acculturation, and her overall beliefs about herself reinforced the shame experience. The Unified Treatment model was effective, as it increased Lexi's awareness of her emotional experience. She was able to understand the function of her emotions, even the difficult ones, and to increase her ability to tolerate those emotions. Lexi was able to identify the thinking traps that persisted in various aspects of her life and that negatively influenced her core beliefs. The UT reinforced opportunities for Lexi to identify alternative appraisals about her experiences and beliefs; resulting in her increased ability to decrease binge eating episodes and enhance her sense of self. The UT model aims to help clients "get better at feeling" rather than just "feel better" in the short term. Following outpatient treatment, Lexi is continuously improving her ability to tolerate her emotions and is getting better at feeling.

References

Barlow, D., Farchione, T., Fairholme, C., Ellard, K., Boisseau, C., Allen, L., & Ehrenreich-May, J. (2011). *Unified protocol for transdiagnostic treatment of emotional disorders: Therapist guide*. New York: Oxford University Press.

Binford, R. B., Mussell, M. P., Peterson, C. B., Crow, S. J., & Mitchell, J. E. (2004). Relation of binge eating age of onset to functional aspects of binge eating in binge eating disorder. *International Journal of Eating Disorders, 35*, 286–292.

Bruch, H. (1962). Perceptual and conceptual disturbances in anorexia nervosa. *Psychosomatic Medicine, 24*(2), 187–194.

Duarte, C., Pinto-Gouveia, J., & Ferreira, C. (2017). Ashamed and fused with body image and eating: Binge eating as an avoidance strategy. *Clinical Psychology and Psychotherapy, 24*, 195–202.

Gay, R. (2017). *Hunger: A memoir of (my) body*. New York: Harper Collins Publisher.

Gilbert, P. (1998). What is shame: Some core issues and controversies. In P. Gilbert & B. Andrews (Eds.), *Shame: Interpersonal behaviour, psychopathology and culture* (pp. 3–36). New York: Oxford University Press.

Gilbert, P. (2002). Body shame: A biopsychosocial conceptualisation and overview with treatment implications. In P. Gilbert & J. Miles (Eds.), *Body shame: Conceptualisation, research and treatment* (pp. 3–54). New York: Brunner Routledge.

Grilo, C. M., Lozano, C., & Masheb, R. M. (2005). Ethnicity and sampling bias in binge eating disorder: Black women who seek treatment have different characteristics than those who do not. *International Journal of Eating Disorders, 38*(3), 257–262.

Jones, L. V., & Guy-Sheftall, B. (2015). Conquering the Black girl blues. *Social Work, 60*(4), 343–350.

Masheb, R. M., & Grilo, C. M. (2006). Emotional overeating and its association with eating disorder psychopathology among overweight patients with binge eating disorder. *International Journal of Eating Disorders, 39*, 141–146.

Maya Angelou Quotes. (n.d.). Retrieved from www.goodreads.com/author/quotes/3503. Maya_Angelou.

National Eating Disorders Association. (2016). *Marginalization and eating disorders*. Retrieved January 7, 2018 from www.nationaleatingdisorders.org/learn/general-information/marginalization.

The National Institute for the Clinical Application of Behavioral Medicine. (2017). *Guilt vs Shame*. Retrieved January 7, 2018 from www.nicabm.com.

Overstreet, N. M., Quinn, D. M., & Agocha, V. B. (2010). Beyond thinness: The influence of a curvaceous body ideal on body dissatisfaction in Black and White women. *Sex Roles, 63*, 91–103.

Striegel-Moore, R. M., Wilfley, D. E., Pike, K. M., Dohm, F. A., & Fairburn, C. G. (2000). Recurrent binge eating in Black American women. *Archives of Family Medicine, 9*, 83–87.

Tejada, K. (2013). Book review [Review of the book *Shame, stereotypes, and Black women in America; For Colored girls who've considered politics when being strong isn't enough*, by M.V. Harris-Perry]. *Humanity & Society, 37*(3), 269–271.

Thompson-Brenner, H., Franklin, D., Smith, M., Brooks, G., Espel-Huynh, H., & Boswell, J. F. (in press). *Unified protocol for eating disorders and comorbidity: An adaptation of the unified protocol*. New York: Oxford University Press.

White, M. A., & Grilo, C. M. (2005). Ethnic differences in the prediction of eating and body image disturbances among female adolescent psychiatric inpatients. *International Journal of Eating Disorders, 38*, 78–84.

15 Food as a Drug

Mental Problem, Spiritual Solution

Joyce Woodson

Introduction

As a member of 12-step programs and minister of the gospel, I witness the miracle of recovery daily. I have endured the five-point cycle of addiction and unhealthy dependencies as outlined in Brand (2017): (1) pain, (2) use of addictive agents to soothe and/or distract, (3) temporary anesthesia, (4) negative consequences, and (5) shame and guilt resulting in more pain. I have also witnessed others stuck in that same cycle. Because I live the 12 steps and minister to people who are dependent on various substances, I know that the dis-ease of addiction must have an agent. I recognize that the most challenging aspect of my recovery is when that addictive agent is food. When I feel discomfort, food is my go-to for self-soothing! The entire process up to and including consumption provides some level of comfort. Shopping for ingredients, looking for recipes, and purchasing and preparing food are all a part of the addiction. However, to be clear, it is not solely the actual consumption of food I find soothing; instead, it is the repeated hand-to-mouth activity that provides the greatest comfort. It is the same reason I smoked cigarettes and drank alcohol excessively. The truth is, the dis-ease of addiction started and ended with food! Before I smoked or used drugs or drank alcohol, I ate addictively. After being delivered from the use and abuse of those substances, food once again became the addictive agent. As I began to address this manifestation of my dis-ease, I came to realize that I did not keep eating because I was hungry or because the food tasted good. I kept eating because something was eating me.

Growing up and now ministering in the Black community, it has been my experience that any type of mental illness is a source of shame and embarrassment and consequently remains hidden, misunderstood, and unaddressed. The dis-ease of food addiction—if recognized at all in the Black community—appears manifested mainly by binge eating or overeating. It is an undeniable problem in this form given the physical evidence of its existence. However, there is a hidden and underserved population of persons with food addictions at the other polarity of this dis-ease. Until very recently, I had no idea Black people were ever considered to have bulimia or anorexia. Many people, especially in the Black community, believe these diagnoses afflict only White persons. This ignorance of the existence of these conditions in Black people, coupled with the purely clinical approach to treatment of mental illnesses, has caused many Black persons to fail to acknowledge that their mental challenges—including disordered eating—exist. I believe that being caught in the grips of this denial or refusal is one reason many Black people tend not to seek help for mental health concerns. Therapy is seen as an undesirable option because it means admitting something is wrong. We will, however, go to the church for help.

Unfortunately, neither approach, therapy or church, is successful or sustainable when attempted in a vacuum. When seeking help from the church, people tend not to fully disclose all of their issues. Consequently, many clergy members do not recognize food addiction when they see or hear it. When taking a purely clinical approach, there are issues in the Black lived experience that contribute to the illness that are not recognized or even broached by White mental health professionals. Fear keeps the disease festering and unaddressed—fear on all sides. Fear of rejection, fear of offending, fear of exposure, fear of incompetence, fear of judgement, fear of embarrassment. Fear in both the sufferer and the mental health professional is a very real barrier to successful treatment of the food-related disorders in the African American community.

During my years in ministerial counseling in the Black community, I have worked with people grappling with a variety of issues and concerns. Studies have revealed that a vast majority of those with food addiction or EDs have suffered some sort of trauma and/or sexual abuse (Briere & Scott, 2007). Most of the Black women I minister to have experienced sexual molestation. This type of abuse is another hidden issue, or one that is not discussed in Black family households or communities as often as it should be. During a women's recovery group session held in my church, I asked everyone in the room to raise their hand if they had ever been sexually abused. In a room of 10 to 15 women, all but one raised her hand. The one woman that did not raise her hand admitted to extreme and traumatic physical abuse by a parent. She also happened to be the only one in attendance that was visibly suffering with morbid obesity.

I came to understand that what happened to me as a child was considered molestation after I was 18 years sober. I had been in therapy for substance abuse for years, but it was in a 12-step meeting, listening to others speak about their experiences, that I actually faced my truth for the first time. That was the beginning of my healing. That was also the beginning of the revelations related to my unhealthy relationship with food. Food kept me from feeling, and I came to understand that I could not heal what I could not feel.

Shanice[1] is another person who stands out particularly and with whom I developed a close ministerial relationship. Although alcohol and drug free for nearly five years, Shanice still battled with depression, PTSD, and suicidal tendencies. Because she had no obvious physical appearance of an eating disorder, it was not until much later that I learned of her food addiction and years of cutting. Shanice had endured horrific physical, mental, and sexual abuse as a child. And after her sexual abuse was exposed, she began to implode. She was referred to one mental health facility after another as a result of her depression and suicide attempts. It was during her treatment in various mental health facilities that she learned more negative coping mechanisms. She learned different ways to restrict and to furtively purge and cut. Now her repertoire of responses to discomfort included binging and purging and restricting and cutting in addition to sexual promiscuity and substance misuse. Shanice continued to suffer with this dis-ease, experiencing many of its comorbid manifestations for years. Unfortunately, there were few treatment facilities near her home in the state where she lived that could provide the intense level of care she needed. Insurance issues and cost of treatment presented an additional barrier, further limiting her options. A facility was located 45 miles from her home, and she was admitted immediately upon assessment.

Once finally in residential treatment, however, she did what she had done previously, which was to not disclose fully to staff her full repertoire of behaviors and history. For example, she had not shared that she had once been a binge eater, without purging, and weighed more than 200 pounds in her small frame. However, by this time, Shanice was restricting, and the focus was on refeeding and gaining weight. Weight gain was a particularly arduous task in this case because not only was there a limited assortment of food items on the facility's menu, but the items seemed foreign and were unappealing to her. In addition, no inquiries were made about a possible history of sexual abuse, which was likely at the root of her issues, at least in part. Sadly, it seemed that treatment employed at this facility was not tailored to the client and appeared woefully inadequate, at least in this case. Shanice felt uncomfortable in this treatment facility, comprised of an all-White treatment team, which served a predominately White client base. The only people of color on staff were technicians responsible for policing the food at mealtime and ensuring patients did not engage in disordered eating activities or self-harm. The team appeared to do their best to treat Shanice using a color-blind approach, which all but assured she would not improve. This meant that in addition to refeeding her with foods that were dissonant to her culture and experience, no one talked with her about important personal issues related to ethnicity such as hair and skin care. The African American staff members secretly spoke harshly to Shanice. They totally bought into the idea that Black people do not have eating disorders, and because there was no visual physical evidence of her problem, they continually asked her why she was there and told her that she simply needed to "eat differently."

Their critical and ostracizing comments only exacerbated her feelings of exclusion and doom. During intake, individual therapy, and groups, there were no questions asked or important discussions raised about racism or microaggressions suffered because of her lived experience as a Black woman. Feeling doubtful about her success, suspicious, and mistrustful, Shanice did not raise any of these concerns. For some time, she didn't talk at all in group or individually to staff about anything. She didn't talk about her inability to have time alone for daily prayer and meditation, which are tools for coping that are encouraged in the 12-step programs. And although 12-step meetings were held at the hospital on certain days of the week, unfortunately, she wasn't able to attend because there was never anyone available or willing to escort her. There was also no mention of or access to church services at the facility. And although the church where she was a member had live streams on the internet, sadly, Wi-Fi on the unit had poor connectivity. Also, the service conflicted with group, adding to her frustration. Because Shanice did not want anyone to know she was being treated for an eating disorder, she didn't disclose this to anyone in her family, at church, or in her 12-step support circles. So her spiritual connection consisted almost exclusively of conversations with me in my ministerial role.

After three months of feeling stuck in the wrong place with the wrong people, Shanice repeated the cycle that she had during previous treatment for depression and suicide attempts. She followed all of the rules carefully, said all the things staff wanted her to say, and succeeded in termination but without measurable improvement. The discharge plan in no way addressed any of the discomforting circumstances that were related to her lived experiences as a Black woman or those that led to her addictive behaviors initially, as they had remained undisclosed during the treatment process. Many of the recommendations that had been at least minimally helpful from 12-steps were discouraged. Specifically, those practices of the 12-step program for food addiction (i.e., weighing food, getting phone numbers, and keeping in touch with fellow sufferers) were strongly discouraged. Feeling more damaged and more defeated, Shanice swore never again to return to inpatient treatment for her addiction dis-ease, considering it pointless. Shanice left the hospital determine to shed the weight that she had gained. She was determined to do it without disordered eating. She went to her physicians to focus on the physical aspect of her threefold illness and all its devastating consequences. Doctors were able to identify and address some physical conditions that resulted from her eating disorder, and for a period of time, she attended meetings, church, and talk therapy along with using medication for her physical conditions, anxiety and depression. While practicing the spiritual principles of the 12-step program in her daily life, attending Food Addicts in Recovery Anonymous (FA) and other 12-step meetings, attending church services and serving in recovery ministry at church, Shanice began to thrive. She had found a therapist she trusted and was getting closer to addressing the causes and conditions for her dis-ease and its many manifestations.

Unfortunately, one of them resurfaced and triggered the use of a different addictive agent. Shanice rekindled a previously failed relationship that again became unhealthy and a source of emotional discomfort. She had stopped attending 12-step meetings, church services, and recovery ministry meetings, opting to spend time with her boyfriend. Her daily prayer and meditation began to dwindle, and her routines and disciplines were broken. In short, she neglected her spiritual conditions, rendering her defenseless to the first addictive bite. Entering once again into the cycle, she was admitted into that same hospital. This time she spent seven months in the facility without adequate treatment, and her prognosis was that she would need to be institutionalized indefinitely. Fortunately, members of Shanice's church family and 12-step support groups joined Shanice and began employing the spiritual instructions and believing the promise found in God's word: "Confess your trespasses to one another, and pray for one another, that you may be healed. The effective, fervent prayer of a righteous man avails much" (Holy Bible NKJV James 5:16). Now refocused on the maintenance of her spiritual conditions and practicing a program of recovery that includes church, therapy, 12-steps and recovery ministry meetings, she is again making good progress, and coping more adaptively with ED triggers. She is healing from her dis-ease of addiction.

My work with others like Shanice provides evidence that hers is not an isolated case. Programming in eating-disorder treatment facilities appears not to have been designed with Black clients in mind. Their unique needs may go unmet at every level: body, mind, and—perhaps most importantly—spirit. Similar to persons who abuse alcohol and other substances, the problem for those who grapple with food addiction is centered inside their minds (*AA Big Book*, 2013). In the *AA Big Book* (2013), it is stated that physical and spiritual components of the malady and its associated consequences are undeniable. It logically follows that the most successful and sustainable treatment plans include tools that address all three components, physical, mental and spiritual (*AA Big Book*, 2013). Recovery is like a three-legged stool. All three legs are needed in order for the stool to be functional. Similarly, a three-cord braided rope is stronger than a single-corded one. It would seem implausible to even momentarily consider healing in the African American culture without including faith. As a practicing minister, I believe that if you leave God out of the treatment plan, sustained healing and contented recovery are virtually impossible. In my ministry, I serve as a guide on a person's journey to and through the vital spiritual experiences and ultimately their healing process. Armed with the Bible, 12-steps, and my own story, I help them envision God in their treatment. I assure them that with God as the head of their treatment team, they can succeed and be free from active food addiction. It has been my experience that when a treatment plan lacks the spiritual element or foundation on which the person relies, the plan will be ineffective, and the person easily returns to what is familiar. This seems to have been at least partially the reason Shanice continued to struggle after termination. The *AA Big Book* (2013) teaches that when healing from the dis-ease, faith has to work twenty-four hours a day, in and through us lest we perish. What makes recovery particularly challenging for a person struggling with food addiction is that unlike those who suffer from alcohol or drug dependency, gambling, or other vices, there is no way to be completely abstinent from the addictive agent. It is often said in 12-step food meetings that we have to take that tiger out of the cage and pet it three times a day! You must have a relationship with food in order to live. We rely on God to manage that relationship. Likewise, we cannot completely avoid emotional discomfort.

Trying to navigate and/or reconcile societal systems, cultural norms, and spiritual beliefs can cause a great deal of discomfort. Moving around in the world as a Black woman with the pressures to conform to systems and standards that were developed without consideration of our natural features, body structures, or ethnic culture produces an emotional tax that others do not experience or understand completely. Just as we rely on God to manage our relationship with food, we must learn to rely fully on God to help us manage our responses to these discomforts and emotional taxes that are uniquely our own.

Fellowship with a group of like-minded people can be a key component to recovery. It is within this fellowship that we share our pain and burdens as well as our triumphs and excitement without the fear of judgement. For not only can pain and frustration trigger disordered eating, but the excitement of success can also spawn a similar response. I was told early on in my recovery that program and fellowship are important, but there will come a time when the only thing that stands between me and that addictive agent is the God of my understanding. Both in church and in 12-step meetings, we are instructed repeatedly to "Ask God for help." The 12-steps help me, Shanice, and countless others like us to develop and maintain the loving and powerful relationships with God that help us cope daily with our addictions. My experience with the dis-ease of addiction and my journey with God uniquely qualify me to help others find or at least begin the search for their own loving, caring relationship with God that will help them practice a manner of living to render them happy and usefully whole. In the 12-steps, we believe that helping others is critical for the sufferer's continued deliverance from their seemingly hopelessly damaged state of mind and body. And it is the attainment and continual practice of the 12th step, "Having had a spiritual awakening as a result of these steps, we tried to carry the message to food addicts and practice these principles in all our affairs" (*Food Addicts in Recovery Anonymous*, 2013), that is intended to encourage us to help and empower others to join us in embracing all of the 12 steps on the journey toward "the Joy of Good Living," which is the very theme and spirit of 12-step recovery. Similarly, it is written, "And they overcame him by the blood of the Lamb and by the word of their testimony, and they did not love their lives to the death" (Holy Bible NKJV Rev. 12:11).

Note

1. A pseudonym is used here, and "Shanice" granted the author permission to write about her experience.

References

Alcoholics Anonymous Big Book (4th ed.). (2013). New York: Alcoholics Anonymous World Services, Inc.

Brand, R. (2017). *Recovery: Freedom from our addictions*. New York: Henry Holt and Company.

Briere, J., & Scott, C. (2007). Assessment of traumatic symptoms in eating-disordered populations. *Eating Disorders, 15,* 347–358. doi:10.1080/10640260701454360.

Food Addicts in Recovery Anonymous. (2013). Woburn, MA: Food Addicts in Recovery Anonymous, Inc.

The Holy Bible: New King James Version. (1989). Scofield, C.I. (Ed.). Nashville, TN: Thomas Nelson Publishers.

16 Creative Training Approaches for Clinicians-in-Training Working With African American Women With Eating Disorders

Jacqueline Conley

Introduction

The National Eating Disorder Association (NEDA, n.d.) reports that 30 million people struggle with an eating disorder in the USA. Eating disorders do not discriminate based on ethnicity, gender, and socioeconomic status; however, data, research, and treatment approaches for African American (AA) women with eating disorders are still limited. The DSM-V identifies various types of eating disorders (American Psychiatric Association, 2013). African American women, however, are more likely to be diagnosed with binge eating disorder (BED). The actual figures on African American women with eating disorders are limited because they are overlooked, undiagnosed by medical and mental health professionals, or African Americans underutilize mental health services (Stone & Conley, 2004).

The literature identifies several culturally contextual issues that must be considered when working with African American women with eating disorders. These issues might be difficult for clinicians-in-training to discuss; however, they need to be present in the clinical space for cultural competency. Culture contributes to one's attitudes, perception, and knowledge and can play a significant role in eating disorders and a person's relationship with food. Factors such as acculturation, stress, oppression, racism, poverty, and trauma have been identified throughout the literature on African American women with eating disorders. A cursory overview of these factors is provided, along with a creative training approach, and process questions that can assist instructors and professionals working with trainees.

Acculturation

Acculturation, as defined by Merriam-Webster (n.d.), is a cultural modification of an individual, group, or people by adapting to or borrowing traits from another culture. Assimilation and acculturation are not unknown to the African American community; however, they have been present since slavery, emancipation, and so on. Strides have been made for African Americans to express their cultural heritage; however, messages still exist that propel them to accept mainstream cultural values, such as BE THIN and HAVE LONG STRAIGHT HAIR. Researchers suggests that acculturation plays a role in the development of eating disorders among women of color (Lynch, 2004; Mastria, 2002). The stress of acculturation, particularly for African American women, if not addressed with health messages, can contribute to unhealthy relationship with food and eating habits.

Stress

Stress is a normal part of life, and it can have a positive and negative impact on an individual. The body can react to stress with physical, mental, or emotional responses. In terms of eating behaviors and stress, food binging, dieting, purging, or starving have served as a sensible means of coping for women of color due to physical and psychic atrocities. Thompson (1996) notes that these atrocities derive from racism, sexism, homophobia, classism, the stress of acculturation, and emotional, physical, and sexual abuse. Typically, for the African American woman to survive in society, she becomes characterized as and assumes the strong Black woman (SBW) ideology or stance. Because of this SBW stance, African American women tend to assume multiple roles of caretaking, financial provision, and emotional support (Woods-Giscombe, 2010; Beauboeuf-Lafontant, 2003). Harrington, Crowther, and Shipherd (2010) note that the SBW role plays a moderating role in women with binge eating symptoms. The "critical mechanisms by which traumatic, stressful, and discriminatory experiences influence African American women's binge eating symptomatology are through increasing the likelihood or severity of emotion regulation difficulties, self-silencing behaviors, and the use of eating to fulfill psychological functions" (Harrington, 2007, p. 122). Barrington, Ceballos, Bishop, McGregor, and Beresford (2012) suggest that perceived stress in many contexts may contribute to obesity by way of biobehavioral processes. Chronic stress results in increased intake of foods higher in sugar and fat, leading to weight gain (Torres & Nowson, 2007). Finally, in general, low-income African American women are at greater risk of physiological stress than either Black men or White women (Geronimus, Hicken, Keene, & Bound, 2006), which may contribute to unhealthy eating patterns. Understanding the relationship between stress and eating is an important factor that trainees need to be aware of when working with African American women.

Trauma (Oppression, Racism, Classism, and Sexual Abuse)

Trauma is defined as a deeply distressing or disturbing experience (Merriam-Webster, n.d.). Trauma, particularly earlier childhood sexual and physical abuse, can play a role in the development of eating disorders. In addition, African American women's experiences with oppression, racism, and classism must be examined when working with African American women with eating disorders. As a result, overeating may serve a as a tool to manage emotions, histories of oppression, victimization, and exclusion (Beauboeuf-Lafontant, 2003; Thompson, 1992). Overall, African American women manage their weight within the context of societal racism, discrimination, and gender inequalities (Everett, Hall, & Hamilton-Mason, 2010).

Socioeconomic Status

The relationship between socioeconomic status (SES) and obesity is apparent. Ogden, Lamb, Carroll, and Flegal (2010) report that 54% of African American women with incomes below the 130% poverty line are obese. Lower socioeconomic status among African American women, who experience racism, can influence the drive to binge as a coping mechanism. Hughes (1997) theorized that the economic and emotional deprivation experienced by African American women with eating disorders may explain a historical relationship with mouth-stuffing habits that serves as a tool to fill emptiness. In addition, due to low socioeconomic status, the inability to afford more nutritional foods leaves a person eating high-caloric and sugar-based foods. Understanding the relationship between SES and eating patterns can assist instructors train students to work with African American women with eating disorders.

Comorbidity

African American women have the highest rates of obesity in the United States and are at increased risk for a variety of comorbid health conditions (Flegal, Carroll, Kit, & Ogden, 2012). Specifically, there is a strong relationship with BED and other comorbid conditions such as severe obesity (Hudson, Hiripi, Pope, & Kessler, 2007; Wilson, Grilo, & Vitousek, 2007), depression (Kessler & Bromet, 2013), and substance disorders (Cheng et al., 2012; Guss, Kissileff, Devlin, Zimmerli, & Walsh, 2002; Swinbourne et al., 2012). Based on the link between BED and obesity, African American women are more at risk for cardiovascular disease, high cholesterol, and high glucose levels (De Franca, Gigante, & Olinto, 2014; Granje, 2018).

Recruiting and Training African American Clinicians and Researchers

Eating disorder professionals have articulated the need to recruit and train African American researchers and clinicians to work in the field of eating disorders (Gayle Brooks, PhD, V.P. and CCO for the Renfrew Center; Cynthia Bulik, PhD, founding director of the University of North Carolina Center of Excellence for Eating Disorders; and Franko et al. (2012)). Furthermore, Talleyrand (2010) suggests that research must examine the contribution of stress to maladaptive eating regulation responses among African American women. Once they are identified, appropriate counseling treatment programs need to be available for African American women. Therefore, it is imperative not only to train African American clinicians but to ensure that all clinicians have a strong foundation in culturally sensitive treatment and understand contextual factors that exist among African American women with eating disorders. Stone and Conley (2004) stated,

> In calling for cultural competency from mental health professionals, it is to be stressed that the professional must possess an understanding of the sociopolitical realities that exist in the United States. Professionals cannot be in denial that specific groups of people are denied access to full participation in economic and social life in our country. These forces that support exclusion are not random, nor are the phenomena of poverty, violence, and involvement in the criminal justice system all attributable to personal irresponsibility.
>
> (p. 371)

Creative Training Approach

In most graduate-level programs, theory- and conceptual-based learning occurs in the classroom. Trainees are taught various theoretical approaches to working with eating disorders such as interpersonal therapy (IPT) and enhanced cognitive behavior therapy (CBT-E), and these approaches have had good success (Tanofsky-Kraff et al., 2013). In addition to theories, trainees are also exposed to evidence-based psychological interventions (EBIs) such as the Body Project and appetite awareness treatment (AAT). Prior to trainees' gaining hands-on exposure, which typically occurs during practicum and internship, creative approaches along with traditional pedagogy can better facilitate the transfer of knowledge among mental health professionals in training (Conley, 2011, 2019; Hill, Roffman, Stahl, Friedman, Hummel, & Wallace, 2008; Neukrug, Bayne, Dean-Nganga, & Pusateri, 2013; Whitelock, Faulkner, & Miell, 2008). The research suggests that there is a training and treatment gap in the field of eating disorders (Austin, Kendrin, & Sonneville, 2013; Kazdin, Fitzsimmons-Craft, & Wilfley, 2017). Clinical training programs can benefit from using both approaches when training students to work with African American women with eating disorders. The lack of diverse training materials on African American women with eating disorders presents challenges.

The emergence of feature films as a training tool has become increasingly valuable to instructors (Badura, 2002). For example, popular films have been used to cultivate multiculturally competent counselors (Shen, 2015) and teach multicultural counseling (Nittoli & Guiffrida, 2018). Tyler and Mathews (1995) state, "Feature films can provide an experience that might have a stronger impact on student attitudes and behaviors than a more traditional approach" (p. 7). Similarly, Pearson (2006) states, "When careful consideration is taken, using the power of film to engage learning on multiple levels can transform learning from an academic exercise into an emotional, intellectual and personal experience" (p. 77). Films featuring African American women with eating disorders are extremely limited. In a blog interview with Patel (2015), Omawale states, "In media there are very few forefront women of color, and there are no forefront women of color struggling with eating disorders in an open platform" (blog). The lack of African American women portrayed with eating disorders in the media could indicate that this disorder does not exist or is minimal within this population. This unknowing stance by the film industry can perpetuate the myth that "Black folks don't have eating disorders" and lead to film not providing a platform to illustrate its existence. In September 2018, film writer, director, and producer Omawale's feature film *SOLACE* made its world premiere at the LA Film Festival. *SOLACE* is based on Omawale's life, which includes her struggle with an eating disorder. (For more information and the movie trailer, see www.solacefilm.com/.) More recently, the use of social media has provided people with the platform to journal their life stories. Thus, social media provides instructors with a plethora of authentic, contextually based material that can be utilized with counselors in training.

After reviewing approximately 50 YouTube channels, the following seven channels were identified because they provided a woman's journey through her eating disorder over a long period of time or a synapse of her story on eating disorders. The channels were not exclusive to binge eating disorder (BED) but were more reflective of eating disorders among African American women:

- A Black Girls Eating Disorder Journey (long journey with multiple posts): www.bing.com/videos/search?q=+eating+disorders+and+aftican+americ an+women%2c+you+tube&&view=detail&mid=67571B8A0A78869A9 C8267571B8A0A78869A9C82&&FORM=VDRVRV
- Anorexia while black (several parts): www.youtube.com/watch?v=ah2Lm XMLTZA
- Lying about my eating disorder (long journey with multiple posts): www. youtube.com/watch?v=7TXI7F9eGB4
- My bulimia and self-harm (synopsis): www.youtube.com/watch?v=QPw TC4BW6mQ
- What you don't know about Jazzmyne (synopsis): www.youtube.com/ watch?v=LnhRcX5y6As
- When Being Curvy Hurts: One Black Woman's Severe Struggle with Body Image: https://abcnews.go.com/Health/curvy-hurts-black-womans-severe-struggle-body-image/story?id=24777077
- Eating disorders are black women's issues too | Young minds (synopsis): www.youtube.com/watch?v=YVqCZCf7Xnc

Process Questions

The following is a short list of questions that were developed to serve as a guide for trainees to critically think about contextual information while watching the YouTube videos. These questions can also be utilized with any training videos that might be developed on African American women with eating disorders.

1. What messages about food has she heard?
2. What messages does she tell herself about food and eating patterns?
3. What factors related to oppression are mentioned?
4. Does she talk about trauma in her life and what survival strategies she has used to cope?
5. What other types of addictive behaviors has she engaged in?
6. Does she have evidence of or talk about comorbidity?
7. What are her triggers to eat, and are they based in culturally contextual issues?
8. Does she identify with being "all" to others (i.e., strong Black woman)?
9. Does she identify with or mention any socioeconomic challenges?
10. Does she hurt herself (i.e., cutting or mutilation)?
11. What parts of the video stood out to you and why?
12. What strengths does she mention to help her deal with her eating disorder?
13. Create questions that were not mentioned in the list.

Conclusion

Eating disorders among African American women have not reached epic proportions; however, as the numbers increase, the need for recruiting and training African American counselors and researchers (and others interested in working with African Americans from a culturally contextual space) is essential. In addition, the limited amount of research and training materials on African American women with eating disorders can hinder instructors' ability to prepare trainees prior to their journey to practicums and internships. Thus, creative approaches become valuable. Feature films and other audiovisual materials have long been used within the training program as an ancillary to traditional materials. Used in conjunction with traditional materials, creative activities can provide a mechanism for instructors to aid students in the transfer of knowledge and emotional understanding. These elements can contribute to the growth and development of future clinicians trained to work with African American women with eating disorders. Due to the nonexistence of training videos, films, or videos that depict African American women with eating disorders, it was the author's intention use social media (i.e., YouTube) to find relevant channels of African American women's journey through their eating disorders. Moving forward, the development of such training videos is a necessity in the field. More importantly, the videos should be an in-depth depiction of a woman's journey through her eating disorder versus a short 30-minute synopsis. Finally, as with any training material, process questions should be provided to guide and assist the trainee to develop a deeper and critical knowledge of the associated contextual issues.

References

Acculturation. (n.d.). Merriam-Webster. Retrieved September 2, 2018 from www.merriam-webster.com/dictionary/acculturation.

American Psychiatric Association. (2013). *Diagnostic and statistical manual of mental disorders* (5th ed.). Washington, DC: Author.

Austin, S. B., Kendrin, R., & Sonneville, K. R. (2013). Closing the "know-do" gap: Training public health professionals in eating disorders prevention via case-method teaching. *International Journal of Eating Disorders, 46*, 533–537. http://doi.org/10.1002/eat.22111.

Badura, A. S. (2002). Capturing students' attention: Movie clips set the stage for learning in abnormal psychology. *Teaching of Psychology, 29*, 58–60.

Barrington, W. E., Ceballos, R. M., Bishop, S. K., McGregor, B. A., & Beresford, S. A. (2012). Perceived stress, behavior, and body mass index among adults participating in a worksite obesity prevention program, Seattle, 2005–2007. *Preventing Chronic Disease, 9*, 120001. https://doi.org/10.5888/pcd9.120001.

Beauboeuf-Lafontant, T. (2003). Strong and large black women? Exploring relationships between deviant womanhood and weight. *Gender & Society, 17*(1), 111–121.

Cheng, C. Y., Reich, D., Haiman, C. A., Tandon, A., Patterson, N., Selvin, E., . . . Kao, W. H. (2012). African ancestry and its correlation to type 2 diabetes in African Americans: A genetic admixture analysis in three U.S. population cohorts. *PLoS One, 7*(3), e32840. https://doi.org/10.1371/journal.pone.0032840.

Conley, J. A. (2011). In treatment: Using a television series as an experiential learning activity for graduate level training in counselling psychology. *International Humanities Review, 2*(2), 29–37.

Conley, J. A. (2019). Using *For Colored Girls* as a creative way to help me understand how empathic I am. *Journal of Creativity in Mental Health, 14*(2), 243–257. https://doi.org/10.1080/15401383.2019.1577198.

De Franca, G. V., Gigante, D. P., & Olinto, M. T. (2014). Binge eating in adults: Prevalence and association with obesity, poor self-rated health status and body dissatisfaction. *Public Health & Nutrition, 17*, 932–938.

Everett, J., Hall, C., & Hamilton-Mason, J. (2010). Everyday conflict and daily stressors: Coping responses of Black women. *Affilia, 25*(1), 30–42.

Flegal, K. M., Carroll, M. D., Kit, B. K., & Ogden, C. L. (2012). Prevalence of obesity and trends in the distribution of body mass index among US adults, 1999–2010. *JAMA, 307*(5), 491–497. https://doi.org/10.1001/jama.2012.39.

Franko, D. L., Thompson-Brenner, H., Thompson, D. R., Boisseau, C. L., Davis, A., Forbush, K. T., . . . Wilson, G. T. (2012). Racial/ethnic differences in adults in randomized clinical trials of binge eating disorder. *Journal Consulting and Clinical Psychology, 80*(2), 186–195. https://doi.org/10.1037/a0026700.

Geronimus, A. T., Hicken, M., Keene, D., & Bound, J. (2006). "Weathering" and age patterns of allostatic load scores among blacks and whites in the United States. *American Journal Public Health, 96*(5), 826–833. https://doi.org/10.2105/ajph.2004.060749.

Granje, J. (2018). Binge Eating Disorder (BED): Nutritional prevention and treatment. *Journal of Food and Nutritional Disorders, 7*(2), 1–12. https://doi.org/10.4172/2324-9323.1000248.

Guss, J. L., Kissileff, H. R., Devlin, M. J., Zimmerli, E., & Walsh, B. T. (2002). Binge size increases with body mass index in women with binge-eating disorder. *Obesity Research, 10*(10), 1021–1029. https://doi.org/10.1038/oby.2002.139.

Harrington, E. F. (2007). *Binge eating and the "strong black woman": An explanatory model of binge eating in African American women.* Master thesis, Kent State University.

Harrington, E. F., Crowther, J. H., & Shipherd, J. C. (2010). Trauma, binge eating, and the "strong Black woman." *Journal of Consulting and Clinical Psychology, 78*(4), 469–479. https://doi.org/10.1037/a0019174.

Hill, C. E., Roffman, M., Stahl, J., Friedman, S., Hummel, A., & Wallace, C. (2008). Helping skills training for undergraduates: Outcomes and predictors of outcomes. *Journal of Counseling Psychology, 55*, 359–370. https://doi.org/10.1037/0022-0167.55.3.359.

Hudson, J. I., Hiripi, E., Pope, H. G., Jr., & Kessler, R. C. (2007). The prevalence and correlates of eating disorders in the National Comorbidity Survey Replication. *Biological Psychiatry, 61*(3), 348–358. https://doi.org/10.1016/j.biopsych.2006.03.040.

Hughes, M. H. (1997). Soul, black women, and food. In Carole Counihan & Penny van Esterik (Eds), *Food and culture* (pp. 272–280). New York: Routledge.

Kazdin, A. E., Fitzsimmons-Craft, E., & Wilfley, D. (2017). Addressing critical gaps in the treatment of eating disorders. *International Journal of Eating Disorders, 50*(3), 170–189. https://doi.org/10.1002/eat.22670.

Kessler, R. C., & Bromet, E. J. (2013). The epidemiology of depression across cultures. *Annual Reviews of Public Health, 34*, 119–138.

Lynch, S. L. (2004). *Eating disorders in African American women: Incorporating race into considerations of etiology and treatment.* Unpublished doctoral dissertation, Widener University, Delaware.

Mastria, M. (2002). Ethnicity and eating disorders. *Psychoanalysis and Psychotherapist, 19*(1), 59–77.

The National Eating Disorder Association. (n.d.). *Statistics and research on eating disorders.* Retrieved from www.nationaleatingdisorders.org/statistics-research-eating-disorders.

Neukrug, E., Bayne, H., Dean-Nganga, L., & Pusateri, C. (2013). Creative and novel approaches to empathy: A neo-Rogerian perspective. *Journal of Mental Health Counseling, 35*, 29–42. https://doi.org/10.17744/mehc.35.1.5q375220327000t2.

Nittoli, J. M., & Guiffrida, D. A. (2018). Using popular film to teach multicultural counseling: A constructivist approach. *Journal of Creativity in Mental Health, 13*(3), 344–357. https://doi.org/10.1080/15401383.2017.1340216.

Ogden, C. L., Lamb, M. M., Carroll, M. D., & Flegal, K. M. (2010). *Obesity and socioeconomic status in adults: United States 1988–1994 and 2005–2008.* NCHS data brief no 50. Hyattsville, MD: National Center for Health Statistics.

Omawale, T. (Producer & Director). (2018). *SOLACE* [Motion Picture]. United States.

Patel, P. (2015). *Filmmaker Tchaiko Omawale is opening a conversation about black women and eating disorders* [Blog post]. Retrieved from www.nationaleatingdisorders.org/blog/filmmaker-tchaiko-omawale-opening-conversation-about-black-women-and-eating-disorders.

Pearson, Q. M. (2006). Using the film *The Hours* to teach diagnosis. *Journal of Humanistic Counseling, Education, and Development, 45*, 70–78.

Shen, Y.-J. (2015). Cultivating multiculturally competent counselors through movies. *Journal of Creativity in Mental Health, 10*, 232–246. https://doi.org/10.1080/15401383.2014.959679.

Stone, D., & Conley, J.A. (2004). A Partnership between Roberts' crisis intervention model and the multicultural competencies. *Brief Treatment and Crisis Intervention, 4*(4), 367–375.

Swinbourne, J., Hunt, C., Abbott, M., Russell, J., St Clare, T., & Touyz, S. (2012). The comorbidity between eating disorders and anxiety disorders: Prevalence in an eating disorder sample and anxiety disorder sample. *Australian and New Zealand Journal of Psychiatry, 46*(2), 118–131.

Talleyrand, R. M. (2010). Eating disorders in African American girls: Implications for counselors. *Journal of Counseling and Development, 88,* 319–324.

Tanofsky-Kraff, M., Bulik, C. M., Marcus, M. D., Striegel, R. H., Wilfley, D. E., Wonderlich, S. A., & Hudson, J. I. (2013). Binge eating disorder: The next generation of research. *International Journal of Eating Disorders, 46*(3), 193–207. https://doi.org/10.1002/eat.22089.

Thompson, B. (1992). "A way outa no way": Eating problems among African American, Latina, and White women. *Gender & Society, 6*(4), 546–561.

Thompson, B. W. (1996). *A hunger so wide and so deep: A multiracial view of women's eating problems.* Minneapolis, MN: University of Minnesota Press.

Torres, S. J., & Nowson, C. A. (2007). Relationship between stress, eating behavior, and obesity. *Nutrition, 23*(11–12), 887–894. https://doi.org/10.1016/j.nut.2007.08.008.

Trauma. (n.d.). Merriam-Webster. Retrieved September 2, 2018 from www.merriam-webster.com/dictionary/trauma.

Tyler, J. M., & Mathews, C. (1995). Understanding the impact of feature films in classroom learning: Blending CEST and transhistorical perspectives. *The Counseling and Human Development Newsletter, 14,* 6–7.

Whitelock, D., Faulkner, D., & Miell, D. (2008). Promoting creativity in Ph.D. supervision: Tensions and dilemmas. *Thinking Skills and Creativity, 3,* 143–153.

Wilson, G. T., Grilo, C. M., & Vitousek, K. M. (2007). Psychological treatment of eating disorders. *American Psychologist, 62*(3), 199–216. https://doi.org/10.1037/0003-066X.62.3.199.

Woods-Giscombe, C. L. (2010). Superwoman schema: African American women's views on stress, strength, and health. *Qualitative Health Research, 20*(5), 668–683. https://doi.org/10.1177/1049732310361892.

Part V

Addressing Special Populations

17 Bulimia

An Attempt to Solve Insoluble Problems

Jennifer Ashby-Bullock

Racism, poverty, homophobia or the stress of acculturation from immigration—
those are the disorders. Anorexia, bulimia and compulsive eating are very
orderly, sane responses to those disorders. So that's why I don't even use the
word "disorder." I'm shifting the focus away from the notion of eating problems as pathology, and instead labeling forms of discrimination as pathological.
—Becky Thompson

I was in the throes of bulimia when I met Becky Thompson. Thompson is an
educator, activist, and author of *A Hunger So Wide and So Deep: A Multiracial View of Women's Eating Problems*. She presented at Grinnell College
when I was a sophomore, and her research on women of color and eating problems was the most profound, insightful, and liberating information I had ever
acquired about eating disorders.

If my interaction with Thompson had occurred five years earlier, maybe
I would not have developed an eating disorder after I encountered racism at
my high school. When I was 14 years old, I enrolled at Francis W. Parker
High School on the Near-North Side of Chicago. At that time, I had no way
of knowing that I would be the only girl in my graduating class who self-
identified as African American. I chose Parker over the University of Chicago
Laboratory High School, the more competitive and proximate school in my
neighborhood, because I thought the philosophy and the pedagogy at Parker
would be more similar to what I had grown accustomed to at my Montessori
elementary school. Neither I nor my parents could have predicted that my decision to attend Parker would result in my experiencing pernicious racism and
social exclusion that would leave me with emotional scars and crippling eating
problems that would take years to shed.

The overwhelmingly White, disproportionately wealthy students I encountered at Parker were unlike any peers I had met or attempted to socialize with
in or out of school. After two years of being taunted with racist slurs such as
"Aunt Jemima" and "Chaka Zulu," being excluded from social gatherings and
events, and having my family's professional, middle-class status regarded as
impoverished, I decided to end the pain and stop the emotional hemorrhaging

by making myself more acceptable, more palatable to my classmates. Although my classmates had given me every indication that I would never find acceptance among them, that reality was too painful to accept. As a result of my deep need to be accepted by my peers, my young and naive self thought the way to achieve greater acceptance was to make myself thinner.

Therefore, I set about achieving my objective with the determination of a sad, marginalized adolescent girl. Every Monday when I returned to school and listened to my classmates recount stories about all the fun they had shared over the weekend, I felt the acute stab of exclusion. I was never invited to their parties and spent every weekend at home with my parents. Desperate to fix the flaws I believed made me unacceptable to my classmates, I decided to become thin, hoping that by altering my body shape, I would elevate my social standing.

My decision to use purging as a means of ending my palpable suffering was a deliberate one. I succeeded in losing weight, at least. In three months, I managed to lose 40 pounds. Though I lost weight, I never found acceptance among my classmates at Parker. Little did I know that my *solution* would become an entrenched and intractable addiction that would take me years to overcome.

During my sophomore year, I began therapy with a wonderful psychologist I have identified as Dr. Y. Dr. Y served as my therapist both before and after I developed bulimia, and she played a key role in my eventual decision to transfer from Francis W. Parker School to the University of Chicago Laboratory Schools for my senior year of high school. While recovering from bulimia took seven years, much longer than I would have ever expected, I recognize in hindsight that my recovery began the day I decided to leave the hostile, toxic, racist environment in which I first attempted to redress the effects of social ills by adopting disordered eating habits.

In hindsight, I also realize all the therapists I worked with over the years to overcome my problematic eating behaviors were White—not by design but by coincidence. As I reflect on what allowed our cross-racial treatment relationships to be healing and successful, I attribute it to the therapists' abilities to accomplish three goals. They acknowledged my oppressions, allowed me to identify the role they had played in my development of problem eating behaviors, and held me responsible for seeking less destructive remedies to those oppressions and assaults. In other words, the therapists first validated my behaviors then sought to change them.

My recovery from bulimia was difficult and not without setbacks. With the help of skillful, compassionate therapists, I developed the courage to let go of habits that were designed to alleviate suffering but were no longer benefitting me. The fact that I was able to give up binging and purging three times per day and take the risk of learning more effective, less self-destructive ways to address the uncomfortable, unfair, painful experiences I first encountered in adolescence is a testament to the work my therapists and I accomplished together. Not only did our work help me heal, it also served as my inspiration to become a psychotherapist.

In my role as a therapist, I now have the honor of helping other women and adolescents struggling with eating problems. My experience has taught me how vitally important it is to build relationships with my clients—to inquire about and understand their experiences around racism, classism, homophobia, and gender identity. These factors almost certainly played a role in their development of eating problems. Equally important, I stay abreast of eating disorders research and incorporate best practice methodologies into my treatment approaches.

18 Disordered Eating Habits of a Black, Deaf Adolescent Female

A Case Study Applying a Cognitive Behavioral Therapy Approach to School Psychological Services

Erica L. Payne

Introduction

Disordered eating habits among adolescent girls vary in type, complexity, and etiology. These habits have become a widespread issue—a mental health crisis that could reach epidemic proportions among school-age youth. Approximately 13% to 20% of American children have a mental health disorder, and that number is on the rise (Centers for Disease Control and Prevention, 2013). According to Cavanaugh and Lemberg (1999), weight consciousness is a gripping concern for girls as young as nine years of age. Furthermore, "[t]here is a significantly high mortality rate among individuals with eating disorders—more than 12 times higher than any other cause of death in females 15 to 24 years old" (Bardick, Bernes, Witko, Spriddle, & Roest, 2004, p. 168). However, limited empirical evidence exists on disordered eating among Black girls (Talleyrand, 2010), and such evidence among Black deaf girls is nonexistent. Therefore, it is hoped not only that this case study sheds light on a growing problem but also that it piques the interest of researchers to delve into the disordered eating behaviors of Black, deaf adolescent girls.

For the sake of this case study, the term "disordered eating" pertains to a significant, pathological pattern of abnormal eating behavior that is associated with an adolescent's thoughts and emotions and that impacts the adolescent's physical, psychological, and social well-being. The most common eating disorders among school-aged youth are anorexia nervosa, bulimia nervosa, and binge eating disorder (NEDA toolkit), all of which are recognized as clinical mental health disorders in the fifth edition of the *Diagnostic and Statistical Manual* (American Psychiatric Association, 2013). This case study focuses on a Black, deaf adolescent female who has an eating disorder and responds well to school-based counseling using short-term cognitive behavioral therapy (CBT) techniques. The intended use of this case study is to inform researchers and school-based practitioners of the need for further investigation of Black deaf females' disordered eating behavior and treatment from a sociocultural frame of reference.

The Role of Self-Image

The way an adolescent female perceives herself plays a role in her mental, physical, emotional, and social development (Reel, 2013; Boes, Ng, & Daviston, 2004). Various factors can impact a person's self-image. For adolescent females, those factors include

- dieting and temperament (e.g., perfectionism, neuroticism, sensitivity, and rigidity; Lawton, 2005),
- extremist thinking, feelings of helplessness, and body dissatisfaction based on mainstream standards of thinness (Merikangas et al., 2011; Steinhausen, 2009; Hudson, Hiripi, Pope, & Kessler, 2007),
- sexual abuse and lack of self-assertion (Battling Eating Disorders, 2006),
- competitiveness, emotional distress, criticism, and conformity (Bardick et al., 2004),
- changes in body weight and shape (Thompson & Digsby, 2004),
- acculturation related to societal norms about thinness (Talleyrand, 2010), and
- stress, depression, drug and alcohol use, and eating patterns (Mugoya, Hooper, Chappie, & Cumi, 2019).

For Black and biracial adolescent females, those factors may also include

- stigmas related to mental health services (Dillard, 2019),
- a negative perception of one's body image, low self-esteem, cultural expectations, a desire for male attention, peer pressure related to sexual intercourse, and gender role confusion (Smart, 2010),
- racial identity and race-related events (Talleyrand, 2010), and
- weight-related criticism and discrimination (Balentine, Stitt, Bonner, & Clark, 1991).

For deaf adolescent females, the issue of disordered eating is exacerbated by race, cultural identity confusion, and acculturation (Aldalur & Schooler, 2019). It is important for educators to consider these factors when providing educational and mental health services at school. Likewise, it is important for researchers to pay close attention to the effect these factors have on body image, learning, and social-emotional functioning.

The School Psychologist

As a certified school psychologist with three postbaccalaureate degrees from Gallaudet University, I have provided educational and counseling services to school-age youth for more than 22 years, including children who are deaf/hard of hearing (DHH). I am a Black, hearing woman who is fluent in American Sign Language (ASL). My school-based counseling approach includes an integrated model influenced by mindfulness and cognitive behavioral therapy.

The Client

Jasmine[1] is a 13-year-old Black female who is enrolled in the eighth grade in a public school. She has mild to moderate, bilateral sensorineural hearing loss resulting from meningitis that was contracted from one of her peers in elementary school. Currently, she receives good benefit from wearing bilateral hearing aids that have been consistently worn since she was nine years of age. Medically, Jasmine has no history of mental health diagnoses, psychotropic medications, hospitalizations, or prior counseling experience. Physically, she is 5 feet, 2 inches tall and weighs 125 pounds. Jasmine is also regarded as a healthy individual.

Further, Jasmine is the middle child of three. She has a younger sister and an older brother—both of whom are talented athletes. Jasmine resides with her parents and siblings in a single-family home with one shared vehicle. They are very close-knit, as they attend church weekly and spend quality time together daily (e.g., eat meals together and participate in community service activities, etc.). Given that Jasmine is the oldest female child, she responsibly assists with caring for her siblings (e.g., babysitting and homework support) and has daily chores. Due to an employment crisis and financial difficulties, her father has been traveling out of state for work for the past six months. Jasmine's mother is an executive secretary at their church.

Equally important, Jasmine is the only deaf individual in her family, falling into the group of more than 90% of deaf children who have hearing parents (Mitchell & Karchmer, 2004). Her educational program includes the use of spoken English and sign language support when needed in noisy environments (e.g., in the cafeteria, gymnasium, or auditorium). Teachers have always regarded Jasmine as a charismatic learner who interacts well with peers and adults. Socially, her friends are hearing, moderate to high achievers, and well liked by peers and teachers. There are no same-aged female D/deaf peers at her school that function at or near her grade or maturity level. At the time she was referred to the school psychologist, Jasmine's academic profile had shifted from that of an average (C) to above-average (B+) student with interests in cosmetology and art to a below average student (D–) who became disinterested in school, career goals, and socializing. More specifically, six weeks before the referral, she complained about not feeling well and went to see the school nurse. Although there were no signs of physical illness, the nurse contacted me and the school social worker because some of Jasmine's peers reported that she was binge eating food she had hidden in her clothing. Upon further inquiry, Jasmine self-reported disordered eating habits and requested adult assistance to stop hurting herself. She was immediately referred to the school social worker for mental health assessment and diagnostic intervention. Subsequent to working with the school nurse and the social worker, Jasmine was referred to me, the school psychologist, due to her psychosomatic symptoms that were believed to be related to anxiety.

Diagnostic Considerations

Jasmine initially worked with the school social worker and was diagnosed with binge eating disorder (BED). The disorder was triggered by anxiety related to her father's out of town employment, negative emotions related to comments and interactions by a male student to whom she was attracted, and a negative body image as she had gained weight. Her binge eating behavior dated back three months, prior to the referral when her father began working out of town to continue financially supporting his family. Her BED was characterized by the following traits:

- eating uncontrollably several times a day for the past three months,
- eating regardless of whether she felt hungry,
- eating in isolation or "in hiding" because she was ashamed, and
- unhappiness (and sometimes disgust) with her eating habits after binging.

Two months after Jasmine was diagnosed, the social worker took a medical leave of absence. At that time, I (the school psychologist) became actively involved in Jasmine's intervention. I began counseling Jasmine once a week for 30 minutes. She immediately took well to me once she learned that I specialized in working with DHH populations. She also reported that she felt more comfortable working with a Black school psychologist, although she showed considerable progress with the social worker, a White woman.

Jasmine reported her lack of control over her eating behavior to the extent that she hides food in her bedroom and in her bookbag. Reportedly, she initially binged one to four times a week, but most recently (a week before she began working with me), her binging behavior increased to four to six times a week with no purging. Furthermore, Jasmine denied a history of alcohol or drug use, abuse, trauma, or suicidal ideation.

The Cognitive Behavioral Therapy Approach

Jasmine's counseling sessions emphasized mindfulness (e.g., guided meditation) and CBT (e.g., body image, belief system, cultural weight standards, self-acceptance, response to criticism, the need to belong, socialization values, dietary restraint, and binge eating behaviors). A core part of Jasmine's counseling sessions included the following tasks:

- in-session activities,
- homework, and

- reframing thoughts, words, and behaviors through the use of I-statements, open-ended questions, and real-life stories of celebrities who conquered their eating disorders.

The first phase of her 22-week counseling experience included baseline (e.g., preintervention) data collection using informal inventories specifically designed for deaf students. Jasmine also defined normal versus dysfunctional eating habits, discussed her beliefs and values pertaining to body image, and set counseling goals. The second phase included weekly school-based counseling (e.g., intervention) for a duration of 30 minutes per session. The third and final phase included a self-advocacy checklist, a continuum-of-care plan for high school (e.g., postintervention), and revisiting goals set during phase one.

The Counseling Process

Throughout CBT counseling sessions, Jasmine responded well to mindfulness practices including guided imagery. Over the course of 22 weeks, her participation in the counseling process revealed more about the sociocultural nature of her binging behavior to include deaf cultural identity confusion related to a dating interest in a hearing peer and trying to "fit in" as a deaf adolescent surrounded by mostly hearing peers. As a result, I used the Minnesota Social Skills Checklist for Deaf/Hard of Hearing Students to provide baseline, descriptive data regarding Jasmine's self-concept/self-esteem, social interaction/friendship, and pragmatic skills as part of her ongoing weekly school-based counseling sessions. The instrument was used as an informal measure rather than for diagnostic purposes and was administered three times during the counseling process as a preintervention, mid-intervention, and postintervention data collection tool. Jasmine's checklist responses yielded the following themes at various phases of her 22-week counseling process:

- identified herself as a deaf/hard of hearing individual (preintervention),
- reported bullying behaviors (preintervention),
- stated the impact of hearing loss in various settings and situations (preintervention),
- experienced social isolation as a deaf individual in predominantly hearing environments (preintervention and mid-intervention),
- reduced participation in social situations (pre- and mid-intervention),
- accepted responsibility and apologized for binging behavior (mid-intervention),
- listed character traits of a friend (mid-intervention),
- listed the characteristics of a role model (mid-intervention),
- stated the consequences of her behavior (mid- and postintervention),
- stated the difference between positive and negative self-esteem (mid-intervention),

- expressed and shared feelings (mid- and postintervention),
- listed and participated in areas of interest (mid- and postintervention),
- listed personal strengths, weaknesses, and values (mid- and postintervention),
- was willing to try new things or take positive risks (postintervention),
- increased participation in social situations (postintervention),
- used self-regulation strategies (postintervention),
- stated the benefits and risks of social media (postintervention), and
- identified the differences between acquaintances and close friends (postintervention).

Moreover, Jasmine attended weekly counseling sessions with the school psychologist for 22 weeks before she was promoted to high school. At the end of her middle-school counseling sessions, she completed the Informal Inventory of Independence and Self-Advocacy Skills for Deaf/Hard of Hearing Students (Clark & Scheele, 2005) to identify her strengths and needs and to determine the level of counseling services she needed in high school. Based on the inventory findings, an action plan was developed to ensure that all key players in Jasmine's life would support and promote her self-advocacy skills. By the end of her eighth-grade year, she approached mastery level in the following skill areas:

- explains her needs to a new teacher, interpreter, or staff member,
- engages with peers on a level that is on par with hearing peers,
- expresses personal opinions concerning current educational program or services,
- notifies the appropriate person to request additional explanation or tutoring or support, and
- informs team members of her specific needs.

In support of her counseling progress and as part of her continuum-of-counseling services (with another service provider) in high school, Jasmine's service hours were reduced to one 30-minute session twice monthly for relapse prevention, self-advocacy skill maintenance, and progress monitoring. In addition, her continuum of care included being assigned a D/deaf mentor provided by a local community organization as a daily or weekly check-in/check-out support service. Last, her care plan included periodic nutritional consultations with the school nurse to monitor her food selections and portion control. Jasmine's binge eating habits were in full remission prior to her enrolling in high school. Her counseling progress is believed to be attributed to various factors including, but not limited to, rapport with the school psychologist, increased personal and interpersonal skills, connections to deaf community events for children with hearing loss and their families, and asserting her need for her father to work locally to allow for increased quality time as a family unit.

Conclusion

This case study focused on short-term school counseling services provided by the school psychologist to address a Black, deaf adolescent female's binge eating behavior. The client's initial diagnosis and counseling services were provided by the school social worker. The client was then referred to the school psychologist, who provided services for 22 weeks during her eighth-grade year. Sociocultural aspects of this binge eating case closely resemble the social and cultural experiences of a D/deaf student who has no family members or close friends with hearing loss. Jasmine's self-disclosed comfort with the school psychologist who is of the same race and has decades of expertise working with DHH populations is believed to have contributed to rapport building and counseling progress. Other factors that contribute to Jasmine's success throughout the counseling process include her self-awareness, assertiveness, and willingness to do the work that was necessary for shifting her dysfunctional eating behavior to a growth mindset and healthy eating habits. Jasmine also created emotional stability. I would be remiss not to mention the highly effective mindfulness and CBT practices that were used by the school counseling staff. Although no quantifiable outcomes were obtained from formal measures, qualitative outcomes were observed and monitored, resulting from informal measures specifically designed for school-aged deaf students. Additionally, weekly counseling sessions resulted in a reduction and eventual remission of binge eating behavior, increased self-awareness and self-assertion, increased peer socialization, functional eating habits, reduced anxiety, and improved parent–child–family relationships. Furthermore, Jasmine's multidimensional counseling plan positively impacted her intra- and interpersonal skills and promoted a renewed sense of identity and self-acceptance that is critical to a Black deaf female's healthy psychological development. Though limited in empirical data, my school-based counseling experience with Jasmine provides a school psychological perspective of the sociocultural factors of the mild to moderate binge eating behavior of a Black Deaf Adolescent female.

Note

1. A pseudonym is used instead of my client's real name, and all identifiable aspects of this case study have been altered for confidentiality purposes.

References

Aldalur, A., & Schooler, D. (2019). Culture and deaf women's body image. *The Journal of Deaf Studies and Deaf Education, 24*(1), 11–24. https://doi.org/10.1093.deafed/eny028.

American Psychiatric Association. (2013). *Diagnostic and statistical manual of mental disorders* (5th ed.). Washington, DC: American Psychiatric Association. https:/doi.org/10.1176/appi.books.9780890425596.

Balentine, M., Stitt, K., Bonner, J., & Clark, L. (1991). Self-reported eating disorders of black, low-income, adolescents: Behavior, body weight, perceptions, and methods of dieting. *American School Health Association, 61*(9), 392–396.

Bardick, A. D., Bernes, K. B., Witko, K. D., Spriddle, J. W., & Roest, A. R. (2004). Eating disorder intervention, prevention, and treatment: Recommendations for school counselors. *Professional School Counseling*, 8(2), 168–175.

Boes, S. R., Ng, V., & Daviston, T. (2004). Unmasking eating disorders in the schools. *Professional School Counseling*, 7(5), 376–377.

Cavanaugh, C. J., & Lemberg, R. (1999). What we know about eating disorders: Facts and statistics. In R. Lemberg & L. Cohn (Eds.), *Eating disorders: A reference sourcebook*. Phoenix, AZ: The Oryx Press.

Centers for Disease Control and Prevention. (2013). Youth risk behavior surveillance— United States, 2005–2011. *Surveillance Summaries, MMWR*, 62(2), 1–35.

Clark, G., & Scheele, L. (2005). *Informal inventory of independence and self-advocacy skills for deaf/hard of hearing students* (Informal inventory reformatted by K. Anderson in 2010). Retrieved from http:/www.handsandvoices.org.

Dillard, C. (2019). Black minds matter: Interrupting school practices that disregard the mental health of black youth. *Teaching Tolerance*, 63, 44–48.

Hudson, J. I., Hiripi, E., Pope, H. G., & Kessler, R. C. (2007). The prevalence and correlates of eating disorders in the National Comorbidity Survey Replication. *Biological Psychiatry*, 61(3), 348–358.

Lawton, S. A. (Ed.). (2005). *Eating disorders information for teens: Health tips about Anorexia, Bulimia, Binge Eating, and other eating disorders*. Detroit, MI: Omnigraphics, Inc.

Merikangas, K. R., He, J., Burstein, M., Sendsen, J., Avenevoli, S., Case, B., & Georgiades, K. (2011). Service utilization for lifetime mental disorders in U.S. adolescents: Results of the National Comorbidity Survey-Adolescent Supplement (NCS-A). *Journal of the American Academy of Child & Adolescent Psychiatry*, 50(1), 32–45.

Mitchell, R. E., & Karchmer, M. A. (2004). Chasing the mythical ten percent: Parental hearing status of deaf and hard of hearing students in the United States. *Sign Language Studies*, 4(2), 138–163.

Mugoya, G. C. T., Hooper, L. M., Chappie, B., & Cumi, K. (2019). Impact of depressive symptoms and alcohol use on disordered eating and suicidality: A moderated mediation study. *Journal of Mental Health Counseling*, 40(1), 26–42.

Paragas, D. (Director). (2006). *Battling eating disorders* [DVD]. Meridian Education Corporation.

Reel, J. J. (Ed.). (2013). *Eating disorders: An encyclopedia of causes, treatment, and prevention*. Santa Barbara, CA: Greenwood.

Smart, R. (2010). Counseling a biracial female college student with an eating disorder: A case study applying an integrative biopsychosocialcultural perspective. *Journal of College Counseling*, 13, 182–193.

Steinhausen, H. C. (2009). Outcomes of eating disorders. *Child and Adolescent Psychiatric Clinics of North America*, 18(1), 225–242.

Talleyrand, R. M. (2010). Eating disorders in African American girls: Implications for counselors. *Journal of Counseling and Development*, 88(3), 319–324.

Thompson, S. H., & Digsby, S. (2004). A preliminary survey of dieting, body dissatisfaction, and eating problems among high school cheerleaders. *Journal of School Health*, 74(3), 85–90.

19 Who Should Be at the Treatment Table? College Students With Eating Disorders and Body Image Issues

Mary M. Churchill

Introduction

The demand for mental health services on college campuses has increased significantly in the last 15 years. Staff working at college counseling centers are faced with an influx of students who have various levels of distress, with eating disorder cases rising at an alarming rate. According to the 2014 American College Counseling Association survey, 94% of counseling center directors reported an upward trend in the number of students with severe psychological problems on college campuses (Gallagher, 2014). The number of college students struggling with food and body image issues has increased. In addition, more Black students are presenting at counseling centers with problems related to eating, restricting, purging, binging, and their associated disorders (e.g., depression, anxiety, substance abuse). Small and Fuller (2016) discussed how race and eating disorders impact Black women attending predominantly White universities. They brought the issue to the forefront and recommended strategies to help therapists of all races and theoretical orientations to provide appropriate treatment for Black students with eating disorders and body image issues. Further, Small and Fuller indicated that the issues impacting eating disorders for Black women include biology, socio-economics, food availability, family constellation, parental issues, and family trauma. The authors recommend that therapists explore issues of skin color, hair texture, body shape, and the significance of being full-figured women in the Black community. In Sally B.'s community and family, "overweight" was not perceived as a deficit or ugly. However, when Sally entered a predominantly White environment where thin and White were the norm for beauty, she felt lost and overwhelmed; thus, she turned to food as comfort but used purging and restricting to maintain her view of a proper body weight and shape. From my clinical experiences working with Black women with eating issues, I suggest that clinicians investigate the dynamics of skin color, hair texture, and body shape to formulate a more comprehensive view of Black women struggling with eating and body image concerns.

College counseling center staff are tasked with learning effective ways to manage the influx of students dealing with eating disorders. Treatment teams have proven to be an effective treatment model, because teams include information from staff from different disciplines and departments. Using a treatment team approach provides students who are dealing with eating disorders and other co-occurring disorders with viable options to manage their disorders. More importantly, this approach helps students accomplish their primary goals: graduating college and getting a job.

The Case: Sally B.

The purpose of this section is to discuss how various departments at the University of Richmond have developed into a cohesive treatment team in an effort to provide services to students presenting with eating disorders and body image concerns. The treatment team is an essential component of treating college students with eating disorders. Following is a summary of the initial case that brought the first eating disorder treatment team together.

Sally B. first came to the attention of staff and faculty after being hospitalized for alcohol intoxication during her second semester of her first year of college. Sally B. is an attractive Black female, measuring 5 feet and 10 inches and weighing 150 pounds. She has light skin, greyish eyes, and long dark hair. Sally B.'s grade point average is a 3.6, and she plans to become a physician. She came from an intact, rural, middle-class Black family from a nearby state. Her parents managed a small second-generation grocery store and bar, and they also managed several rental properties owned by Sally B.'s maternal grandfather. Sally B.'s mother attended three years of college before she returned home to help with the family business. While in her late 20s, she met Sally B's father, who was a high school graduate. Sally B.'s extended family— grandparents, aunts, uncle, and cousin—lived nearby and was a good support system. The family was very proud that Sally B. was attending the University of Richmond and were supportive of her goal to become a physician. Finances were never a problem; Sally B. never had to worry about money for clothes and transportation. Moreover, Sally B.'s church played a major role in the family and the community. Her mother, grandmother, and aunts were active members in the church. Sunday church dinners were a staple in Sally B.'s family. Growing up in her family, food was always a centerpiece at all family gatherings.

The team initially received information from a professor about Sally B. The professor noted that Sally B.'s academic performance had declined due to absences and not turning in assignments on time. On several occasions, Sally B. had to leave the classroom unexpectedly, missing two quizzes. The professor completed a form titled "Conveying a Concern About a Student" and sent it to the Dean of Women's office, which is a common practice at UR if a faculty member is concerned about a student. Sally B. was asked to schedule an appointment with an assistant dean to discuss her performance. However, prior to the meeting, a UR Police report was generated that indicated that Sally B. had been taken to a local hospital the night before due to alcohol intoxication, her second trip to the hospital. One of Sally B.'s friends found her passed out in a residence hall dorm. When the campus police arrived, they assessed Sally B., and she was transported to the hospital by ambulance. She was treated for alcohol intoxication and released the next day. Her discharge plan instructed her to make an appointment at Counseling and Psychological Services and to meet with a member of the Dean of Women's staff. The next day, she met with the assistant dean of women. The dean was able to convince Sally B. to schedule a meeting at Counseling and Psychological Services (CAPS).

Appointment at CAPS

Once Sally B. came to CAPS, she was put on my schedule for an intake appointment. Prior to the first meeting, students are required to complete several computer-generated surveys and documents indicating their presenting complaints and problem areas. For example, CAPS uses the Counseling Center Assessment of Psychological Symptoms (CCAPS) that generates 10 scales and the Alcohol Use Disorders Identification Test (AUDIT), which is a 10-item screening tool developed by the World Health Organization to assess alcohol consumption, drinking behaviors, and alcohol-related problems. Sally B.'s CCAPS scales were elevated for generalized anxiety, eating concerns, family distress, and substance use. She indicated thoughts of harm to self but was assessed not to be a danger to herself. On the Audit that has four levels or zones that indicate the severity of alcohol use, she scored 16, indicating a recommendation of advice plus brief counseling and continued monitoring. At her initial intake meeting, we discussed limits of confidentiality, her answers on our intake surveys, her understanding of why she had been referred to CAPS, and her goal for counseling. During this session, we identified her problem areas and developed a plan of action to help her change behaviors. At that point, she was given provisional diagnoses of generalized anxiety disorder, substance use disorder, and transitional issues.

Counseling and Psychological Services receives various reports and phone calls about students' behaviors generated by faculty, staff, parents, and other concerned individuals. I reviewed Sally B.'s intake information, a referral from the Dean of Women's office, a UR Police report on her transportation to the hospital for alcohol intoxication, Student Health documentation about her physical complaints and physical health, a professor's reports on her declining academic performance, written transcripts of phone calls and emails from her parents, and a report from two of her friends. It soon became apparent that talking to key UR staff would provide a clearer understanding of Sally B.'s problem and that gathering us in the same room would be beneficial.

The First Treatment Team Meeting

At the first team meeting, members shared information they had gathered about her behavior. It became evident that staff and faculty members each held more key pieces of information that had not been included in their written reports. In isolation, these pieces of information painted an incomplete picture, but combined, they pointed to a student with a serious eating disorder. We found that working across departments allowed us to draw a clearer picture of behaviors that were impacting this student's performance and functioning.

An unusual piece of information came from the housekeeping department. The University of Richmond is primarily a residential campus, with the majority of the undergraduate students living on campus. As a result, UR can be viewed as a small city with its own post office and zip code and various services. For example, it has a fully licensed and accredited police department with staff trained in mental health first aid. Furthermore, UR offers housekeeping services that includes cleaning dormitory bathrooms and other community areas in the dormitories, such as hallways and laundry rooms. Soon after Sally B.'s third hospitalization, her dorm's housekeeping staff made a report to their supervisor that the sink in the basement of the dorm was full of regurgitated material. The sink was found stopped up and the floor wet with vomit. This had happened several weeks in a row, resulting in a report to the supervisor. Just by happenstance, the same housekeeper had also been assigned to the CAPS office building and found regurgitated material in that bathroom sink. Eventually, through coordination among housekeeping, UR Police, and the Dean of Women's office, Sally B. was identified, and this information was made available to CAPS, which helped identify Sally B.'s eating disorder.

The Origin of the Treatment Team Concept

The idea for a treatment team came from my graduate school training. In my second year of clinical psychology training, I was assigned as a graduate intern to work at a treatment center for children. Later in my professional career, I worked as a forensic psychologist at a state mental hospital with individuals found not guilty by reason of insanity. In both settings, one with children and the other with adults, each client was assessed by medical, social services, psychology, occupational therapy and physical therapy. Each department member submitted written reports and met as a team to discuss the best treatment plan. The head of the treatment team in both settings was a psychiatrist who collaborated with the team members. In the forensic unit of the state mental hospital, the more savvy treatment teams sought input from the ward staff who interacted with patients daily for extended periods of observations and care. I found the information that the ward staff provided very illuminating and protective. For instance, if the ward staff advised me that a patient was not amendable to talking and advised me to come back, I adhered to the staff's advice. Some of my colleagues ignored the non-professional staff's advice, and some were physically challenged or assaulted by patients.

Today, at UR, we have a similar treatment team format based on my graduate school experiences working in clinical settings that used teams to provide services to students with eating and body image concerns. Each person possesses different perspectives and opinions on how best to treat students. The new team is also dealing with more mandatory reporting guidelines such as the Clery Act, Title IX, and more strict circles of confidentiality.

Review of the Literature

Writing this article required me to review the literature to determine if what we are doing at the University of Richmond is "best practice." The literature provided me with support to recommend the continued use of the interaction between and among departments to help find the best results for students at this juncture in their development.

Many articles discussed the benefits of a treatment team and what disciplines should compose the team. Most articles advocate for a core team that consists of a physician, a nutritionist, and a psychologist, with the duties spelled out for each specialty. In addition to ensuring that UR was adhering to best practice in treating students with eating disorders, I had to evaluate whether treatment models existed in the literature to treat Black women with eating disorders on college campuses. While I did not find articles on treatment teams designed to treat Black women, I found several publications that confirm that what we have been doing is "best practice" in treating eating disorders of college students, including treating Black women.

Patrick, Hebert, Green, and Ingram (2011) examined treatment teams in an outpatient setting focused on patients in the military. They discussed a "coordination team of professionals" and identified their roles. For example, a psychiatrist evaluates medication needs; a psychologist conducts testing and talk therapy; a pain specialist assesses pain management; and the substance abuse counselor assesses alcohol and drug use. The core group scheduled weekly meetings to discuss the cases. They concluded that collaboration resulted in well-coordinated and integrated care, particularly when dealing with difficult resistant patients who present with multiple comorbidities.

The team approach has also been used for treating persons with mental illness and substance abuse. Teague, Drake, and Ackerson (1995) discussed the use of the continuous treatment team. This is a coordinated multidisciplinary team that provides not only treatment but also case management and rehabilitative services. This approach was useful for us at the university, particularly the emphasis on case management. Just as the authors found that the continuous treatment team was useful for their population of people with severe mental illness and substance use disorders, we also found it effective for our students struggling with both an eating disorder and substances use problems.

In terms of addressing issues related to college students, Casey N. Tallent, National Collegiate Outreach Director for Eating Recovery Center, published an informative brochure entitled "Campuses Collaborating for Eating Disorder Recovery: Establishing Eating Disorders Treatment Teams, Guidelines, and Referral Practices for Providers in Educational Settings" (2017). She provided rationale for why colleges and universities should treat students with eating disorders and identified who should be on treatment teams. Tallent advocated for a multidisciplinary treatment team, which is what we have at UR. She recommended that different offices on campus collaborate in developing and executing treatment plans and referrals for students struggling with eating disorders. Furthermore, she gave suggestions on how to create a treatment team meeting, organize outreach events, and establish treatment team guidelines.

Treatment teams have been found to be effective in other settings as well. Epstein (2014) reported that in-hospital teams limited adverse events for patients, improved outcomes, and added to the patient's satisfaction. She further discussed the treatment team concept as a "team sport" that resulted in improved medical and surgical care.

The use of teams in the primary care setting was advocated by Bodenheimer (2019), who discussed the advantages of using teams to ensure that patients received evidence-based treatment while reducing clinical work for patients with diabetes, hypertension, depression, and uncomplicated musculoskeletal problems.

Mitchell, Klein, and Maduramente (2015) worked with college students using interdisciplinary treatment teams. They found that the treatment team was more therapeutically effective than individual or group treatments.

In summary, using a treatment team model to work with college students with eating disorders and body image issues is a "best practice" approach. The team must have flexible membership, which allows the team to have information from multiple sources that will help in identifying and planning a successful outcome. In addition, training of all faculty and staff is a key element in this process. Finally, not only is it important to ask the hard questions when designing a treatment plan for Black women, it is also essential to expand the membership of the treatment team, using all the information necessary to plan the student's success in graduating from college and having a healthy lifestyle.

References

Bodenheimer, T. (2019). Building powerful primary care teams. *Mayo Clinic Proceedings, 94*(7), 1135–1137.

Epstein, N. E. (2014). Multidisciplinary in-hospital teams improve patient outcomes: A review. *Surgical Neurology International, 5*(Suppl. 7), S295–S303. https://doi.org/10.4103/2152-7806.139612.

Gallagher, R. P. (2014). *National Survey of College Counseling Centers 2014.* Sponsor: American College Counseling Association. The International Association of Counseling Services, Inc. Monograph Series Number 9V.

Mitchell, S. L., Klein, J., & Maduramente, A. (2015). Assessing the impact of an eating disorders treatment approach with college students. *Eating Disorders, 21*(1), 45–59.

Patrick, V., Hebert, C., Green, S., & Ingram, C. L. (2011). Integrated multidisciplinary treatment teams: A mental health model for outpatient settings in the military. *Military Medicine, 176*, 986–990.

Small, C., & Fuller, M. B. (2016). In the shadows of eating disorders. *iaedp™ Foundation Membership Spotlight,* 1–4.

Tallent, C. N. (2017). *Campuses collaborating for eating disorder recovery: Establishing eating disorders treatment teams, guidelines, and referral practices for providers in educational settings* (2nd ed.). Eating Recovery Center. Retrieved from www. eatingrecovery.com.

Teague, G. G., Drake, R. E., & Ackerson, T. H. (1995). Evaluating use of continuous treatment teams for persons with mental illness and substance abuse. *Psychiatric Services, 46*(7), 689–695.

20 Evolution of the Fluffy Ideal in Jamaica

Venecia Pearce-Dunbar
and Caryl James Bateman

Effects of Eurocentric Ideals on Afrocentric Ideals: An Overview

Despite it being 150 years since slavery has been abolished and 57 years since Jamaica has gained its independence, its people continue to struggle for a sense of identity (Ward & Hickling, 2004). Understandably so, like many other countries with a history of a plantation society and where the majority of its people are of African descent, this developing country whether implicitly or explicitly is often influenced by the more dominant Western European culture (Akbar, Chambers, & Thompson, 2001). These influences go beyond the governance of its society to the very physical existence of their being. When compared to European characteristics, which are revered as "good," "beautiful," and "superior" people of African descent are classified as "Black" and represent a more inferior race, which is considered to be "evil," "ugly," and "undesirable" (Jackson-Lowman, 2014, p. 158). These societies are faced with a constant reminder that the European characteristics of "very fair skin, straight blonde hair, blue eyes, Nordic facial features, thin bodies" (Jackson-Lowman, 2014, p. 158) represent the standards of beauty, and any other characteristics outside of these represent the opposite. Such messages are embedded in the social institutions of a society (government, church, family/peers, school, media and business industries; Awad et al. 2015). Despite this, there was a period after independence in which movements of Garveyism and Rastafarianism allowed Jamaicans to become more conscious and accepting of their African heritage and physique (Palmer, 2014). Jamaicans became proud of their skin color and embraced voluptuous, full-bodied females (Ichinohe et al., 2004). Despite the Western media's influence on other ethnic groups, reports of body dissatisfaction were at the time seen as an anomaly for the country.

Black pride, although deemed a protective mechanism for Jamaicans, in recent times has been infiltrated by the European standards of beauty. Evidence of this is seen in an elevation in the reports of body dissatisfaction. Even though they seem to predominantly be among women, it is important to note that males, to a lesser extent, should not be excluded. Body dissatisfaction is seen through empirical findings of the skin bleaching epidemic (Charles,

2003; Peltzer, Pengpid, & James, 2016), increased rates of disordered eating behaviors (Harrison et al., 2019), and an increase in the incidences of eating disorders (Samms-Vaughan, 2002; White & Gardner, 2002; Sewell, Martin, & Abel, 2010). Though not negating these challenges, of grave concern is the obesity epidemic and the economic, social, and psychological implications that this may have for Jamaica.

Obesity and Weight Perception

Obesity is a global epidemic that affects both developed and developing countries (Ellulu, Abed, Rahmat, Ranneh, & Ali, 2014). It is associated with ethnic and gender disparities, in which females (McCarty et al., 2009; Ogden & Carroll, 2010) and Blacks reportedly have a higher prevalence in comparison to their White counterparts (Ogden & Carroll, 2010). Unfortunately, the Caribbean is no exception, and with the increasing rates, particularly among females and the youthful population, this brings the annual costs of the disease to an estimated $68.5 billion and a disease burden estimated at $88.2 million (Traboulay & Hoyte, 2015). Finding solutions to treat and stem its prevalence therefore becomes a priority. These solutions have to take into consideration the complexity of obesity, which includes both physical and psychological complications (Collins & Bentz, 2009). While not discounting the high morbidity and mortality rates associated with obesity, equal attention must be given to the psychological factors associated with the illness, as these play a critical role in intervention (Collins & Bentz, 2009). One of the psychological factors that strongly influences obesity is weight perception. Weight perception can be viewed from the individual's perception of his or her weight (Assari & Caldwell, 2015) or society's perception of the individual's weight (Sutin & Terracciano, 2013). With regard to the individual's perception of weight, researchers have shown that actual weight perception plays a major role in the intention to lose weight. For example, one study showed where perceived actual obesity mediated the intention for weight loss in Caribbean Black males but only partially mediated the intention for weight loss in Caribbean Black women (Assari & Caldwell, 2015). This same study also showed that, next to African American women, Caribbean Black women had the second-highest rates of obesity when compared to other ethnic groups (Assari & Caldwell, 2015).

Culture and Body Ideals

Perhaps the partial mediation along with the higher prevalence in Black women can be explained by the influence of culture and body ideals. In that, research has found a difference between the body ideals embraced by White and Black women. For instance, studies show that White women are more likely to embrace the thin ideal and have higher rates of body dissatisfaction

(Van Vonderen & Kinnally, 2012). In these societies, obesity is frowned upon, and the stigmatization leads to the development of other psychological distress such as substance abuse and anxiety disorders (Sutin & Terracciano, 2013). In predominantly Black societies, the body ideals are different, in that Black women are more likely to embrace a much larger body ideal (Kernper, Sargent, Drane, Valois, & Hussey, 1994) and are more satisfied with their body types (Roberts, Cash, Feingold, & Johnson, 2006). It is interesting that while these women chose a larger body size as their preferred silhouettes, when it comes to them describing their actual body size, they chose smaller silhouettes (Gordon, Castro, Sitnikov, & Holm-Denoma, 2010; Kernper et al., 1994) and were two times more likely than White women to describe themselves as thinner and seven times more likely to say they are not overweight (Kernper et al., 1994). This underestimation of their body size may influence their lack of regulation for food intake, and could explain why there is a high prevalence of obesity and binge eating disorder among Blacks in America and Caribbean Blacks (Taylor et al., 2013). Binge eating disorder (BED) is one of the three subtypes of eating disorders next to anorexia nervosa (AN) and bulimia nervosa (BN) and is the most prevalent of the eating disorders; it is strongly associated with obesity. Although being obese does not necessarily mean that the individual will also be diagnosed with BED, Blacks also have higher rates of BED and are less likely to engage in under-eating and weight compensatory behaviors (Taylor, Caldwell, Baser, Faison, & Jackson, 2007). These behaviors seek to further maintain high rates of obesity and myriad associated mental health issues which, in addition to BED, include distorted body image, low self-esteem, and depression (Ivbijaro, 2010). One study found depression to be most prevalent among Caribbean women who were obese (Assari & Caldwell, 2015).

Historical Context for the Bigger Ideal in Jamaica

> The body is a "site of enormous symbolic work and symbolic production . . . its deformities are stigmatic and stigmatizing, while at the same time, its perfections, culturally defined, are objects of praise and admiration."
>
> (Turner, 1984, p. 190)

The Black woman is by nature curvy and voluptuous (Gentles-Peart, 2018). People of the Caribbean, and Jamaicans in particular, hail from strong African ancestry (Gray & Frederick, 2012). Traditionally, people of African heritage are believed to have heavier/larger body sizes. Comparable to the African ancestry, there is cultural discourse on Jamaicans' social acceptance of heavier body weights (Ichinohe et al., 2004; Sobo, 1993). Larger bodies were a mark of an ethnic identity and social status common in the rural areas, where there was high value on fatness, which represents health, fertility, childbearing abilities, happiness, and an indication of social status, as opposed to thinness (Brewis, Wutich, Falletta-Cowden, & Rodriguez-Soto, 2011; Sobo, 1993). A thin body would be commonly referred to as "mauger" ("mawga"; "maga") and seen as powerless or represented illness (Sobo, 1993). Weight loss was a signal of social neglect (Sault, 1994) to the point where

> a Jamaican seeing someone grow thin wonders about the sorts of life stresses that have caused the weight loss (rather than offering congratulations for it and attributing it to a "good" diet, as many middle and upper-class people in the United States do).
>
> (Sault, 1994, p. 136)

A full-figured, plump, thick, curvy, or voluptuous female was therefore considered more physically attractive compared to others with a slender or thin physique (Savacool, 2009; Sobo, 1993). Sobo (1993) in her ethnographic finding posits that "the concept of thinness goes hand in hand with ideas antithetical to those associated with 'good fat'" (p. 35). This gives the impression that historically, Jamaicans value larger bodies (Anderson-Fye, McClure, Dreyer, Bharati, & James, 2017). The larger, voluptuous body, then, was a signal of Black femininity (Gentles-Peart, 2018). A respected adult, for instance, is often called a "big man" or a "big woman" (Sault, 1994). Jamaicans also have a tendency to separate fat into "good fat" and "bad fat" (Sobo, 1993), where fatness at its best was associated with qualities of moistness, fertility, and "kindness" (a social and giving nature), happiness, vitality, and bodily health in general (Sobo, 1993). Bad fat is considered sloppy or lack of pleasant qualities. These suppositions are argued to be a chief contributor to the cultural aesthetic preference for a plump body and curvaceous figure (Anderson-Fye et al., 2017); specifically, the "Coca-Cola-bottle shape"—the larger buttocks and bust (Savacool, 2009).

The influence of the European and North American Western ideals on the Jamaican population today is pervasive, and with the media, globalization, and tourism, Jamaica continues to have ongoing exposure to the Western way of life (Ichinohe et al., 2004). Nonetheless, studies suggest that while a significant portion of the population is classified as overweight or obese, Jamaicans are of the opinion that their weight is acceptable, and this results in low motivations for weight loss (Ichinohe et al., 2004; Jamaica Health and Lifestyle Survey-II, 2008). The current body preferences of Jamaicans ranges from a medium, "average" body, "not too fat or too slim" (Pearce, Dibb, & Gaines Jr, 2014; Barned & Lipps, 2014); the voluptuous and curvaceous body or thick (Gentles-Peart, 2013); and the fuller and even slender figure (Anderson-Fye et al., 2017). The preference for fatness or fuller bodies stands in stark contrast to the White "thin ideal" and seems to contradict the notion that as the society becomes more modern, there is a general shift towards thinness (Becker, Smith, & Ciao, 2005).

The Term "Fluffy"—Where Was the Term Derived From? What Does It Mean?

The cultural tolerance for fatness in Jamaica is central to expressions of endearment for larger body sizes. The term "fluffy" became prominent locally in the early 2000s as a term used to describe heavier women who are attractive, sexy, secure, and confident despite their body size (Barned & Lipps, 2014; Pearce et al., 2014). Fluffy women, from a medical perspective, are considered to be overweight or obese based on the body mass index (BMI) and are at risk for non-communicable disease (Barned & Lipps, 2014; Pearce et al., 2014). The colloquial adjective for larger women was made popular by Miss Kitty, a radio/TV personality and entertainer who gained prominence over the past few years. Miss Kitty herself was at the time a full-bodied lady with a flamboyant personality. She famously became known as the one to coin the term "fluffy diva." Though the use of "fluffy" has been widely associated with Jamaica, the term is not of Jamaican origin. This label seemingly originated with Sharlyne Powell in the 1980s to describe a set of plus-size women (who exercised at a gym in Florida, USA) in a more positive light rather than the negative word—"fat" (Semler, 1988). The term later re-emerged in the Jamaican landscape as a sign of body positivity in response to weight stigma.

The unpacking of what it means to be "fluffy" therefore does not only entail the physical size of the body but requires a deeper look at the psychological and social representations. For Barned and Lipps (2014), fluffy is not just about the physical body, but it entails traits of charisma, confidence and a bubbly personality which made larger-bodied women amiable. "Fluffy," then, conveyed an important social message that a fuller-bodied woman should not be demonized but should be seen as normal, attractive, worthy and serving to preserve an ethnic identity and cultural acceptance of larger body sizes. A nationwide approval and use of the term signifies some resistance to anti-fat attitudes or the framing of obesity or fatness as a weakness. Destigmatizing heavier bodies and use of positive labels may favor fortifying strengths of women with larger bodies rather than accepting stereotypes or weight stigma. Arguably, such terms could be viewed as a means of reducing fat shaming and promoting acceptance of larger-bodied women and health at every size. The discourse on "fluffy," hence, may reflect beliefs that heavier Jamaican women can assert themselves and see themselves as worthy, healthy, and happy.

How Is a Larger Ideal Being Transmitted Through the Local Media?

The expansion of American and European media outlets has proliferated and promoted the thin female body (Anderson-Fye, 2004) as the beauty ideal. Nevertheless, certain socio-cultural messages still transmit local body ideals in Jamaica. These messages are important in understanding body presentation in certain cultural contexts (Anderson-Fye et al., 2017). The body preferences endorsed by Jamaicans may be influenced by the local media through music videos as well as dancehall music. Several references have been made by male artistes in popular music for the most part towards an admiration of fatness or fluffy or larger body sizes. The references made to a bigger ideal are not unusual considering that research has shown that Black males prefer their ideal female partner to have a larger mid-section and bottom (Celio, Zabinski, & Wilfey, 2002). Some examples include the song "Bedroom Bully," sung by Busy Signal (2013), in which he expresses his love for fat, voluptuous-bodied women. Similarly, in the song "Fluffy Anthem" by RDX (2014), the singers emphasize that larger bodied women should not be underestimated because of their size. Additionally, in the dancehall culture, larger-bodied women are recognized for their ability to perform seductive dances equally well, as evident in songs such as "Lifestyle" by singer Yanique (2017) (who also goes by the name "The Curvy Diva") and "Bubble" by singer Charly Black (2008).

The adoration of larger, curvy women extends to the wider society and is evident in popular soca lyrics such as "I Want a Rolly Polly" by Mr. Killa (2013), where he sings about his love for larger women and highlights that larger women are God's creation, describing these women as clean and healthy. These songs, however, do not negate preferences for slender frames. Lyrics such as "tuck in yuh belly" by Leftside & Esco (2005) or the featuring of smaller women in music videos and carnival costumes signifies some aversion to an apple shape or big stomachs. Notwithstanding this, the inclusion of varying body sizes in the local media may in essence be promoting diversity. Gillen and Lefkowitz (2011) argue that individuals who are from cultures that are more tolerant of bigger body sizes will in general have more flexibility for body ideals which are more attainable than the slender, perfect body that is depicted in Western media.

So What Is Ideal?

But do Afrocentric people really demonstrate this flexibility? If we fight against the thin ideal and embrace the fluffy ideal, does this make us healthier? We have seen where fluffy served to defy fat stigma and promote body positivity and also encouraged negligence towards addressing the negative health consequences of being overweight or obese. Further, there seem to have been some descriptive complexities when the term fluffy has been used interchangeably with the thick ideal. While this may have brought some confusion as to which ideal one subscribes to (Duncan & Robinson, 2004), the thick ideal seems to also have its own set of complications (Awad et al., 2015). More recently, the thick ideal has been given its own definition and has been clearly delineated from the fluffy ideal. Thick is defined as a middle ground between thin and fluffy as "not fat or skinny but like both mixed together" (Burk, 2013, p. 504). While this ideal seems to encourage a healthy, balanced lifestyle which incorporates a variety of foods along with exercise (Ristovski-Slijepcevic, Bell,

Chapman, & Beagan, 2010), it also emphasizes the Coca-Cola-bottle shape, where fat is distributed in the "right places": smaller waist, thick in hips (Wise, 2018), bigger butts (Pace, 2016). Emphasis on these ideal shapes may serve to discriminate against those who do not fall within this category and may perpetuate the cycle of body dissatisfaction among Black women (Chithambo & Huey, 2013; Overstreet, Quinn, & Agocha, 2010). With the thick ideal being the most recently embraced and advocated for among Blacks, care has to be taken that it is not perceived as "the healthy alternative" and that it doesn't further perpetuate the prevalence of body dissatisfaction (Pace, 2016).

Anderson-Fye's (2004) findings from her study on Belize women advocates an ethno-psychological construal of local culture which resulted in women refusing to abandon their identity regardless of Western exposure. While we may advocate for our bodies, we have to do so in a kind and flexible manner, taking into account that there are unique bodies of different shapes and sizes. That we may need to evict from our vocabularies this notion of "ideal"; as women, our bodies go through seasonal changes, through menarche, childbearing, menopause, medical illnesses, and aging. It is imperative that we accept, admire, and celebrate our bodies, and as we evolve in our life cycle we add a more loving embrace towards a more positive body image.

References

Akbar, M., Chambers Jr, J. W., & Thompson, V. L. S. (2001). Racial identity, Afric-entric values, and self-esteem in Jamaican children. *Journal of black Psychology*, *27*(3), 341–358. https://doi.org/10.1177/0095798401027003006.

Anderson-Fye, E. P. (2004). A "Coca-Cola" shape: Cultural change, body image, and eating disorders in San Andrés, Belize. *Culture, Medicine and Psychiatry*, *28*(4), 561–595. https://doi.org/10.1007/s11013-004-1068-4.

Anderson-Fye, E. P., McClure, S. M., Dreyer, R. E., Bharati, A., & James, C. (2017). On body economics and fitting in: Upward mobility and obesity stigma in Jamaica. *Ethnicity and Health*, 1–15. https://doi.org/10.1080/13557858.2017.1395815.

Assari, S., & Caldwell, C. H. (2015). Gender and ethnic differences in the association between obesity and depression among black adolescents. *Journal of racial and ethnic health disparities*, *2*(4), 481–493. https://doi.org/10.1007/s40615-015-0096-9.

Awad, G. H., Norwood, C., Taylor, D. S., Martinez, M., McClain, S., Jones, B., . . . Chapman-Hilliard, C. (2015). Beauty and body image concerns among African American college women. *Journal of Black Psychology*, *41*(6), 540–564. https://doi.org/10.1177/0095798414550864.

Barned, C., & Lipps, G. E. (2014). Development and validation of a measure of attitudes toward Fluffy Women. *West Indian Medical Journal*, *63*(6), 626–633. https://doi.org/10.7727/wimj.2013.321.

Becker, C. B., Smith, L. M., & Ciao, A. C. (2005). Reducing eating disorder risk factors in sorority members: A randomized trial. *Behavior Therapy*, *36*(3), 245–253. https://doi.org/10.1016/S0005-7894(05)80073-5.

Brewis, A. A., Wutich, A., Falletta-Cowden, A., & Rodriguez-Soto, I. (2011). Body norms and fat stigma in global perspective. *Current Anthropology*, *52*(2), 269–276.

Burk, B. N. (2015). Black girls' perceptions of health and ideal body types. *Journal of Gender Studies, 24*(5), 496–511. https://doi.org/10.1080/09589236.2013.856750.

Celio, A. A., Zabinski, M. F., & Wilfey, D. E. (2002). African American body images. In T. F. Cash & T. Pruzinsky (Eds.), *Body image: A handbook of theory, research, and clinical practice* (pp. 234–242). New York: Guilford Press.

Charles, C. A. (2003). Skin bleaching, self-hate, and black identity in Jamaica. *Journal of Black Studies, 33*(6), 711–728. https://doi.org/10.1177%2F0021934703033006001.

Chithambo, T. P., & Huey, S. J. (2013). Black/white differences in perceived weight and attractiveness among overweight women. *Journal of Obesity, 2013.* https://doi.org/10.1155/2013/320326.

Collins, J. C., & Bentz, J. E. (2009). Behavioral and psychological factors in obesity. *The Journal of Lancaster General Hospital, 4*(4), 124–127.

Duncan, M. C., & Robinson, T. T. (2004). Obesity and body ideals in the media: Health and fitness practices of young African-American women. *Quest, 56*(1), 77–104. https://doi.org/10.1080/00336297.2004.10491816.

Ellulu, M., Abed, Y., Rahmat, A., Ranneh, Y., & Ali, F. (2014). Epidemiology of obesity in developing countries: Challenges and prevention. *Global Epidemic Obesity, 2*(1), 2. http://doi.org/10.7243/2052-5966-2-2.

Gentles-Peart, K. (2013). West Indian immigrant women, body politics, and cultural citizenship. In *Bodies without borders* (pp. 25–43). New York: Palgrave Macmillan. https://doi.org/10.1057/9781137365385.

Gentles-Peart, K. (2018). Controlling beauty ideals: Caribbean women, thick bodies, and white supremacist discourse. *WSQ, 46*(1–2), 199–214. https://doi.org/10.1353/wsq.2018.0009.

Gillen, M. M., & Lefkowitz, E. S. (2011). Body size perceptions in Racially/Ethnically diverse men and women: Implications for body image and self-esteem. *North American Journal of Psychology, 13*(3), 447–467.

Gordon, K. H., Castro, Y., Sitnikov, L., & Holm-Denoma, J. M. (2010). Cultural body shape ideals and eating disorder symptoms among White, Latina, and Black college women. *Cultural Diversity and Ethnic Minority Psychology, 16*(2), 135. https://doi.org/10.1037/a0018671.

Gray, P. B., & Frederick, D. A. (2012). Body image and body type preferences in St. Kitts, Caribbean: A cross-cultural comparison with U.S. samples regarding attitudes towards muscularity, body fat, and breast size. *Evolutionary Psychology, 10*(3), 631–655. https://doi.org/10.1177/147470491201000319.

Harrison, A., James Bateman, C., Younger-Coleman, N., Williams, M., Roke, K., Clato Day-Scarlett, S., & Chang, S. (2019). Disordered eating behaviours and attitudes among adolescents in a middle-income country. *Eating and Weight Disorders-Studies on Anorexia, Bulimia and Obesity.* https://doi.org/10.1007/s40519-019-00814-5.

Ichinohe, M., Mita, R., Saito, K., Shinkawa, H., Nakaji, S., Coombs, M., & Fuller, E. (2004). Obesity and lifestyle in Jamaica. *International Collaboration in Community Health, 1267,* 39–50. https://doi.org/10.1016/j.ics.2004.01.070.

Ivbijaro, G. O. (2010). Mental health and chronic physical illnesses: The need for continued and integrated care–World Mental Health Day 2010. *Mental Health in Family Medicine, 7*(3), 127.

Jackson-Lowman, H. (2014). An analysis of the impact of Eurocentric concepts of beauty on the lives of African American women. In *African American women: Living at the crossroads of race, gender, class, and culture* (pp. 155–172). San Diego, CA: Cognella Academic Publishing.

Kernper, K. A., Sargent, R. G., Drane, J. W., Valois, R. E., & Hussey, J. R. (1994). Black and white females' perceptions of ideal body size and social norms. *Obesity Research, 2*(2), 117–126. https://doi.org/10.1002/j.1550–8528.1994.tb00637.x.

McCarty, C. A., Kosterman, R., Mason, W. A., McCauley, E., Hawkins, J. D., Herrenkohl, T. I., & Lengua, L. J. (2009). Longitudinal associations among depression, obesity and alcohol use disorders in young adulthood. *General Hospital Psychiatry, 31*(5), 442–450. https://doi.org/10.1016/j.genhosppsych.2009.05.013.

Ogden, C. L., & Carroll, M. D. (2010). Prevalence of overweight, obesity, and extreme obesity among adults: United States, trends 1960–1962 through 2007–2008. *National Center for Health Statistics, 6*(1), 1–6.

Overstreet, N. M., Quinn, D. M., & Agocha, V. B. (2010). Beyond thinness: The influence of a curvaceous body ideal on body dissatisfaction in black and white women. *Sex Roles, 63*(1), 91–103. http://doi.org/10.1007/s11199-010-9887-y.

Pace, D. (2016). *"You look like a skinny white girl": Black cultural effects on the body image of thin black women.* Doctoral dissertation.

Palmer, C. A. (2014). Identity, race and black power. In F. W. Knight & C. A. Palmer (Eds.), *The modern Caribbean.* Chapel Hill, NC: UNC Press Books.

Pearce, V., Dibb, B., & Gaines Jr, S. (2014). Body weight perceptions, obesity and health behaviours in Jamaica. *Caribbean Journal of Psychology, 61*(1), 43–61.

Peltzer, K., Pengpid, S., & James, C. (2016). The globalization of whitening: Prevalence of skin lighteners (or bleachers) use and its social correlates among university students in 26 countries. *International Journal of Dermatology, 55*(2), 165–172. https://doi.org/10.1111/ijd.12860.

Ristovski-Slijepcevic, S., Bell, K., Chapman, G. E., & Beagan, B. L. (2010). Being 'thick' indicates you are eating, you are healthy and you have an attractive body shape: Perspectives on fatness and food choice amongst Black and White men and women in Canada. *Health Sociology Review, 19*(3), 317–329. https://doi.org/10.5172/hesr.2010.19.3.317.

Roberts, A., Cash, T. F., Feingold, A., & Johnson, B. T. (2006). Are black-white differences in females' body dissatisfaction decreasing? A meta-analytic review. *Journal of Consulting and Clinical Psychology, 74*(6), 1121.

Samms-Vaughan, M. (2002). Eating disorders. What's new? *West Indian Medical Journal, 51*(1), 1–3.

Sault, N. L. (1994). *Many mirrors: Body image and social relations.* New Brunswick, NJ: Rutgers University Press.

Savacool, J. (2009). *The world has curves: The global quest for the perfect body.* New York: Rodale.

Semler, D. G. (1988). *Women at large: A new video reaches a new venue.* Retrieved November 14, 2019 from https://books.google.com.jm/books?id=H_7Rn5d6FhAC&pg=PA53&lpg=PA53&dq=&redir_esc=y#v=onepage&q&f=false.

Sewell, C. A., Martin, J. S., & Abel, W. D. (2010). Eating disorders: An emerging pathology. *West Indian Medical Journal, 59*(6), 589–590.

Sobo, E. J. (1993). *One blood: The Jamaican body.* Albany, NY: State University of New York Press.

Sutin, A. R., & Terracciano, A. (2013). Perceived weight discrimination and obesity. *PLoS ONE, 8*(7), e70048. https://doi.org/10.1371/journal.pone.0070048.

Taylor, J. Y., Caldwell, C. H., Baser, R. E., Faison, N., & Jackson, J. S. (2007, November). Prevalence of eating disorders among Blacks in the National Survey of American Life. *International Journal of Eating Disorders, 40*, S10–S14.

Taylor, J. Y., Caldwell, C. H., Baser, R. E., Matusko, N., Faison, N., & Jackson, J. S. (2013). Classification and correlates of eating disorders among Blacks: Findings from the National Survey of American Life. *Journal of Health Care for the Poor and Underserved, 24*(1), 289. https://doi.org/10.1353/hpu.2013.0027.

Traboulay, E. A., & Hoyte, O. P. A. (2015). Mini-review: Obesity in Caribbean Youth. *The West Indian Medical Journal, 64*(3), 250.

Turner, B. S. (1984). *The body and society: Explorations in social theory.* Oxford: B. Blackwell.

Van Vonderen, K. E., & Kinnally, W. (2012). Media effects on body image: Examining media exposure in the broader context of internal and other social factors. *American Communication Journal, 14*(2), 41–57.

Ward, T., & Hickling, F. (2004). Psychology in English speaking Caribbean. *The Psychologist, 17*(8), 442–444.

White, V. O., & Gardner, J. M. (2002). Presence of anorexia nervosa and bulimia nervosa in Jamaica. *West Indian Medical Journal, 51*(1), 32–39.

Wilks, R., Younger, N., Tulloch-Reid, M., McFarlane, S., & Francis, D. (2008). *Jamaica Health and Lifestyle Survey (JHLS-II) 2007–8: Technical report.* Mona, Kingston: University of West Indies Press.

Wise, J. (2018). *The curvy girl handbook vs. the industry: A unique body image in a one-track business.* MA Thesis, Georgia State University.

About the Editors

Charlynn Small, PhD, CEDS-S, is from Washington, DC, and is a licensed clinical psychologist (LCP) on staff at the University of Richmond's Counseling and Psychological Services (CAPS) in Virginia, where she is chairperson of the Eating and Body Image Concerns team. She received her PhD in school psychology at Howard University. Dr. Small is also licensed as a professional counselor (LPC) in Washington, DC. She is a frequent speaker at national and international conferences, advocating for the awareness of eating disorders affecting Black women, persons of color, and other underrepresented groups. Dr. Small is a member of the board of directors of the International Association of Eating Disorders Professionals Foundation (iaedp™) and is a certified member and Approved Supervisor (CEDS-S) of iaedp™. She co-founded the Foundation's African-American Eating Disorders Professionals (AAEDP) Committee and currently serves on the board of the Richmond chapter of iaedp™. She has also served on the advisory board for the National Association of Anorexia Nervosa and Associated Disorders (ANAD).

Mazella Fuller, PhD, MSW, LCSW, CEDS-S, is a clinical associate on staff at the Counseling and Psychological Services of Duke University. Dr. Fuller provides clinical services, consultation, and training for social work and psychology interns. She has worked in education for many years as a high school teacher, adjunct instructor, consultant, and clinician. Dr. Fuller is an integrative health coach, and graduate of Duke Integrative Medicine. She is a certified member and approved supervisor (CEDS-S) of the International Association of Eating Disorders Professionals (iaedp™) and completed the Mindfulness-Based Stress Reduction Program through the Duke Integrative Medicine/Duke University Medical Center. Clinical focus areas are brief individual/student developmental framework, couples, gender and social justice, equity and inclusion, and women's leadership development. Dr. Fuller is a graduate of Smith College for Social Work in Northampton, Massachusetts, and completed her clinical training at the University of Massachusetts, Amherst. Dr. Fuller has served as a member of the advisory board for the National Association of Anorexia Nervosa and Associated Disorders (ANAD).

Contributors

Jennifer Ashby-Bullock, MSW, LCSW, is a social worker on staff at the Counseling and Psychological Services of Duke University. Ms. Bullock is a graduate of Smith College School for Social Work in Massachusetts and completed her social work internship at Duke. She has also worked as a social worker at Duke Hospital and as a psychotherapist in private practice. Ms. Bullock enjoys working with university students, recognizing their unique potential for discovery, growth, and change. She has particular interest in students who are marginalized in one or more of their identities. Her theoretical underpinnings are psychodynamic, and she approaches students and their challenges using a collaborative, interpersonal, developmental approach that incorporates elements of cognitive behavioral therapy and mindfulness. Clinical areas of interest include depression, anxiety, grief/bereavement, and couples therapy. Ms. Bullock has a strong commitment to social justice and to helping those impacted by racism and other forms of discrimination and oppression. When not working, she enjoys reading, running, and playing with her children.

Chantelle Bernard, EdD, is a licensed professional counselor (LPC) at Randolph Macon College in Ashland, Virginia. Dr. Bernard has more than 15 years of experience promoting and facilitating educational, interpersonal, and professional growth opportunities for students in a higher education environment. She earned her doctoral degree in education from Liberty University's School of Behavioral Sciencew. She holds a master's in human services as well as an educational specialist degree. Dr. Bernard possesses a bachelor of arts degree in psychology from the University of North Carolina–Charlotte, and her research interests include examining the effects of anxiety and loneliness on brain chemistry, as well as the impact of prolonged exposure to social networking sites on the emotional and social development of emerging adults (age 18–22). She is trained in mindfulness, meditation, CBT, and various solution-focused techniques. In her spare time, Dr. Bernard actively volunteers on campus working with student groups, as well as with national organizations serving the Mid-Atlantic Region and the greater Richmond community.

Mary M. Churchill, PhD, is a licensed clinical psychologist (LCP). She has been on staff at the University of Richmond's Counseling and Psychological Services (CAPS) in Virginia since 1989. She serves as the university's disabilities advisor and is a member of the university's Eating and Body Image Concerns team. Dr. Churchill earned her BA in social work and her MA and PhD in clinical psychology from the University of Cincinnati. Prior to joining the university, she was a psychologist in the Forensic Unit at Central State Hospital. Before her employment at Central State Hospital, she was the employee assistance program director at the Washington Hospital Center in Washington, DC. She has also worked with various companies and corporations providing management development, diversity training, and assessments. Dr. Churchill enjoys spending time with her family and friends and considers herself a lover of good food. She believes in four essential elements to help people cope with change: SEEP—sleep, eat, exercise, and plan to sleep, eat, and exercise. She maintains the following tenets: your past does not define your future; people can change but change requires work; and counseling provides a safe space to work on issues. She is a member of the Association of Higher Education in Disabilities.

Carolyn Coker Ross, MD, MPH, CEDS, is an author, speaker, and expert in using integrative medicine for the treatment of food and body image issues and addictions. She is board certified in preventive medicine and also in addiction medicine and is a graduate of Dr. Andrew Weil's fellowship in integrative medicine. She consults with treatment centers around the US that want to include her unique integrative medicine approach to treat eating disorders and addictions. She is the author of three books; the latest is *The Food Addiction Recovery Workbook*. Dr. Ross is the CEO of The Anchor Program™, an online coaching program for food and body image issues. Dr. Ross's belief that addictions and eating disorders are a wake-up call to change not only on the physiological and behavioral levels but also on the mental and spiritual levels is a compelling thread that runs through all of her work with clients.

Jacqueline Conley, PhD, is a native of Chicago, Illinois. She is the department chair of Social and Behavioral Sciences at Edward Waters College in Jacksonville, Florida. Dr. Conley received her PhD in counseling psychology at Howard University and her master's in clinical psychology at the University of Illinois, Springfield. In Florida, Dr. Conley is a licensed clinical mental health counselor (LCMHC) and works part-time at her private practice, Life Changing Strategies. In her role as approved clinical supervisor, Dr. Conley does consultation as a certified forensic mental health and child custody evaluator and Florida Circuit Court Family Mediation. In addition, she is a licensed clinical professional counselor (LCPC) in Illinois. With more than 20 years of teaching experience and 25 years of clinical experience, Dr. Conley has a variety of interests including eating disorders, addictions, adult mental health, and graduate student training. Dr. Conley has published in peer-reviewed journals and taught college in both the US and the Caribbean. Dr. Conley also serves on the Northeast Florida Council on Alcoholism and Drug Abuse.

Anisha Cooper, MEd, NCC, LPC, EAS-C, CCTP, is the owner of Wishing Well Counseling & Consulting, a holistic trauma recovery practice that treats trauma as a spiritual injury in collaboration with other disciplines. She is a licensed professional counselor with a specific interest in helping gender and sexual minorities on their healing journeys. She's also recognized as a certified clinical trauma professional and board-certified counselor. Anisha received her bachelor's in biology, minor in chemistry, with a concentration in psychology as well as her master's in counselor education and supervision from Georgia Southern University. She specializes in working with sexual trauma and relearning touch/intimacy after recovery. Alongside these concerns, she has experience in providing training related to professional development for minority communities, and she provides workplace training for diversity and inclusion practices. At home, she often dances with her seven-year-old daughter, who reminds her makeup is not necessary, bellies are homes, and stretch marks make room for beautiful things. In her spare time, Anisha enjoys reading, writing poetry and short stories, and playing board games with her family.

Goulda Downer, PhD, FAND, CNS, LN, RD, is an associate professor and program director in the College of Medicine at Howard University. Prior to her faculty appointment at Howard, Dr. Downer served as assistant clinical professor and director of Public Health Nutrition at Georgetown University Medical School; as the director of Medical Education for the National Organization on Fetal Alcohol Syndrome; and as nutrition faculty in the School of Public Health and Health Services at George Washington University. A recognized expert in the field of nutrition and food security, Dr. Downer has served as food security and nutrition advisor to the United States Agency for International Development (USAID) and as nutrition expert to the US Department of Justice, as well as the DC Superior Court. She received postdoctoral training at Georgetown University's eating disorders clinic and has been licensed in Washington, DC, as a cognitive behavior therapist.

Paula Edwards-Gayfield, MA, LCMHCS, LPC, CEDS, NCC, is the regional assistant vice president at The Renfrew Center, overseeing clinical and administrative operations at several locations. A licensed professional counselor (LPC) in Oklahoma and LPC supervisor in North Carolina, she received her master's degree in counseling from UNC–Charlotte. Ms. Edwards-Gayfield has extensive experience working with adolescents, adults, and families, with special interest in the treatment of eating disorders, women's issues, relationship concerns, mood and anxiety disorders, and life adjustments. A national certified counselor, she is a member of the American Counseling Association, the Oklahoma Counseling Association, and the Oklahoma Eating Disorder Association, and is certified with the International Association of Eating Disorder Professionals (iaedp™). Ms. Edwards-Gayfield is a frequent presenter at local and national conferences with a primary focus on eating disorders and diversity.

Rashida Gray, MD, is a board-certified psychiatrist in Richmond, Virginia. She has practiced for nearly 20 years. Dr. Gray treats a wide variety of psychiatric conditions, from anxiety to schizophrenia. Dr. Gray believes in the power of utilizing a range of therapeutic modalities in addition to medications in order to provide optimal mental health for her patients. She is a proud graduate of Xavier University—number one producer of African-American physicians—and Drexel University College of Medicine. She completed her residency at the University of Pennsylvania. Dr. Gray is a strong advocate for the prevention and treatment of child abuse and neglect and serves on the Greater Richmond board of directors of SCAN (stop child abuse now). She is also a member of Sisterfund, an African-American women's giving circle.

Abigail Harrison, MBBS, DM Paed, is a lecturer at the University of the West Indies (UWI) and consultant pediatrician and adolescent medicine specialist in the Department of Child Health at the University Hospital of the West Indies (UHWI). She is the founder and director of the Teen and Young Families clinics at UHWI. Her research interests include adolescent health screening and disordered eating behaviors in adolescents. She is a member of the Paediatric Association of Jamaica (PAJ) and a member of several organizations that take special interest in the physical and mental health of adolescents, including the Society for Adolescent Health and Medicine (SAHM) and the International Association for Adolescent Health (IAAH), where she currently holds a position on the Executive Committee. As the first adolescent medicine–trained physician in Jamaica, she has as one of her goals the continued improvement of adolescent health care in Jamaica and the Caribbean, to be achieved through national and regional collaborative efforts.

Caryl James Bateman, BSc (Hons), MSc, PhD, is a clinical psychologist and eating disorder specialist in Jamaica. She is also a senior lecturer and the psychology unit coordinator at the University of the West Indies, Mona. She has a passion for helping people, particularly people of the Caribbean. Through her research and her work with her patients, she has recognized that culture plays a significant role in the way in which individuals seek and receive treatment. Within the Caribbean context, she has done research in areas such as eating disorders, body image, sleep, the lived experiences of psychiatric patients, traditional medicine, sexuality, depression, and trauma. She is an advocate for raising eating disorder awareness in the Caribbean and, as such, pioneered the first international conference in the Caribbean: Dying to be Beautiful: Body Image, Eating Behaviours and Health in the Caribbean. She works diligently with eating disorder sufferers and family members. In the international community, Caryl actively informs about the

Caribbean culture and its impact on the presentation and treatment of eating disorders.

Eulena Jonsson, PhD, hails from Barbados and is the associate director of Assessment in Campus Life at Duke University. A main facet of this role involves supporting the strategic and assessment planning processes and professional development of the array of departments housed under the umbrella of Duke's Campus Life. These include Duke's identity and cultural centers as well as student-facing University Campus Activities & Events offices. Dr. Jonsson's professional mission is to serve as an assessment distiller, connector, and guide; to provide direction and guide reflection around research and data needs and findings so that any recommendations made are targeted and actionable. Her expertise and leadership in higher education assessment are bolstered by passionate advocacy of thoughtful evidence-based decision making and a strong foundation of quantitative and qualitative research methods. Dr. Jonsson received PhD and MA degrees in social psychology from the University of North Carolina at Chapel Hill and her BS degree in biology from Wake Forest University.

Warrenetta Crawford Mann, PsyD, is a licensed clinical psychologist whose career was inspired by a passion for people, places, and politics. This passion is fueled by her early life growing up in a family of educators in Atlanta, Georgia. She found her love for these areas came together in an unlikely way at her alma mater, Vanderbilt University, when she discovered the field of psychology. It was there that she decided to pursue graduate studies in psychology with a focus on the impact cultural contexts have on how people grow, develop, and interact with their environments. While completing her master's degree at the University of Louisville and her doctoral degree at Spalding University, she worked with a wide range of diverse populations spanning age, income, educational, racial, ethnic, religious, geographic, and resource backgrounds. It was in this work that she became keenly aware of the juxtaposition of personal and institutional privilege and power. Throughout her time completing her doctoral work, she found herself focusing on both individual and organizational interventions aimed at strengthening multicultural competence and creating inclusive environments. Her understanding of the essence of the common human condition has been instrumental in creating her unique ability to help any individual or group to identify their core values, goals, and potentials for greater success. Dr. Mann has spent the last 15 years working in higher education as an instructor, advisor, counselor, and administrator. She came to the University of South Carolina in August of 2017 and currently serves as director of counseling and psychiatry in Student Health Services. She lives in Columbia with her husband, her teenage daughter, and their dog.

Dawn McMillian, MS, RD, is a registered dietitian with almost 18 years of experience providing individual and group nutrition counseling and diet instruction in many topic areas, including hypertension, heart disease, and weight management. Ms. McMillian works with diverse populations in both clinical and public health settings and has worked in various US regions including Maryland, Delaware, North Carolina, and Georgia. In Maryland, she provided medical nutrition therapy to hospital patients and developed a nutrition curriculum for Harbor City High School and the Paquin School for Expectant Teenage Mothers through a partnership with Maryland General Hospital. Ms. McMillian also worked with Christiana Care, serving three school-based wellness centers in Newark, Delaware, providing students and staff with nutrition counseling regarding weight management and diet modification. In North Carolina, she provided nutrition education and counseling to pediatric, adolescent, and prenatal patients in both English and Spanish while working for Wake County Human Services in Raleigh, North Carolina. Ms. McMillian worked as a public health nutrition consultant for the North Carolina Division of Public Health and is currently a member of the Emory Health Promotion & Wellness team specializing in nutrition counseling, group nutrition education, and health promotion for employees of Emory Healthcare and University. Ms. McMillian holds two bachelor's degrees, one in biological sciences and the other in nutrition and dietetics, from the University of Delaware. She completed her dietetic internship/residency and obtained her master's degree in clinical nutrition at the University of Memphis.

Sasha Ottey, MHA, MT (ASCP), is a clinical and research microbiologist with a bachelor's degree in clinical laboratory science from Howard University and a master's in health administration from the University of Phoenix. She is the founder and executive director of PCOS Challenge: The National Polycystic Ovary Syndrome Association, in response to dissatisfaction with the availability of support resources for women with the condition. As executive director of PCOS Challenge, Ms. Ottey built a coalition of more than 70 major national and international health organizations. She led the first successful legislative advocacy effort in the US Congress to recognize the seriousness of PCOS, the need for further research, improved treatment and care options for a cure for PCOS, and to designate September as PCOS Awareness Month. Ms. Ottey also created the PCOS Awareness Symposium, which is the largest event globally dedicated to polycystic ovary syndrome. The Awareness Symposium has educated thousands of patients and health care professionals about PCOS since 2013. In 2018, she helped organize the first International Conference on PCOS in India for both patients and health care providers. Prior to founding PCOS Challenge, Ms. Ottey was a contract research microbiologist at the National Institutes of Health (NIH).

Erica L. Payne, PhD, is a veteran educator with more than 23 years of combined career experience as a school psychologist, administrator, and entrepreneur. She is a three-time graduate of Gallaudet University, is fluent in

American Sign Language, and enjoys advocating for D/deaf children and families. Currently, Dr. Payne serves as a school psychologist and social entrepreneur in the Mid-Atlantic region of the United States. She enjoys reading, traveling, and writing poetry and prose.

Venecia Pearce-Dunbar, BSc (Hons), MSc, PhD, is a Jamaican, a research psychologist, and a lecturer in psychology in the Department of Sociology, Psychology and Social Work at the University of the West Indies, Mona. She's a graduate of the University of the West Indies, Mona, where she received her BSc in psychology and MSc in applied psychology. Venecia completed her doctoral studies at Brunel University London in the United Kingdom. Her research interests include body weight perceptions, perceptions of fluffy women, cultural differences in weight perception, body image, social media, eating disorders, and health-enhancing behaviors—specifically, physical activity. She's an advocate for healthy living at any size and reducing weight stigma. She currently teaches social psychology, interpersonal and group dynamics, research, and other related courses. She also supervises undergraduate and graduate research projects. She's an author and presents at several conferences locally and overseas. She is currently a member of the iaedp™ international chapter in Jamaica.

Becky Thompson, PhD, is a scholar, poet, and senior yoga teacher who wrote *A Hunger So Wide and So Deep*, the first book on eating problems and recovery from a multiracial perspective. Her edited and authored books also include *Teaching With Tenderness, Making Mirrors: Righting/ Writing By and For Refugees*, *Survivors on the Yoga Mat: Stories for Those Healing From Trauma*, and *Zero is the Whole I Fall Into at Night*. She has been a Rockefeller Fellow in African American Studies at Princeton University and was awarded fellowships by the National Endowment for the Humanities, the American Association for University Women, the Ford Foundation, Political Research Associates, and the Gustavus Myers Award for Outstanding Books on Human Rights. She is the chosen mother of two adult children and lives in Jamaica Plain in Boston. See also http://becky thompsonyoga com.

Kena Watson, LPA, is a master's-level psychologist in Charlotte, North Carolina. She provides therapy for young adults and young adult couples and has a passion for working with women of color, especially college and early-career professionals. Her specialties include body image and eating disorders among people of color, anxiety, and coping with life transitions, particularly those affecting the Gen Z and Millennial demographic. She has four years of experience working at an eating disorder treatment facility, where she provided individual and family therapy as well as facilitated acceptance and commitment therapy (ACT), body image, self-care, and media awareness groups for patients. In addition to therapy, Kena also hosts private therapeutic vision board events that are geared to help individuals and couples connect with their values as they plan their vision for the year. Kena is a co-owner and administrator of an eating disorder culinary consulting company, Kalon Collective, LLC. At Kalon Collective, the mission is to provide support to those in eating disorder recovery with assistance with meal support, grocery shopping, basic cooking skills, fear food exposure, and restaurant meal support.

Joyce Woodson, MBA, was born and raised in the Southeast quadrant of Washington, DC. Mrs. Woodson earned degrees in economics and business administration from the University of Maryland. During her employment with John Snow, Inc., a contracting firm for the US Agency for International Development (USAID) and the Department of Health and Population, her work took her to each region of Africa, including Madagascar. While there, she learned much about the politics of body image and the striking differences between those cultures and US culture regarding body image and food and eating patterns. In her current position as program director of Enterprise Production Operations for the Nature Conservancy, part of her duties include serving as co-lead for the Diversity Equity and Inclusion African American Affinity Group, where she promotes the use of nature for improved mental health. Mrs. Woodson is also a licensed minister and is co-coordinator of the Women's Recovery Ministry. She has 30 years of experience with 12-step recovery programs and mentors women living and recovering from a variety of addictions, including food addiction.

Index

Note: Page numbers in *italics* indicate a figure on the corresponding page.